British planning policy in transition

The Natural and Built Environment series

Editors: Professor Michael J. Bruton, University of Wales, Cardiff
        Professor John Glasson, Oxford Brookes University

1. *Introduction to environmental impact assessment*
   John Glasson, Riki Therivel, Andrew Chadwick

2. *Methods of environmental impact assessment*
   Peter Morris & Riki Therivel (editors)

3. *Public transport*, 3rd edition
   Peter White

4. *Planning, the market and private housebuilding*
   Glen Bramley, Will Bartlett, Christine Lambert

5. *Housing policy in Britain and Europe*
   Gavin McCrone & Mark Stephens

6. *Partnership agencies in British urban policy*
   Nick Bailey (with Alison Barker and Kelvin MacDonald)

7. *British planning policy in transition*
   Mark Tewdwr-Jones (editor)

8. *Urban planning and real estate development*
   John Ratcliffe & Michael Stubbs

9. *Controlling development*
   Philip Booth

British planning policy in transition

PLANNING IN THE MAJOR YEARS
EDITED BY
Mark Tewdwr-Jones
Department of City and Regional Planning
University of Wales Cardiff

© Mark Tewdwr-Jones and Contributors 1996

First published in 1996 by UCL Press

UCL Press Limited
University College London
Gower Street
London WC1E 6BT

and

1900 Frost Road, Suite 101
Bristol
Pennsylvania 19007-1598

The name of University College London (UCL) is a registered
trade mark used by UCL Press with the consent of the owner.

British Library Cataloguing-in-Publication Data
A catalogue record for this book is available from the British Library.

Library of Congress Cataloging-in-Publication Data are available

ISBNs: 1-85728-421-6 HB
       1-85728-422-4 PB

Typeset in Times Roman and Optima.
Printed and bound in Great Britain by Page Bros. (Norwich) Ltd.

Contents

PART TWO
Changing institutional and legal frameworks 99

7 Planning policy implications of local government reorganization 100
John Clotworthy & Neil Harris

8 A future for strategic planning policy – a Manchester perspective 124
Ted Kitchen

9 Interpreting planning law 137
Ian Gatenby & Christopher Williams

Preface

In compiling any set of essays on current policy matters related to the statutory land-use planning system in Britain, one is immediately handicapped by the extent to which public policy alters significantly over relatively short timescales. Any attempt to consider in some depth the current statutory planning policy process at work often fails to recognize the degree to which land-use planning as policy formulation and policy implementation is never stationary. The only picture that can emerge, therefore, is one of a snap-shot, a glimpse of a process currently operating which could, and will, change over time.

This book aims to consider the statutory planning policy system in Britain at the present time (1995) and predominantly takes as a starting point the development of the current processes in the period since 1989–90. The choice of time period for the study is deliberate and has been governed by two main issues. First, it coincides with the publication in 1989 of a government White Paper on the future of development plans. This paper had immense implications for the statutory planning system and effectively precipitated a new era for the future framework of planning policy. Secondly, 1990 marks the end of Margaret Thatcher's period as Prime Minister and, since we are discussing British planning policy within the context of changing political climates, it is appropriate to assess the statutory planning process under John Major's administration. The resultant essays which have been assembled therefore take the planning policy changes of the last five years as the focus of study and provide a context within which an in-depth analysis of intergovernmental planning relations may occur.

Aside from these principal parameters, the period since 1989-90 has witnessed a number of other changes to the role and status of central and local government planning policies in Britain. These changes, which are detailed in the chapters that follow, include: the publication of proposals to abolish structure plans; the introduction of new legislation to speed up development plan preparation; the increased weight afforded to development plans in local authority decision-making; the increase of central government planning policy guidance to local government; the emergence of the environmental agenda and its direct effect on land-use planning; the increase in influence of the European Union and EC directives, and the proposed local government reorganisation for all parts of Britain. These issues have affected the statutory planning framework and are continuing to give rise to uncertainty within both government and the private sector. The current and future framework of planning policy in Britain, the nature of the relationships between different levels of planning policy and planning agencies, and the role and status policy statements take, are the principal themes of the book.

Changes to the statutory planning policy framework are of direct interest to both academics and practitioners, since it is these which set the parameters for state and market intervention in the future planning of the built and natural environment. But as a result of the rapidly changing political and legal context within which planning operates, current statutory policy is a subject which is never well covered in existing planning literature. This problem has been experienced at a personal level in both my teaching and my research, as I constantly search for the most up-to-date texts to inform students of "current planning issues in practice". Although there is no substitute in the end for practical experience to inform graduates of what planning is (or is supposed to be) and how the process operates, students must be prepared for the bureaucratic and legalistic nuances that exist in such a heavily administrative and political profession as land-use planning. As an academic with planning practice experience (I worked for a local planning authority until 1991), I feel it is worthwhile to provide students with as many first hand accounts of planning practice experience as possible. Such accounts are immensely invaluable to students, academics and practitioners and provide insights into those problems currently causing concern in the public policy arena.

The specificity of the book's topic dictates that, in providing these accounts of current planning policy problems, the essays must be a collection of authoritative papers by acknowledged experts. The contributors have been deliberately drawn from both academic research institutions and planning practice, and I consider this provides a unique collection of essays based on informed opinion. Given the problems of securing a unified and coherent collection of papers written by a diverse range of individuals, two themes are necessary to underlie the book. First, the book seeks to enrich the planning literature by drawing upon relevant debates contemporary to planning practice. In other words, the topicality of the work will hopefully attract a great deal of interest among researchers and policy analysts. All the contributors are familiar with the legal and policy requirements of the current statutory planning system and are capable of relating them to debates concerning relationships between central government, local government, and other implementation agencies.

Secondly, the book as a whole explores the links between planning policy at the various administrative levels, and questions what factors and issues are affecting planning policy formulation and implementation at the present time. This means drawing upon current practice to inform and guide future direction. Each contributor recognizes the important role the planning system takes in society to ensure quality in the environment. In drafting papers, therefore, each author was encouraged to promote positive new ideas to enrich our understanding.

Contributors were required to develop their essays in relation to the following four points:

- to identify (with reasons) the most important issues, and perspectives on them, in their field of inquiry
- to relate their professional experiences to the subject by use of empirical findings, attempting as far as possible to identify the constraints and opportunities within the system
- to examine their topic in the context of contemporary planning policies, assessing the current state of land-use planning and practice in Britain
- to illustrate how contemporary discussions in relation to changing governmental structures and networks may assist, or link with, the discussion of planning policy.

The book is divided into three main sections, each reflecting a broad category of analysis. Part One considers the statutory planning policy framework, detailing each level of planning policy currently operating and the relationships between different planning agencies in the policy arena. Each chapter has been prepared by a planning practitioner who is best placed to discuss what is occurring in their respective professional areas. Part Two assesses recent institutional and legal changes to the statutory planning process that will have an impact on the planning policy process. Part Three considers the current constraints and opportunities on the planning policy framework, highlighting political, social, economic and environmental dilemmas facing practitioners at the present time. These chapters are more social scientific in their approach, having been prepared by policy analysts and researchers. In assessing the future of planning policy, specific attention is paid to emerging trends and possible new directions within the 1990s. Although all the chapters are interrelated, they are also self-standing to enable an easy reading style for reference purposes.

I make no claims to provide a "theoretical" text or one which provides "good recipes" for successful policy processes. Rather, I attempt to provide planning students, academics and practitioners with a broad overview of debates current to planning practice, a descriptive volume with some analysis and evaluation. Generally, it is my hope that the book will be recognized as a concise set of essays detailing current statutory planning policy and procedures. What the contributors and I recognize as both important and relevant are inevitably biased views of the current planning system, its roles and its agencies. But I hope the resultant work provides some assistance in explaining and interpreting current practice which readers are encouraged to reconsider as time progresses and new experiences and opportunities are shared.

Acknowledgements

I would like to thank all those colleagues and friends who have participated on this project in some respect. First, a thank you must be extended to all those participants at the "Planning Policy in the 1990s" conference at the University of Wales Cardiff in March 1994 who, unwittingly, provided me with the inspiration for the book. Secondly, I obviously extend my gratitude to the contributors to the book who painstakingly prepared chapters to impossible deadlines, worked on redrafts and had to suffer my unending stream of reminder letters and phone calls. The central and local government practitioners deserve special credit for preparing extended papers aside from their professional duties during an uncertain time within government. Certain individuals deserve special mention, however, for their advice and support during writing. Particular thanks go to: Mick Bruton and Jeremy Alden at Cardiff for their unstinting support and professional comments; Roger Jones, Nick Esson and Kate Williams at UCL Press for progressing the text from manuscript to published work so smoothly; Marilyn Jones for her superb typing skills and for amending paragraphs during the minimum of time; Janice Cole for excellent copying, drawing and revising of the figures; and, finally, Nick Phelps, Gary Higgs, Sean White, Patrick McVeigh and Gareth Jones at UWCC who provided "the Brains". I take full responsibility for any omissions in the overall collection and themes of the paper.

Mark Tewdwr-Jones
Cardiff, March 1995

Contributors

JEREMY ALDEN
Department of City and Regional Planning, University of Wales Cardiff

KEVIN BISHOP
Department of City and Regional Planning, University of Wales Cardiff

JOHN CLOTWORTHY
South Somerset District Council

H.W.E. DAVIES
Department of Land Management and Development, University of Reading

SUE ESSEX
Leader, Cardiff City Council; Department of City and Regional Planning, University of Wales Cardiff

IAN GATENBY
McKenna & Co., Solicitors

NEIL HARRIS
Department of Environment and Planning, Vale of Glamorgan Borough Council

KEITH HAYTON
Centre for Planning, University of Strathclyde

RICHARD JARVIS
Clwyd County Council

ALAN JONES
Newbury District Council

TED KITCHEN
Manchester City Council

CHRIS OFFORD
Northumberland County Council

MATTHEW J. QUINN
Planning Directorate, Department of the Environment

MARK TEWDWR-JONES
Department of City and Regional Planning, University of Wales Cardiff

HUW THOMAS
Department of City and Regional Planning, University of Wales Cardiff

ANDY THORNLEY
Department of Geography, London School of Economics

CHRISTOPHER WILLIAMS
McKenna & Co., Solicitors

CHAPTER 1

Introduction: land-use planning policy after Thatcher

Mark Tewdwr-Jones

Introduction

The planning process operates in Britain as a predominantly administrative system. Planning agencies and organizations responsible for the management of the built and natural environment agree on policies and programmes to instigate change, promote sites and prepare for development. Fundamental to this administrative role of planning agencies in facilitating or "enabling" is: the preparation and implementation of policies, the allocation and organization of goals, and the mediation of conflicting interests by those organizations competing for the allocation of scarce resources.

The statutory planning policy process is therefore concerned with the preparation of land-use plans and the control of development. Although planning, broadly defined, is something much more than plan-making and policy control, Britain has experienced a planning framework devoted almost entirely to a quasi-legal administrative system concerned with policy and control. Since the implementation of the Town and Country Planning Act 1947, when development plans and development control were first introduced in this country, successive governments have laid particular emphasis on the need to prepare land-use plans and ensure state control of the physical environment. These roles have been delegated to local government, with advice from central government and legal parameters established by courts of law. Even today, the main substance of the planning system is administered by governmental professional planning officers, either within forward planning teams (responsible for preparing planning policies) or development control teams (responsible for determining applications for planning permission by individuals and organizations).

Development plan preparation allows the community and those interested in physical change to participate in drafting policies of promotion or conservation. The resultant policies within development plans must be viewed therefore as an agreed set of principles to guide decision-makers on the future of the built and natural environment and as a means through which development opportunities are advertised to the private sector. Planning in Britain equates to physical land-use development, and the promotion and control of that development rests with government. Planning policy, consequently, is fundamental to the future social and economic wellbeing of any spatial area, since it is the essential nexus between the state's requirement to review the need for physical change in an area while controlling unacceptable development and conserving the best quality landscapes.

Given that planning policy can affect the future economic prosperity of an area, it cannot be viewed as an independent statutory function of the state; it is inherent in all governmental activities. Government, either centrally or at the local level, certainly prepares policies, redrafts plans, negotiates with other interested parties, and liaises with developers. But planning policy is more than an administrative exercise: it is a product of a long process of bargaining, negotiation and political compromise, which encompasses the views and activities of a wide range of organizations, including central government, local planning authorities, statutory bodies, the market and the public. All these agencies influence the planning policy process in some respect at various stages of policy formulation and implementation. The extent of influence wielded by these different interest groups varies between governments and between different situations and groups within government. Policy planners will attempt to draft and implement the most appropriate policies for the administrative area they are responsible for, having taken into account the different opinions voiced, but ultimately a plan containing those policies can never be used as a blueprint; there will always be scope for amendments, for other factors to be taken into account, and for exceptions to the rule – a clear sign of the political component that is so intrinsic in the British planning process.

Planning policy is closely tied to the fields of public administration and politics. It operates as *a means of negotiation* between market choice (the desires of the individual) and political choice (the desires and actions of the state). The activity of selecting and amending policies as part of the formulation and implementation of plans can never be a technical problem-solving exercise undertaken by professional urban and regional managers possessing perfect knowledge and high skills with community backing. Planning policy marries the technical issues of physical land-use planning with behavioural actions and choices between different options. Policy planning, as a political process, encompasses both the technical and the ethical; values underlie decisions to an extent equal to technical characteristics. Given this relationship, it is inevitable that conflicts frequently occur, between different arms of the state, between interested organizations, and between individuals. If anything characterizes the turbulence of planning policy, it is the source of argumentation over land use.

Within this introductory chapter, I briefly outline the context for the chapters that follow, indicating the administrative framework of planning policy and the changing political actions that have affected the process over the past 15 years. It is not my intention here to provide a descriptive or analytical account of planning under two different administrations; that is something upon which the other contributors have focused. Rather, this chapter will "set the scene".

The administrative system for land-use planning in Britain

The land-use planning process currently operating in Britain emerged following the enactment of parliamentary legislation in the early 1970s (for a review of the statutory planning system prior to 1971, see Cullingworth & Nadin 1994). In England and Wales, the provisions of the Local Government Act 1972 enacted a three-tier system of local authorities: 47 county councils and 333 district councils, with many community, town or parish councils at the lower level. All of these local authorities are autonomous organizations and, with exception to the parish or community councils, are responsible for a range of state services upon whom specific powers are conferred. The planning framework operated by these local authorities was introduced by the Town and Country Planning Act 1968, subsequently replaced by the Town and Country Planning Act 1971 to bring the system in line with the revised structure of local government. This legislation introduced new forms of development plans to be formulated and implemented by the county and district local government structure. County councils are required to prepare structure plans, broad strategic documents containing policies on a range of issues to apply across the county, whereas district councils were encouraged to prepare district plans, detailed forward planning and development control plans containing policies for specific land-use allocations. The district plans could comprise many different types of documents, including district plans, action area plans and subject plans, according to the needs and development pressures existing for each area. The successfulness of this two-tier planning framework has been analyzed in many studies of the time (e.g. Cross & Bristow 1983, Bruton & Nicholson 1987, Healey et al. 1985) and is not worth repeating here. However, by the mid-1980s, questions were beginning to be asked – predominantly by central government – of both the appropriateness of the planning system to deal with development pressures of the time, and of the local government structure operating the planning system. Thornley (1993) provides one of the most authoritative accounts of the political climate for land-use planning during the 1980s – under so-called "Thatcherism" – and details the changes experienced by the system as the Conservative Party in government "rolled back the frontiers of the state", allowed the market to develop and enterprise to flourish.

During the 1980s, one of the most important reforms initiated by the Conservatives that affected the statutory planning framework was the abolition of the county councils in the seven largest metropolitan areas of England. Under the

3

Local Government Act 1985, the metropolitan county councils for London, Birmingham, Liverpool, Manchester, Sheffield, Newcastle and Leeds were abolished, and their statutory powers transferred to the lower tier authorities: the metropolitan districts and the London boroughs. The planning system was also transferred to the new authorities, with a new statutory system introduced for metropolitan planning. To replace the structure plan and district plan in each authority, a new development plan – unitary development plan – would gradually be introduced, comprising the functions of both former plans: strategic and detailed policies. Outside these metropolitan areas, the two-tier structure plan and district plan would remain in operation as the statutory planning system. The new planning arrangements within the metropolitan authorities after 1986 have been subject to assessment by analysts (e.g. Thew & Watson 1988), although some commentators have focused more on the resultant lack of strategic planning policy to operate across the former metropolitan county areas (Williams et al. 1992).

The local government system and associated statutory planning arrangements in Scotland also underwent reorganization in the early 1970s when a slightly modified administrative pattern emerged. The Local Government (Scotland) Act 1973 created 9 regions, as opposed to "counties" south of the border, 53 districts and 3 island authorities, although only 49 of the local authorities in Scotland possess planning powers, mainly because of the high number of sparsely populated areas. Thus, within six regions, planning is divided between regions and districts; in the remaining three regions the districts possess no planning responsibilities; whereas in the three islands planning is carried out in a unitary local government structure.

Planning policy and Thatcherism

The effects of Thatcherism on the statutory planning system during the 1980s were widespread. The reforms, or deregulation of planning, not only affected the local governmental administrative framework and its duties but also the statutory planning system itself. Forward planning functions and development control powers of local authorities have been amended significantly following the passing of several Acts of Parliament, White Papers and government Circulars. In particular, the forward planning duties of urban authorities were removed in certain areas as the government introduced Enterprise Zones and Urban Development Corporations, which removed planning restrictions and allowed the market to regenerate urban areas such as Bristol, Cardiff, Sheffield, Liverpool and London Docklands without bureaucratic control (see Imrie & Thomas 1993a for a comprehensive review of the policies and effects of UDCs).

On the development control side of local authorities' work, the reduction in control was almost as marked. In the mid-1980s, the government reduced the status of development plans in local authorities' determination of planning applications. A White Paper, "Lifting the Burden" (HM Government 1985), was published which relegated development plans – and ultimately the policies within those plans – in favour of other material considerations, the most prominent of which was the encouragement to create employment. Following this paper in the two to three years to 1987, local authorities were unable to control development effectively in their areas, particularly for large scale housing initiatives and out-of-town retailing development. This period of time has become known as the "appeal-led" planning process, as developers often appealed to the Secretaries of State to overturn the unfavourable decisions of local authorities and allow their proposals to go ahead.

The planning system experienced further uncertainty upon the publication of a government Green Paper in 1986, *The future of development plans* (DOE/WO 1986). The Secretary of State for the Environment at the time, Nicholas Ridley, issued a consultation paper advocating the abolition of structure plans and their replacement with "county planning statements" and the introduction of district-wide unitary development plans, as had just been introduced to the metropolitan areas following the abolition of the metropolitan counties. The amount of criticism the proposals attracted was widespread, and further disillusioned the planning profession and local authority associations.

By 1987, local authorities were beginning to object to the undermining of local democracy in this respect and harassed the government to return to a local authority-led planning system. Additionally, the Planning Inspectorate – responsible for arranging and determining appeals to the Secretary of State – was coming under increasing pressure as the number of appeals against local authority decisions reached an all-time high. Simultaneously, the government received a great deal of criticism from Conservative voters in the rural south and their own members of parliament for not acting to control the possible development of new housing settlements in the South East. As a consequence of this pressure, the government acknowledged the problems operating within the statutory planning system and as a first step announced that, in future, where a development plan was up-to-date and relevant to the development needs of an area, it would be accorded enhanced weight as a decision-making tool, within both local authorities and at appeal, the Secretary of State at the time espousing "local choice" and the need for communities to determine the scope for future development within their own localities.

Although this may have marked a watershed for the Conservatives' policy towards statutory planning, it did not halt additional reforms and proposals to amend the planning framework further. The 1986 Green Paper's proposals were carried through into *The future of development plans* White Paper of January 1989 (HM Government 1989), which again proposed the abolition of structure plans. But by the winter of the same year, the government's enthusiasm towards radical planning reform was diminishing. The replacement of Nicholas Ridley as Environment Secretary with Chris Patten resulted in a change in direction for

Conservative policy towards planning. In the autumn of 1989, Patten announced that the most controversial element of the White Paper's proposals – to abolish structure plans – had been scrapped, but reiterated that further legislation was required. The 1988–9 period was also notable for the government's embrace of "green politics", as the major political parties developed policies for environmental protection (McCormick 1991). Environmental issues, which can be effectively co-ordinated only by the state, was seen by the government as an ideal means through which popular support could be accumulated, and recognized that action on green issues could only be secured with the support of local government. The Environmental Protection Act 1990 set the seal on a move towards state concern for green issues, and indirectly had the effect of bolstering the functions of local authorities as guardians of the environment.

Planning policy during the Major administration

The renaissance of planning policy, or at least the bolstering of local planning authorities' functions, had already occurred in the form of scrapping the White Paper's proposals, and concern for the environment by the time Margaret Thatcher was deposed as leader of the Conservative Party in the autumn of 1990. Consolidating legislation to replace the 1971 Town and Country Planning Act was introduced through parliament. The 1971 Act had been severely hampered by many amendments up to 1990, mainly as a consequence of legislation but also as a cause of changing statutory procedures as detailed in White Papers, Circulars and other statutory instruments. Given the plethora of documentation existing, legislation was required to bring together all these different amendments into one set of planning acts. In 1990, therefore, the government legislated for consolidation of the town and country planning statutes, encompassing all the revisions and amendments to the planning system that had occurred in the previous 20 years. Rather than one parliamentary act, however, the consolidating legislation was divided between three bills: the Town and Country Planning Act 1990, detailing the principle legal requirements on planning policy; the Planning (Conservation Areas and Listed Buildings) Act 1990, which focused on the built heritage, and the Planning (Hazardous Substances) Act 1990, which covers pollution and waste material. Although Chris Patten had stated that further legislation was required, this was not what he had in mind, and the remainder of the 1989 White Paper's proposals remained on the table for discussion for the time being. Therefore, the change in government policy towards the statutory planning system was already under way in 1989, over one year before Mrs Thatcher left office, although this had not been enacted in legislative changes. The pace of change and modified policy stance of the government towards the planning framework was more marked, however, following John Major's appointment as Prime Minister and Michael Heseltine's reappointment as Secretary of State for the Environment.

The first principal change occurred in the form of amending the administrative framework of statutory planning. Following the government's decision to strategically review local government, following the decision to abandon the community charge or "poll tax" and increase public sector accountability, Michael Heseltine announced in the autumn of 1990 that a comprehensive review would be undertaken of local government structure and functions in each of the three countries of Britain. The exact reasons why the government announced the impending reorganization of local authorities remain a point of speculation, a decision that has been described as "against all reasonable expectation, and perhaps against reason itself." (Young 1994: 83).

The reorganization of local government would proceed separately in each of the three countries: England, Wales and Scotland. In England, the Secretary of State announced the establishment of an independent Local Government Commission to consider local government reform and the associated planning framework in separate regions of the country, whereas in Wales and Scotland, reorganization would be pursued by the Secretaries of State and the relevant government departments. Planning as an administrative function of local government would be directly affected by the reform.

Meanwhile, the government announced that the long-promised legislation for the future of the planning system would be tabled for parliamentary time in the 1990–91 session. The resultant statute, the Planning and Compensation Act 1991, which received Royal Assent in July 1991, made widespread reforms to the planning process, but had particular effect on the provisions for statutory planning. Some elements of the 1989 White Paper relating to development plans were included in the bill. The most important reforms concerned the speeding up of development plan preparation, to remove the need for Secretary of State approval for structure plans, to require district authorities to mandatory prepare district-wide local plans for the whole of their administrative areas, and to increase the weight afforded to development plan policies for decision-making purposes (the so-called "Section 54A" requirement).

Other important measures stepped up or introduced at this time included the issuing of national planning statements by the government in the form of Planning Policy Guidance Notes (PPGs) and the preparation of Regional Planning Guidance Notes (RPGs) by county councils within each region.

The release of coherent national and regional planning policy documents, associated with the provisions of the 1991 Act, resulted in the establishment of a new framework for the planning system. The then Chief Planning Adviser at the Department of the Environment stated that the planning system would now comprise of a coherent and interlocking framework of planning policy (Wilson 1990) across the country. Figure 1.1 illustrates this revised planning policy framework for England, Wales and Scotland, together with the co-ordinating level of government responsible for each.

The impact of the provisions of the Planning and Compensation Act 1991 and

PLANNING AGENCIES	PLANNING LEVEL & INSTRUMENTS	SPATIAL COVERAGE
NATIONAL		
Central Government Departments	Parliamentary legislation, Statutory instruments, Judicial judgements, White Papers, Ministerial statements, Circulars, Planning Policy Guidance Notes Minerals Planning Guidance	Britain
REGIONAL		
Integrated regional government offices Scottish Office Welsh Office	Regional Planning Guidance Notes Strategic Planning Guidance Notes (metropolitan areas) National Planning Policy Guidance Notes (Scotland) Planning Policy Guidance (Wales)	English regions Metropolitan England Scotland Wales
LOCAL		
UNTIL APRIL 1996		
Metropolitan and London Boroughs	**Development Plans** Unitary Development Plans (Metropolitan areas)	Metropolitan England
County Councils County Councils Regional Councils	Structure Plans	English counties Welsh counties Scottish regions
District Councils District Councils District Councils	Local Plans	English districts Welsh districts Scottish regions/districts
National Parks Urban Development Corporations	Local Plans	Peak/Lake/Broads Metropolitan England
County Councils County Councils District Councils	Minerals Local Plans Waste Local Plans	England/Wales England Wales
AFTER APRIL 1996		
Metropolitan and London Boroughs Unitary Councils	Unitary Development Plans	Metropolitan England England/Wales *
County Councils Unitary Councils	Structure Plans	English counties Scotland
District Councils Unitary Councils	Local Plans	English districts Scotland
County Councils County Councils	Minerals Local Plans Waste Local Plans	English counties English counties

* Certain areas in England will also undergo local government reorganisation in the period 1996–97. The Secretary of State for the Environment will announce the planning policy dramework for these areas in due course.

Figure 1.1   The planning policy structure in England, Wales and Scotland.

the effects of the PPG and RPG documents are continually being felt in local authorities and by the private sector across the country, and it is this new planning policy system upon which contributors to this book have focused.

Although the administrative framework of statutory planning was radically overhauled at this time, the effect of substantive government policies within planning has not been so marked. Indeed, to some extent, the policy of the government towards land-use planning concerns such as retailing, housing and economic development has been one of stability and consensus, an extension of Thatcherite policies. Planning during Mr Major's period as Prime Minister has not been as ideologically radical as it was under his predecessor. The changes to the statutory planning policy framework that have occurred, therefore, have been very much a continuation of Thatcherite policy. As Kavanagh (1994: 9) remarks, "Major has continued with much of that Thatcher legacy" and views the period since 1990 as one of consolidation after a decade of radical change.

Certainly, in land-use planning terms, although there have been some important policy amendments emerging, these changes have not been as significant as the Thatcher reforms of the 1980s. If one scrutinizes the statutes and policy statements made by government ministers since 1990, one is hard pushed to find anything that has radically altered the planning agenda. The revisions to Planning Policy Guidance Notes on "Town Centres and Retail Development", "Transport" and "Renewable Energy", to name but three, have had a significant bearing on local authorities' planning policies. But none of these have created as much angst for planners as the statements and papers of the previous decade. The introduction of the pro-development plans legislation, the Planning and Compensation Act 1991, has been welcomed by planners, and once plans are in place for the whole of the country, Britain will have a comparatively stable planning framework, epitomizing Whitehall's desire for a coherent planning system from the national planning guidelines down to the locally determined development plans, with a publicly accountable development control system meeting performance targets.

However, there are three particular areas that can be identified which possess a unique Major administration stamp. First, the review of local government, the single most important issue that will have a direct effect on statutory planning policy, was certainly conceived by the Major government, although at the time of writing (March 1995) the future of the process remains uncertain. Secondly, and more distinctly for the government and Mr Major himself, was the launch of the Citizen's Charter (HM Government 1991), which was the Prime Minister's personal initiative. The charter, with its concern for performance indicators, monitoring, competition and value for money in the public sector, has had a direct effect on planning, especially the development control function. The third area of planning transition is with environmental politics, although a cynic might argue that the environmental planning changes that are affecting the statutory planning process in Britain originate from Europe and international treaties.

British planning policy in transition

The planning policy system now in operation is currently very different to that operating just a few years ago. Indeed, John Major's period as Prime Minister has been accompanied by frenzied changes to the statutory planning framework, to relations between central government and local government, and to the performance of the planning process as a public sector service.

These changes have not only focused on the implementation of new structures, but also on the improvement of existing structures and relationships that have affected each and every individual planning service operated by both Whitehall and the town hall. Central government planning policy has shifted to some extent on individual substantive areas, for example in relation to retailing policy, to transport and the environment, which in turn have had an effects on local authorities' actions as the formulators of development plans for the local area. As Planning Policy Guidance Notes have been released covering those areas currently of concern to planning practice, the government has also made efforts to ensure the quality and consistency of its guidance is improved further, as Matthew Quinn stresses in Chapter 2. Although commentators and official reports have made criticisms of PPGs for their ambiguous guidance and lack of clarity (see, for example, Tewdwr-Jones 1994b, House of Commons Environment Committee 1994, House of Commons Welsh Affairs Committee 1993), there is widespread belief in practice that PPGs provide a useful role in guiding the actions of local planning authorities and are a vast improvement on the government planning documents previously released. However, questions still remain on the consistency of the series and on their status compared to other planning policies.

The Regional Planning Guidance Notes implemented by the county councils across the country have also made an impact into the formulation of structure plans, and the local authorities in each region have progressed their own RPG exercises autonomously. Given that all regions of England have recently seen an RPG note in place, questions now arise as to the effectiveness of the exercises and whether procedures and policies can be improved for their revision. In Chapter 3, Chris Offord and Jeremy Alden outline the history of regional planning guidance since the 1989 White Paper and assess its impact by considering how the RPG exercise was established in the northern region of Britain.

Structure plans and the future of strategic policy have always occupied a central role in the statutory planning policy framework to ensure consistency and the future social and economic demands of subregions are met. Although strategic policies can only be developed in terms of physical land use, local authorities are particularly concerned to ensure that strategic policies following any local government reorganization are integral to the planning policy process and can be developed as a co-ordinating mechanism for the successful economic regeneration of regions. The strategic policy exercise in Wales has been developed separately from that for England, and the principality's unique existence as both a country and a region has led to a close relationship between central government and the Welsh local authorities, as Richard Jarvis outlines in Chapter 4. This Welsh strategic policy element is of particular importance at the present time given the imminent establishment of a unitary local government structure. Similarly,

Ted Kitchen outlines in Chapter 8 how Manchester City Council has skilfully utilized strategic policy to regenerate the old industrial region of the North West. In particular he illustrates how strategic policy has provided a focus for the city's entrepreneurial bid to host both the Olympic and the Commonwealth Games.

The improved development plan procedures introduced by the Planning and Compensation Act 1991 has affected the work of district planning authorities markedly, notably on the preparation for district-wide local plans and on the plan-led development control process. Associated with the government's requirements for quality, customer care and financial and managerial pruning, the new planning process within the districts has led to changes to local planning authorities' procedures and to new methods of working. Alan Jones considers the extent to which the planning policy process has been affected by these changes in Chapter 5, by illustrating recent developments within his own district authority, Newbury.

The picture of planning policy and relationships in Scotland has been one of consensus, even during the Thatcher years. The country has taken an independent line on planning over the past 20 years, by enacting separate legislation covering local government structures and the planning system. Scotland has also benefited from the integrated role provided by Scottish Enterprise and the Scottish Development Agency towards land-use planning. As Keith Hayton discusses in Chapter 6, the tri-partite relationship between central government, local government and the private sector has fostered a very different planning policy system to that operating south of the border. To what extent can the Scottish system provide us with good examples and ideas for cross-policy transfer, and how will local government reorganization in Scotland affect these relationships?

The reorganization of local government in England and Wales has also been at the forefront of discussions regarding the future of planning policy. To many, the variety of different local government structures recommended by the Local Government Commission have been a fiasco. What role will planning policy take after reorganization, and how will a mixed planning policy process operate within the same country? We are likely to witness the emergence of new styles of development plans and a modified role for strategic policy guidance. What effect will this have on the role of planning departments, and how will changing structural frameworks affect planning policy relationships between different levels of government? John Clotworthy and Neil Harris consider these questions in Chapter 7 by assessing the reorganization processes in both Wales and the South West of England, illustrating the reactions of local people and policy planners to the different recommendations of the Welsh Office and the Local Government Commission.

Turning attention away from the structural statutory framework for land-use planning policy in Britain and on to more transient areas of policy concern, it is possible to identify a range of matters that will affect the planning policy process over the next few years. Although none of these issues could be described as substantive land-use policy concerns, they are subjects that will affect the parameters of the planning system.

The legal requirements introduced by the new legislation have caused a great deal of ambiguity, none more so than the plan-led clause or "Section 54A". Section 54A introduced a changed decision-making process on the part of local authorities, and has also highlighted questions on the future role and status of different policy documents and relations between different levels of government. The uncertainty existing has also raised important questions on the relationship between planning law and planning policy. Ian Gatenby and Christopher Williams assess the legal effects of recent changes to the statutory policy framework in Chapter 9 and consider how local authorities should react to the new requirements. They illustrate the distinction between planning law on the one hand and planning policy on the other, the differences that exist and the problems these differences cause for planning decision-makers.

The years since 1990 have also seen the increased scrutiny of local authorities' roles as policy-makers and decision-takers in the planning system, with the introduction of "planning charters" and quality performance indicators. These changes have had a direct effect on the way local government politicians and professional officers conduct planning policy business. Recent "problem cases" around Britain and the issuing of official reports have added to an unfair portrayal of this part of the planning system as being either corrupt or else dominated by sleaze, as Sue Essex points out in Chapter 10. The implementation of effective planning policies by local government actors is now, more than ever, under close scrutiny by the government, the Audit Commission and the local government ombudsman.

Planners also need to consider the ways local planning authorities incorporate the "public" in planning decisions and in the policy process in particular. Huw Thomas outlines in Chapter 11 methods through which the public are encouraged to participate in planning in their local communities. Is the current statutory planning process limiting the opportunities for community involvement? With new practices being developed in the field of participation, there are increasing opportunities for planners to learn new methods of working, and to base their actions on truly democratic support.

In Chapter 12, Andy Thornley considers how the market has been affected by the changes to the planning system since Mrs Thatcher's departure. In particular, he questions the political relationship as it now exists between the government, local authorities and the private sector. If the new policy system has created greater local choice, does this represent a "thawing out" of Thatcherism towards planning or the emergence of a stable planning structure?

One of the main areas in which statutory planning policies have altered significantly during the Major administration is in the area of environmental planning, as Kevin Bishop highlights in Chapter 13. In particular, he questions the extent to which the government has been prepared to espouse sustainability while encouraging and supporting non-sustainable development projects involving trade and industry, energy and transport. This contradiction, which is omnipresent as a state political choice, is apparent at the global level and at the local level, and it relates just as much to the future of the countryside as it does to the need to reduce global warming. Local authorities are directly concerned with implementing environmentally friendly policies, and the planning policy system is the principal means through which this can be achieved. The transition to a green policy system is one of the most pressing concerns for statutory planning in the immediate future. Some local planning authorities are taking the opportunity to reassess their statutory planning policies and truly integrate the environmental agenda in their policy and decision-making requirements.

Increasingly, planning as a state activity to co-ordinate the attraction of resources and regional funding is being by-passed in some areas of the country in favour of European structural funds. With political uncertainty existing in the British government towards increasing European powers, to what extent are local authorities and developers in Britain utilizing these opportunities to progress major development projects and attract investment to revitalize run-down areas? In Chapter 14 Lyn Davies assesses the history of the influence Europe has had on planning in Britain and, since 1992, views a greater interest in the concept of spatial planning in member states, an interest that is bound to increase and demonstrably affect the policies and practice of planning in Britain.

Within this introductory chapter some of the principal changes to the planning policy system have been briefly reviewed. The chapters that follow are devoted to considering in greater detail the current and possible future state of planning policy in Britain.

PART ONE

The statutory planning policy framework

CHAPTER 2

Central government planning policy

Matthew J. Quinn

This chapter explores the role of central government policy in the operation of the planning system in England and Wales. It describes the main function of guidance as to promote consistency and quality in the operation of the system and to ensure that decisions contribute positively to national objectives while retaining their essentially local character.

The chapter explores the key direction of current policy, most notably its role in translating the principles of sustainable development into development plans and, in turn, decisions. The chapter goes on to discuss the preparation of guidance and to debate criticism of its content and operation. It concludes that, although there is scope for improvement, the ability to accommodate national goals within a locally operated system through national guidance is an essential strength of planning in Britain and will stand the system in good stead for present and future challenges.

Introduction

In many countries there would be little point in a chapter on central government planning policy. Often, physical planning will be restricted to regional or local level, with limited co-ordination or sense of wider objectives. The driving force for planning in such circumstances is competition between local authorities to increase the local tax base by attracting development. The resulting approach as often as not comprises strict control over detailed design of buildings and physical separation of activities, with little or no influence over broad spatial patterns.

It can be tempting at times to criticize national guidance as a denial of the responsibility vested by statute in local authorities for the day-to-day operation of the planning system. But individual decisions can have impacts far wider than their local areas. They can harm nationally or internationally important nature sites. They can create demand for transport over large areas. They can prevent or deter important investment. They can undermine the proper functioning of the system and reduce people's faith in its operation.

National concerns have a legitimate place in local decision-making. To deny national issues is to a real extent to deny the potential importance of land-use planning for the way we live. National issues need to be reflected in local decisions and, if they could not be, the system as a whole would be the poorer.

The planning system in England, Scotland and Wales has always given a clear role for central guidance. This chapter explores the current role of that guidance and the extent to which it is meeting its objectives.

Why central guidance?

A local system

Individual local planning authorities are charged by law with responsibility for drawing up development plans for their area and for making planning decisions, through the refusal or granting in full, or subject to conditions of planning permission for development. Although there are reserve powers for the relevant Secretary of State to take individual planning decisions, to direct changes to plans, and even to make plans in part or in their entirety, these are very rarely exercised. Some planning applications are granted by the relevant Secretary of State or by independent planning inspectors on appeal against the local planning authority's decision, or after its failure to decide an application. But even allowing for these decisions, over 95 per cent of planning permissions are given by local planning authorities.

The role of guidance

Within the context of a very locally based system of decision-making, central guidance serves two main functions:
- to ensure national concerns (for example, for the environment or for key elements of national infrastructure) are properly pursued or defended in local decisions, and
- to promote consistency and quality in practice and decision-making.

These are limited and legitimate aims. Without a form of common guidance, some individual local decisions might undermine national aims or commitments, especially those towards the environment, housing or the economy. Much guidance is focused on providing for these national needs:
- maintaining an adequate supply of employment land to assist national competitiveness and avoid excessive costs to UK industry

17

- maintaining an adequate supply of housing land to provide homes for people across the country at reasonable cost
- promoting more sustainable development to contribute to the nation's international commitments, and avoiding damage to our precious natural resources.

The quality of decisions is central to the effectiveness of the system as a whole. People legitimately expect clarity, fairness, flexibility, professionalism and avoidance of bias or favour. Securing these goals is a legitimate concern of government if the system is to meet its aims in a cost-effective manner and command respect.

Avoiding inconsistency in decisions or practice is also a key concern. Inconsistency can not only undermine overall objectives but can be costly and confusing for both developers and the public. It can lead to one authority's measures being undermined by action in a neighbouring authority. Problems can be shunted from one area to another rather than tackled by the authority to which they are most relevant. Ultimately, inconsistency and lack of quality in decisions can risk bringing the whole system into disrepute.

A clear set of national policy guidelines should be in the interest of all users of the system:

- they should ensure that everyone knows what is expected of them and what is likely to be permissible, and
- they should enable decisions to be taken at the local level while still ensuring that national concerns are reflected.

The existence of central guidance does not change the fact that the essence of the system lies at local government level and in the locally prepared development plans. It is for local planning authorities to determine how best their areas should be developed in the light of national guidance and local concerns, following public consultation. This remains a genuinely locally based system. That it has remained so stems in no small part from its ability to reflect effectively the concerns of the different interested parties, including central government.

National guidance and the planning system

National planning policy for England and Wales has been delivered in several forms over the years, but the bulk is now found in the Planning Policy Guidance Note series (the PPGs) (compare the situation in Scotland with NPPGs; see Keith Hayton's discussion in Ch. 6). PPGs were introduced in 1988 to provide a concise and readily accessible source of guidance to replace the various government Circulars that until then had been the main vehicle for advice. Circulars are still used but are generally confined to more technical or administrative issues. There is a separate series of minerals planning guidance notes (MPGs).

National government also issues regional and strategic guidance to guide development in specific areas (see Ch. 3 for a discussion of regional planning).

Guidance and plans

National, regional and strategic guidance must by law be taken into account by local planning authorities when they are preparing their development plans, which set out the policies for development over the coming years in their areas.

Since changes to the primary legislation (Town and Country Planning Act 1990) introduced by the Planning and Compensation Act in 1991, development plans (the structure plan at county level; the local plan – which must be in general conformity with the structure plan – at district level; and the two-part unitary development plan covering both strategic and local issues in metropolitan boroughs) are now the primary consideration in determining applications for planning permission. Decisions must now accord with the plan unless there are overriding reasons to the contrary. This has been rightly dubbed the "plan-led system". In this way, the plan is the main determinant of decisions. Because national guidance is a major influence on plans, it thereby has a major indirect effect on individual decisions.

National government has the opportunity to comment on plans in preparation to ensure that they are consistent with national policy. This helps to avoid confusing clashes between local and national policy. Comments will also be made on the quality of plans. Where necessary, central government will make formal objections to policies, and ultimately it can direct modification to a plan before it can finally be adopted. This role has been increasingly actively pursued since the introduction of the new legislation.

Objections to local plans or unitary development plans will be considered at a local inquiry by an independent inspector whose task is to report to the local planning authority on the plan. For the more strategic county structure plan, which until 1992 had to be formally approved by the relevant Secretary of State, an independent panel will consider views on the plan in an Examination in Public and offer advice to the authority. The objections made by central government to local plans are varied, but the principal objections relate to the function of national involvement in planning:

- the clarity of the wording of plans (quality)
- conflict with individual national policies (consistency).

Guidance and individual decisions

National guidance has no statutory role in individual decisions beyond its influence on the development plan, but it has developed a strong role in case law. The Courts have held that the government's statements of planning policy are material considerations that must be taken into account, where relevant in decisions on planning applications.

In addition to this backing in common law, the existence of a right of appeal for an aggrieved applicant against the decision of a local planning authority helps to ensure a degree of consistency and conformity with both local plan policy and

19

national guidance. Planning inspectors in appeals will take decisions based on the provisions of the local development plan, informed by relevant national guidance and other material considerations raised by the parties to the appeal.

Likewise, the existence of a legal requirement for notification of proposed local decisions that do not accord with the adopted development plan provides the relevant Secretary of State with the opportunity to take the decision away from the local planning authority. It must then be judged in the same statutory context against the plan and national policy framework.

Together, these legal checks ensure that the national guidance is properly taken into account in the production of structure and local plans and in individual decisions.

The current policy direction: sustainable development

The national commitment to sustainable development can only be properly pursued if the key principles are consistently applied at a local level. This is not possible with ad hoc decision-making. It demands an overall and spatial approach to planning that reflects both national and local aims, so that the implications of individual development for the whole are fully weighed.

This common inheritance

The present direction of UK Government planning policy traces its origins to the Environment White Paper, *This common inheritance* in 1990 (HM Government 1990). *This common inheritance* was the UK's first comprehensive environmental policy statement. It committed the government to pursue the principles of sustainable development as set out by the Brundtland Commission for the United Nations.

The 1990 strategy set out a key role for land-use planning to contribute to sustainable development objectives. The planning system recurs throughout the strategy as a tool for implementing sustainable development.

Sustainable development

Sustainable development is a much abused term, but at its heart, sustainable development is about:
- conserving natural resources
- enabling development and economic growth to take place in ways that preserve or enhance the environment overall, and
- maintaining quality and opportunity for future generations.

These objectives demand the effective and positive management of change, promoting economic development and a better environment.

The planning system embraces all these aims. It has been concerned since its inception with balancing environmental and economic issues when making individual decisions. It has also always been concerned with looking to the future and making long-term strategic decisions about the release of land for development. Most important of all perhaps, it has done all of these in the context of a descending hierarchy of strategic objectives set by the different tiers of government. The environmental slogan "think globally, act locally" seems made for the tiered operation of the planning system.

Reviewing national policy

The 1990 strategy committed the government to review the first series of national Planning Policy Guidance to ensure that it contributed to the goal of more sustainable development patterns. All of the original guidance notes have now been reviewed and the process of revision has been completed in England with the publication of a revised PPG2 on green belts (DoE 1995). Table 2.1 sets out the process of review for the PPG series in England and Wales.

Table 2.1   Process of review for the Planning Policy Guidance Notes.

PPG		90	91	92	93	94	95
1	General policies and principles			3			
2	Green belts						3
3	Housing			3			
4	Industrial & commercial development and small firms			3			
5	Simplified planning zones			3			
6	Town centres and retail developments				3		
7	Countryside and the rural economy			3			
8	Telecommunications			3			
9	Nature conservation					3	
12	Development plans and regional planning guidance			3			
13	Transport					3	
14	Development of unstable land	3					
15	Planning and the historic environment					3	
16	Archaeology and planning	3					
17	Sport and recreation		3				
18	Enforcing planning control		3				
19	Outdoor advertisement control			3			
20	Coastal planning			3			
21	Tourism			3			
22	Renewable energy				3		
23	Planning & pollution control					3	
24	Noise					3	

3 = up to date

21

Formulating guidance

The original batch of Planning Policy Guidance Notes were issued as a synopsis of the advice previously contained in government Circulars in 1987. Subsequent revisions have been subject to an extensive consultative process.

A typical planning policy guidance note now goes through six public stages:
- research, establishing the need for new guidance or the success of existing guidance judged against the criterion of sustainable development
- consultation, seeking views on a draft revision to the guidance and issued usually alongside the research
- revision and publication of the guidance in the light of consultation
- dissemination of the revised approach using seminars and conferences
- a good practice guide, promoting consistency and best practice for local authorities; and
- further research and monitoring, to see how the policies are being applied and to test their impacts.

In addition to this public work, PPGs must also be agreed by the interested government departments before they can be issued for consultation or in final form. They thus reflect the collective view of government, although most will only be under the signature of one or two Secretaries of State.

Research

Most recent PPGs have been informed by specific policy research. This seeks to identify any problems with the existing guidance or to identify needs for additional advice. The Department of the Environment planning research programme is some £1 million per annum and is focused on addressing practical and policy concerns. Among recent research reports are:
- *The effectiveness of green belts* (DoE 1993g), a study on the effectiveness of green belts and their relationship to sustainable development principles which informed the revision of PPG2
- *Reducing transport emissions through planning* (DoE 1993e), carried out by ECOTEC for the Department of the Environment and the Department of Transport and published by HMSO in April 1993 – a study of the relationship between land-use patterns and transport demand which informed the preparation of the draft PPG13
- *Alternative development patterns: new settlements* (DoE 1992a), prepared by University of Reading and David Lock Associates, which informed the guidance on settlements contained in PPG3 (DoE 1992e) and PPG13 (DoE/DoT 1994).
- *The potential economic effects of PPG13*, carried out by Land Use Consultants and Roger Tym for DoE and DoT to inform the revision of draft PPG13 in 1993/4 and to be published early in 1995.

Current work that may inform future guidance includes:
- a study of the effectiveness of PPG7 *The countryside and rural economy* on rural development, and
- a study of the housing capacities of urban areas.

In order to ensure that the guidance is reflecting the concerns of practitioners, relevant developers and local authority representatives are involved both in advising on the topics for research and in steering or commenting on the progress of individual research projects. This ensures that there is an opportunity to shape the work, which will inform future guidance.

The final product is made public, usually through publication by HMSO. It is generally published alongside the draft PPG in order to inform discussion of the consultation draft of the revised guidance; or it may be published in advance and itself be the subject of comment and consultation to inform the direction of the policy response.

Consultation

All significant new or revised guidance is issued for public consultation. The recent focus has been to ensure that this is not just a paper exercise. To achieve this more informed debate typically involves not just the issuing of the draft text but also discussion and seminars with interested groups and the active involvement of the local authority and professional associations.

PPG13 provides a good example of recent experience. This benefited from over 800 written comments that were collated and discussed before revisions could be made. In addition, over a dozen seminars and discussion groups were held. Some of these were organized by the Department of the Environment, but most were organized with the Department's participation and support by professional bodies such as the Royal Town Planning Institute and the Institution of Civil Engineers, or by planning practices whose clients had an interest in the topic. Together, these meetings helped to ensure that all sides fully understood the issues involved and the reasons behind decisions or comments.

Revision and publication

From consultation draft to final PPG can take over a year. Half of this time may be taken up with consultation, but the remainder is occupied by the task of reflecting the views expressed in consultation and seeking agreement to the necessary changes. The full results of consultation are always reported to ministers who then determine what changes are needed from the consultation draft. There is usually no secondary consultation, although, when there are long delays in taking forward guidance or very substantive changes, this may sometimes prove of benefit.

23

Dissemination

The government has come some way from the days when guidance was issued in Circulars, and local authorities were left to make of it what they could. The issuing of the final guidance is now accompanied by seminars and presentations explaining its significance and discussing the issues it raises with practitioners.

Seminars not only help practitioners to come to grips with the new policy but also serve to point up problems with the new guidance and hence the need for any additional advice, explanation or support for implementation. They have become an essential part of the PPG process.

A successful series of regional seminars has been held in England with the RTPI to discuss a succession of new planning policy guidance shortly after its publication.

Good practice

PPGs may be followed by a fuller good practice guide, offering examples of the way in which the policies have been or can be implemented.

PPG12 on the development plan system has now been accompanied by two good practice guides: one on development plan preparation itself (DoE 1992c) and one on the environmental appraisal of plans (DoE 1993b). These have formed part of a common house series.

PPG6, *Town centres and retail development* (DoE/WO 1993) has been supplemented by the publication of *Vital and viable town centres* (DoE 1994h), a guide to town centre success by URBED for the Department of the Environment. PPG13 will benefit from its own good practice guide in the course of 1995. These two documents are more promotional and have a wider potential audience than planning professionals and so are in a more highly designed and illustrated format. Professional and representative and governmental bodies have also prepared their own guidance, often with the support and assistance of the Department of the Environment in order to inform the work of their members.

None of these guides represent policy or have a statutory status, but they can be very helpful in promoting consistency, quality and understanding in the delivery of planning services.

Further research and monitoring

A PPG is not there for its own sake. It exists to produce an outcome, so monitoring of its implementation is vital. This has two aspects: monitoring the implementation itself to see whether it is happening, and looking at the effects of implementation to see whether they are those intended.

Current research and monitoring includes a study of PPG13's impact on plans and decisions and a broad look at developing key indicators for the overall performance of the system in delivering land-use objectives.

Criticisms of the PPGs

The PPGs were intended to offer a clear, concise and readily available source of guidance. They have since been charged with setting a clear framework for promoting sustainable development in the UK. This is a tall order and it is hardly surprising if there are criticisms:
- lack of clarity in the expression of objectives
- set out conflicting objectives without resolving them
- leave unresolved conflicts and inconsistencies between different PPGs
- are too lengthy and do not distinguish policies and discussion clearly enough
- do not cover a consistent range of topics
- present a moving target as a result of constant revisions
- lack a clear relationship to other government programmes, and
- are subject to amendment through ministerial statements.

Clarity

One aim of the PPG series is to provide clear and accessible advice. Clarity avoids unnecessary debate and allows all parties to be sure of their ground. It thereby reduces uncertainty and potential costs. A fudged or ambiguous statement is likely to lead to the opposite. Developers will generally say that they dislike uncertainty more than they dislike clear advice, even if that advice means they have to rethink their approach. In practice, developers may seek to steel a march over rivals by exploiting the wording of policy to improve their case.

Under very close examination, not all PPGs seem as clearly expressed as decision-takers might sometimes wish. PPGs are policy statements, with all the subtlety and balance that entails, but they are often examined at public inquiry with forensic zeal as if they were some form of contract. This is an examination that they often cannot stand.

The fault for the apparent uncertainty of PPGs may lie less with the PPG than with the advocate's desire to look at the detailed expression of policy rather than its intent (or indeed at the intent rather than the wording), but it does suggest that those of us who draft PPGs may have to pay more attention than has sometimes been the case in the past to the way in which a text may be exploited.

Lack of clarity should not be confused with the proper expression of complex and multiple objectives. It is the nature of planning for there always to be competing priorities to weigh in the balance and it is right that PPGs should set these out.

25

Conflict

When there are a wide range of conflicting objectives to balance, some would like to see the PPGs setting out how to do that balancing act.

Each PPG covers a separate topic and the balance between potentially conflicting objectives is left to the interpretation of those making decisions. This seems perfectly proper. If national guidance were to set out a hierarchy of the importance of different issues, there would be very little left for the system to undertake. Of course, each case or area will require a different weight to be placed on those different priorities, depending on the local priorities and the national objectives. Other than those actions required by law, the system is essentially discretionary – shades of grey rather than black and white.

The PPGs have been revised over several years. This inevitably means that the exact wording or policy emphasis of PPGs may not be entirely consistent. Although more might be done to relate PPGs and to ensure they are as up-to-date and consistent as possible, policy development and the need to keep advice fresh inevitably means that there will be some differences.

Length and expression of policy

It is not always easy to pick out key policy points from PPGs or determine the weight to be attached to them. There is little point in having policy if it is unclear. In recent PPGs an attempt has been made to draw attention to the key objectives of the guidance and to distinguish new policy emphasis by setting out the key aims on the opening page and making greater use of bullet points.

PPGs are also perceived as becoming longer and a little more discursive. There may be several reasons for this:

- new policies can require more explanation than the continuation of existing policies
- improved consultation leads to more points needing to be addressed
- sustainable development is a more complex subject to convey than were the previous objectives
- the creation of the PPG series leads to expectations of comprehensive coverage of issues.

In principle, PPGs could simply set out overall aims on a page or two and leave the rest to local planning authorities. There is some attraction to this "bullet point" approach, but there are risks too. It might for example result in the need for subsidiary guidance to ensure consistency and effective implementation. It might also risk giving too much weight to the fewer words offered. One of the shortest Circulars ever issued was Circular 14/85, which in a page and a half stressed the presumption in favour of development and the importance of economic growth and then suggested that little weight should be given to an out of date development plan (DOE 1985). Rightly or wrongly, that Circular, which preceded the legislation introducing the plan-led system by some six years, was widely viewed as the cause of a substantial increase in the number of planning appeals and in the overturning of local decisions.

Coverage

Many people would like to see a PPG on their topic. PPGs are understandably seen as the premier league of advice, with Circulars at best struggling for promotion. Among current PPGs:

- there are two on general principles and practice (PPG1 and PPG12)
- the core PPGs are on key things for which the planning system should provide, such as housing (PPG3), retailing (PPG6), industry and commerce (PPG4)
- there are others about what the system should protect, such as PPG9 on nature conservation, PPG2 on green belts, PPG15 on heritage, and PPG24 on noise
- there are others on cross-cutting themes such as transport (PPG13)
- the remainder cover some quite technical topics such as telecommunications, renewable energy and pollution control.

Much of the material in the more technical PPGs is less about policy than practice. This does not make it any less useful. Indeed, in areas that the average local planning authority comes across rarely, it is an important aid to quality and consistency of procedure and decision-making.

Moving target

The planning system in England and Wales has always produced its moving targets. Because it is based on a hierarchy of policy, there is always the danger that one part of the system is more advanced or delayed than another, with local plans prepared ahead of revised structure plans, and national policy rarely coming out at the right time for everyone. This has been exacerbated by the near-simultaneous commitment to revising the national policy guidance at the same time as committing local planning authorities to prepare local plans to be in place by the end of 1996.

Change is disruptive for everyone in a system. The goal for the next few years is to achieve a degree of consistency and to stick with the published policy so far as that is sensible in the light of objectives and understanding of the issues. Research and monitoring continue and the logic of the current iterative approach is that revisions will occur. This simply needs to be tempered by the realism that policy often has to settle down to be effective. The emphasis on sustainable development (which commands all-party support) should ensure a higher degree of continuity than has sometimes been the case in the past.

27

Relation to other programmes

Planning can only set the framework for development and help to facilitate it. Other measures may be necessary to deliver the objectives. Since the move to the plan-led system, greater emphasis has been placed on bringing other activities together with planning objectives. There should be no inconsistency between government programmes and the plan-led system, because all the programmes must work within the local planning framework. If the framework is effective, it should help to channel activity and support into those areas that will help to see it implemented.

This is true across a range of activities:

- local authority transport programmes should flow from their development plan policies
- economic and housing strategies should also be consistent with plans and so funding in these areas should support plan aims
- regeneration agencies such as English Partnerships are charged with working within the development plan framework

Achieving consistency in these areas is primarily the task of the local authorities that are responsible for developing the different strategies and bids. These will generally be the same authority that prepares the local plan.

Inevitably, there will sometimes be the perception that one arm of government is pursuing policies that can make the planning task more difficult. Some changes – most notably the increasing privatization and deregulation of services – do make the planning task different from that of previous years. That does not make them inconsistent, it simply means that planning has to address the challenges of finding new approaches to achieving objectives.

Ministerial announcements

Ministerial announcements have long served as a means of updating or clarifying published guidance. Although it can make policy less accessible, it is an essential tool to provide for rapid response to emerging issues. Such statements will generally be incorporated into published guidance at an early opportunity to ensure that they are widely known.

Testing success

In 1994, the Department of the Environment decided to commission research to assess how successful the PPGs were in meeting their objectives.

Land Use Consultants carried out the research in three main stages:

- an initial questionnaire to all local planning authorities seeking their views

on PPGs in general and the value of each PPG in particular
- detailed interviews with practitioners, including central government departments
- detailed interviews with selected authorities plus a seminar with elected members.

The research will report later in 1995, but its main general findings were:
- a surprisingly high degree of support for the effectiveness and clarity of the PPG series among planning officers, with some 60% rating them very highly on those counts
- a fairly predictable variation in the use made of the different PPGs, mainly depending on their date of issue and the likelihood of encountering the topic
- a lack of penetration by the PPGs beyond the planning professionals, with few elected members having read one and fewer still members of the public, and
- a feeling among professionals that more could be done to meet the objectives of sustainable development, although a recognition that a useful start had been made.

The broad picture then is one of encouraging success in achieving consistency and quality for the planning professionals, a reasonable start on the sustainable development objectives but less success, perhaps inevitably, in one of the original 1987 objectives of the PPG series – making them accessible to the general public.

Conclusion

The planning system's survival, in much the same basic form as that in which it was created in the 1940s, owes much to its inherent flexibility and the wide respect that it commands. That flexibility and respect in turn rest in the structured role given to each participant in the system: central and local government, the local inhabitant, the developer. Resolving the potentially conflicting interests of these different groups within the same system is both the constant challenge and, I believe, the greatest strength of planning in Britain. With the plan-led system and the goal of sustainable development, the planning system is starting a new and very healthy era. The planning system cannot and will not deliver everything, but we all have the right to expect it to deliver as much as it can to make life a little better for us all now and in the future.

29

CHAPTER 3

Regional planning guidance

Jeremy Alden & Chris Offord

The rise of regional planning in Britain

Although the 1980s saw many debates on the north/south divide and regional problems in this country, the focus of planning policies was largely upon the inner city. The solution to regional problems in the 1980s was seen by the government as being provided increasingly via the market mechanism. However, in the 1990s, regional issues and the need for regional-strategic planning guidance has emerged at the top of the planning agenda for several reasons. These have included increasing disparities both between and within regions: inflationary pressures, green issues and development pressures in the southern half of Britain; the impact of the 1992 European Community Single Market and opening of the Channel Tunnel in 1994; and the need for strategic thinking and solutions to several regional questions, which have usually involved large-scale investment projects.

One of the main features of regional planning in this country until the 1990s had been its weak institutional framework within the statutory planning system. This situation has surprised many observers of this country's planning system. As Minay (1992) has noted, regional planning has never quite achieved the importance in our country's planning practice that its attention in academic textbooks and advocacy by many influential writers might suggest. It is certainly worth remembering that regionalism is not a new idea of the 1990s, nor indeed of the 1960s and 1970s, which saw the publication of several strategic plans for specific regions (e.g. 1970 Strategic Plan for the South East, or 1977 Strategic Plan for the Northern Region). It is rather a revival of interest from that shown in the first decade of this century. The need for a regional approach to government and decision-making at both central and local levels was recognized and forcibly argued by the work of the Fabian Society (1904), Geddes' *Cities in evolution* (1915), Fawcett's *Provinces of England* (1916), G. D. H. Cole's *The future of local government* (1921) and, of course, the pioneering work of Patrick Abercrombie in the preparation of many city–regional development plans. It is worth noting here that 1994 saw the fiftieth anniversary of one of this country's most famous development plans, namely the Greater London Development Plan of 1944. It is appropriate that the fiftieth anniversary memorial lecture for Patrick Abercrombie was given by Professor Peter Hall in Liverpool in December 1994 to mark the contribution of one of this country's most influential urban–regional planners.

It should also not be forgotten that this country contains some of the earliest examples of regional plan preparation in the world. Planners in this country have inherited a substantial legacy of regional planning. Any review of the world's most famous and earliest regional plans would include a reference to the 1921 South Wales Regional Survey, widely recognized as the first serious attempt at regional planning in this country. The South Wales Regional Survey Committee, of which Patrick Abercrombie was a member, had the task of preparing a strategy for the distribution and location of housing in the South Wales region, having regard to the region's future development. Since the 1920s, major regional planning initiatives seem to have occurred in 20-year cycles, with the preparation of city–regional development plans in the 1940s, regional plans and White Papers for specific regions in the 1960s, and then the official encouragement and recognition given to regional planning in the latter 1980s, as illustrated by the 1986 Green Paper, *The future of development plans* (DOE/WO 1986) and the subsequent White Paper, *The future of development plans* in 1989 (HM Government 1989).

Developing regional planning guidance in the 1980s

The 1986 Green Paper on *The future of development plans* stressed that development plans were an essential part of a national planning system since they provided the framework for development control. They were also seen as an effective means of co-ordinating the needs of development and the interests of conservation. In considering possible changes to improve the system, the government's objectives were to cut out the unnecessary and wasteful overlap between county and district functions in plan preparation, reduce the need for detailed ministerial supervision, simplify the form and content of development plans, and speed up the procedures for preparing and adopting them. The 1986 paper outlined proposed changes in England and Wales in the arrangements for planning at regional, county and district levels. The main change was the introduction of stronger regional guidance as an integral element of the statutory planning system. Regional planning was no longer to be purely advisory: it was to be given a statutory status. The paper recommended that there should be a wider coverage of regional or subregional strategic guidance issued by the Secretary of State after consultation with local authorities in the area (ibid.: paras 40–44).

Following the abolition of the Greater London Council and the metropolitan county councils in 1986, the Government envisaged arrangements that enabled

31

local planning authorities in those areas to work together to advise the Secretary of State on the need for strategic guidance to assist them in the preparation of their Unitary Development Plans. Outside the metropolitan areas and the South East of England, which had established SERPLAN (the South East Regional Planning Conference), the Green Paper noted several examples of local planning authorities co-operating to consider strategic issues affecting their areas. The government welcomed local authorities elsewhere in the country making similar arrangements.

However, the Green Paper emphasized that any such arrangements would not represent a formalized regional structure, nor would there be a return to the type of large-scale regional planning attempted in the 1960s and 1970s.

The White Paper, *The future of development plans*, issued in January 1989, set out the government's proposals for the reform of the development plan system, following feedback from the 1986 Green Paper. The objectives of the White Paper proposals were to provide a clear policy framework for local planning decisions, to simplify and speed up the preparation and review of plans, and to define the responsibilities of counties and districts more clearly. The government stated in the White Paper that it was "committed to maintaining an effective planning system that meets both the needs of development and the interest of conservation". (HM Government 1989: para. 2).

The government intended to achieve its planning objectives through a five-pronged approach, identified in paragraph 4 of the White Paper:

- publishing national guidance on planning policies (already well advanced through its Planning Policy Guidance Notes and Minerals Planning Guidance Notes)
- providing regional planning guidance where necessary to assist in the preparation of new statements of County Planning Policies and District Development Plans (as had been published in PPGs 9, 10 and 11 (DoE 1988a, 1988c, 1988b))
- introducing a single tier of District Development Plans to replace the present two-tier system of structure and local plans
- simplifying procedures while continuing to provide for effective public participation in plan preparation
- reducing the need for ministerial authorization and intervention.

By May 1990, the government had decided not to replace structure plans with the county policy statements suggested a year earlier, but the momentum for regional planning guidance gained in strength, particularly in relation to the need for strategic and visionary aspects of the plan process.

The "new system" for planning was presented in Part 2 of the White Paper. Paragraphs 2.5–2.8 covered regional planning guidance in England, and paragraph 2.9 guidance in Wales.

The White Paper noted that the Secretary of State for the Environment had already published guidance for some regions. For example, regional guidance was issued in July 1986 following consultation with SERPLAN, and had been reproduced in PPG9. The White Paper confirmed that future guidance would be published in the PPG series.

The White Paper did not require all local authorities to co-operate and produce regional strategies. In paragraph 2.7 of the White Paper it stated that:

> such arrangements may not be needed in all areas but local authorities are free to take the initiative in setting up similar arrangements where there are matters that can usefully be addressed on a regional or subregional basis.

However, the role of regional planning guidance was given some "force" following the statement in paragraph 2.8, that:

> where guidance is issued by the Secretary of State, the counties must have regard to it in preparing their statements of county planning policies and the districts in preparing their development plans; both the statements and development plans must be consistent with any relevant national and regional planning guidance.

In Part 5 of the White Paper (i.e. Summary and Conclusion), the first main proposal to be identified was the wider coverage of regional planning guidance, issued by the Secretaries of State after consultation with the local planning authorities in the area.

By the end of the 1980s, regional planning had become firmly established as an integral element of the "new system" for planning for England and Wales.

Regional guidance within PPG15 and PPG12

In May 1990, the Department of the Environment published PPG15, *Regional planning guidance, structure plans and the content of development plans* (DOE 1990). This was followed by PPG15 (Wales) in October 1990 with a slightly different title, *Strategic planning guidance in Wales, structure plans and the content of development plans* (WO 1990b). PPG15 emphasized that county structure plans continued to be a key element in the development plan system. The PPG also provided guidance on the counties' role in the preparation of regional planning guidance. PPG15 noted in paragraph 4 that "its general purpose is to clarify the counties' strategic planning function, both under the present system and for the longer term." PPG15 confirmed the view expressed in the 1989 White Paper that there was to be a wider coverage of regional planning guidance, the primary function of which was to provide the necessary framework for the preparation of structure plans (para. 5). The Department of the Environment considered that regional advice should limit itself to land-use matters in line with the recommendations of PPG15. Neither the Department of the Environment nor the Welsh Office were anxious to see the embryonic regional planning system develop into a more effective form of regional planning that took account of other non land-

33

use matters. This point was also one of the main conclusions of Davies (1991) in her assessment of regional planning guidance. The scope and content of regional planning guidance has continued into the mid-1990s to be a controversial subject.

In PPG15, local authorities were encouraged to join together in Standing Conferences to prepare advice on which the Secretary of State could base his guidance (para. 6). Although the lead role was given to the county councils, it was emphasized that both district councils and national park authorities should be closely involved in the process (para. 7). Although the timing for regional planning guidance was not seen as the same in all regions, the Secretary of State's view aimed to have guidance in place "for most regions during the early 1990s" (para. 12). The conclusion of PPG15 (para. 32) was very robust in urging county planning authorities to "press ahead, in the light of this advice, with co-operation over the preparation of regional planning guidance".

In Wales, the development of strategic planning guidance for the principality was initiated by the Welsh Office with PPG15 (Wales). It is tempting to ask the question why the term "regional" has not been issued in Wales for the exercise, in contrast to the English regions. As Alden (1992) has noted, although part of the reason may be the nomenclature of describing Wales a region rather than a nation, it may also be partly owing to the Welsh Office view that it did not wish to see the "new" style of regional planning as a re-run of the "old" style as contained in the 1967 White Paper, *Wales: the way ahead* (HM Government 1967). At that time, many planners in Wales viewed that White Paper as being a regional plan. The Strategic Planning Guidance in Wales exercise focused upon the Assembly of Welsh Counties (AWC) taking the lead in co-ordinating the contributions of district councils, national park authorities and other interested parties in assessing the existing framework and in providing advice on the main strategic issues likely to affect Wales in the next 10–15 years, and Richard Jarvis provides a detailed account of this process in Chapter 4.

The thrust of the 1989 White Paper and PPG15 was supported by the report published by the County Planning Officers' Society in April 1990 on Regional Guidance and Regional Planning Conferences (CPOS 1990). The report supported the concept of regional guidance and the use of planning conferences for its formulation throughout England and Wales. It also noted the distinctive arrangements that were necessary in Wales, and the urgency of preparing regional guidance where none existed for regions without metropolitan areas. The report concluded by stressing the value of keeping under review the need for a mechanism whereby best practice can be identified and shared between regions.

In May 1991, the Royal Town Planning Institute published a discussion document on *The regional planning process* (RTPI 1991a, prepared for the Council of the Institute by the Regional Planning Working Party of the South West Branch). This was followed in June 1991 by a statement from the Town and Country Planning Association aimed at improving current procedures for regional guidance (TCPA 1991). Both the RTPI and TCPA were calling for a strengthening of the regional dimension in our country's planning system from its, hitherto, weak position. The RTPI document is of some interest because it discussed what may be regarded as some of the key elements of good practice that should be followed in preparing regional planning guidance. The Working Group Report concluded that regional guidance is just a step in the right direction, and that the only effective approach to the process is through the preparation of regional plans prepared in accordance with simple statutory procedures.

The main conclusions of the Working Group's Report were that:

- the government should proceed as soon as possible to a system requiring the preparation of regional plans (as opposed to issuing regional guidance)
- there should be separate secretariat–technical groups that can independently prepare the professional and technical input into the regional planning process
- the government should require the monitoring and review of regional plans
- consideration should be given to the appropriateness for regional planning of the areas of the standard regions
- the timescale of regional plans should be 20–30 years
- the aims of regional planning should be:
  - the identification of realistic levels of changes
  - provision of input to national planning and compatibility on inter-regional issues
- provision of a regional framework for structure plans, and
- securing of objectives to implement regional objectives.

One of the useful contributions of this report on the regional planning process was to emphasize the link between strategic plan-making at European Community level with that at national, regional, subregional (i.e. both structure plans and unitary plans) and local level.

Following the introduction of the Planning and Compensation Act 1991, the 1990 PPG15 was replaced by PPG12, published separately for England and Wales in February 1992 as *Development plans and regional planning guidance* and *Development plans and strategic planning guidance* respectively (DOE 1992b, WO 1992a). Both documents describe the role of development plans in the planning system, and cover structure plans, local plans, and unitary development plans. They also referred to national guidance through the form of PPG notes. However, in addition, both PPGs 12 emphasize that the government's regional planning guidance sets broad strategic policies for land-use development where there are issues which, although not of national scope, apply across regions or parts of regions and need to be considered on a scale wider than the area of a single authority (see para. 1.6 of PPG12).

Paragraph 2.1 of both PPG12 and PPG12 (Wales) states that "the primary function of regional guidance is to provide the necessary framework for the preparation of structure plans". Section 2 of PPG12 covers the preparation, content, timing and progress of regional planning guidance in England. On the preparation of regional planning guidance, PPG12 covers the following points:

- The Secretary of State considers that each region should have up-to-date regional guidance, as a result of reasonably frequent review.
- The county councils, and organizations representing other local authorities, will generally have a leading role in considering and advising on regional planning matters.
- Before advice is submitted to the Secretary of State, regional conferences should carry out appropriate consultation.
- When the Secretary of State decides to issue regional guidance, it will be published in draft and then consideration will be given to any representations received before finally issuing the guidance.
- Once regional guidance has been issued, local authorities are expected to take it into account in preparing their plans.

On the content and timing of regional planning guidance, PPG12 notes that:

- Regional guidance will normally cover those issues that are of regional importance, or that need to be considered on a wider geographical basis than that of individual structure plans.
- Regional planning guidance will be limited to matters that are relevant to the preparation of development plans.
- Topics covered will depend on the individual circumstances of each region.
- Guidance will suggest a broad development framework for the region over a period of 20 years or more.
- Regional guidance will cover priorities for the environment, transport, infrastructure, economic development, agriculture, minerals, waste treatment and disposal. Other topics covered will depend on regional circumstances, although the scale and distribution of provision of new housing would normally be expected to be included
- The Secretary of State hopes to have guidance in place for most regions by the end of 1993.

Progress achieved with regional planning guidance

The 1992 PPG12 notes that strategic guidance is already in place for all the former metropolitan counties and London. As at February 1992, regional guidance had been published under three PPGs and six Regional Planning Guidance Notes (RPGs). During the past 18 months, guidance has also been published for four further areas, leaving just three regions to be covered by RPGs (see Table 3.1 for an overview of the current RPG situation).

RPG9 for the South East (DoE 1994g) illustrates very well the new approach to regional-strategic planning in the 1990s and beyond. The RPG note is issued by the Secretary of State for the Environment and covers the period 1991–2011. The guidance sets out government policy as contained in both PPGs and MPGs. It

Table 3.1   The Regional Planning Guidance Notes.

Title	Date of issue
PPG10 Strategic Guidance for the West Midlands	September 1988
PPG11 Strategic Guidance for Merseyside	October 1988
RPG1 Strategic Guidance for Tyne and Wear	June 1989
RPG2 Strategic Guidance for West Yorkshire	September 1989
RPG3 Strategic Guidance for London	September 1989
RPG4 Strategic Guidance for Greater Manchester	December 1989
RPG5 Strategic Guidance for South Yorkshire	December 1989
RPG6 Regional Planning Guidance for East Anglia	July 1991
RPG7 Regional Planning Guidance for the Northern Region	September 1993
RPG8 Regional Planning Guidance for East Midlands	March 1994
RPG9 Regional Planning Guidance for the South East	March 1994
RPG10 Regional Planning Guidance for the South West	July 1994

Notes: List correct at March 1995; those guidance notes presently in draft are excluded.

provides county councils in the South East region with a framework for structure plan reviews. It also provides an overall context for investment decisions and the production of revised strategic planning guidance for London and for the proposed further guidance on the East Thames Corridor. The guidance emphasizes the vital role of South East England in the development of the UK economy, its concern for protecting the quality of the environment, and on the need for balanced development between the west and east of the region. The guidance also stresses that the South East cannot be viewed in isolation from the rest of the country; planning policies for all regions must reflect clear and consistent national objectives. Most of the other RPG notes follow this pattern. We now move on to consider the formulation of regional planning guidance in practice by examining work on the preparation of the guidance for the northern region.

The northern region

Background

The Department of the Environment's Northern Regional Office first wrote to the three county councils of Cleveland, Durham and Northumberland in 1989. To those working in the system it seemed a recipe for delay, certainly to get to the stage of actually allocating specific land uses on a plan. To avoid delay, the Department of the Environment suggested an early start on regional guidance. The letter of invitation included the following paragraph:

We would hope that the three County Councils would jointly take the lead in preparing advice for the Secretary of State and that when finalized the joint advice would be sent to the Secretary of State through whatever administrative arrangements the councils decide to establish for this purpose. This

37

procedure would, we consider, best reflect the strategic nature of regional planning guidance and ensure tight and effective working arrangements.

Regarding the role of the district councils, the regional office stressed that they would have an important part to play, first by providing input, through the existing county/district officer liaison arrangements that operate, to the advice that the county councils would prepare. Secondly, they maintained, the district councils would have ample opportunity, along with all the other interested parties, to express their views at the formal consultation stages by the Secretary of State.

The Department of the Environment envisaged two consultation stages, with in each case a six-week period for comment. The first would be when the Secretary of State consults on the advice given by the county councils. The second would be after consultation on the draft regional planning guidance. Once the guidance was published, local authorities would have to take it into account in preparing their structure plans. As an incentive to do this, PPG12 reminds local authorities that failure to do so could result in more intervention by the Secretary of State.

On the question of timing, the office suggested that the preparation of the advice should proceed as quickly as possible to enable a submission of the advice as soon as possible after the proposals in the White Paper are brought into force. This necessitated the three authorities making the necessary arrangements to undertake the work jointly and an early start would ensure that work could be better programmed, thereby avoiding undue delays later on.

In the subsequent months county structure plans found their way back into favour, but county councils saw the regional guidance as an essential part of the process. In view of the three levels of plan required, it was apparent to the three northern county councils that the process had to strike an appropriate balance of joint involvement without over-elaborate and cumbersome procedures.

Organization

Discussions took place between the three councils and a special members' Regional Guidance Steering Group was formed. This consisted of five councillors from each authority, together with a district councillor for each county area and Gateshead Metropolitan Borough Council for the Tyne & Wear authorities. This was supported at management level by the chief planners from the counties and three districts and Gateshead MBC, together with the Principal Planner at the DOE Regional Office. The real work was done by a six-person officer group drawn from the three counties, with occasional participation from an officer from Gateshead and the DOE. The six officers were all from planning or environment departments of the county councils. Cleveland County Council took responsibility for chairing the steering, management and working groups.

The approach

By the time the administrative arrangements were sorted out it was June 1990, some 11 months after the initial invitation by the DOE. The aim of the working group was to produce a consultation draft for approval by the councils within six months. This was not as demanding as it sounds. Over the years the councils in the northern region (including Cumbria) had prepared regional reports that were strongly economics-based but analyzed a range of land-use issues. They provided a basis for representations to government, for securing financial allocations and grant, and as an information base for a variety of activities. It was not as though they had to start from scratch or re-invent the wheel.

After the initial meeting the officers went their separate ways to write draft chapters, returning to weld it together and fill in relevant data and other information. As well as being responsible for certain environmental topics, Northumberland County Council had the task of writing the housing chapter. This is, of course, central to all regional guidance. A major problem at the time was the lack of up-to-date census data, which added to the uncertainty.

The officers were keen that the guidance should have a regional flavour and not just be a repetition of other planning and mineral policy guidance, with the odd place-name thrown in. There was a conscious effort to write this into the advice to the Secretary of State. In addition, the management group agreed to produce a two-page vision statement that preceded the main text but set a regional context for what followed.

Some problems

One major problem was to educate the councillors into thinking of regional guidance as part of the development plan process. They were familiar with the regional reports, which had a strong economic emphasis, and thought that regional planning guidance would be a continuation of this exercise. To stress the importance of environmental matters, the officers' working group did propose that the environment sections in the advice drafts featured prior to those relating to economic matters, but members would not accept this. Interestingly, the Secretary of State placed the environmental section first in the final guidance released.

As stated above, the housing forecasts were not straightforward. Ideally, regional planning guidance on housing figures should be based on population, household formation, dwelling stock replacement and other such standard factors as vacancy rates and second homes. A technical meeting was therefore held between regional DOE and county officers to discuss how best to proceed. As a result, the counties produced new figures based on the 1991 Census results using the standard method that had been used in preparing both the original advice and draft guidance figures. These formed the basis for the housing requirements figures included in the final guidance note. Table 3.2 compares the housing figures

Table 3.2   Input of housing figures to the RPG drafting process.

	Advice	Draft guidance	Guidance
Cleveland	13 000	10 000	14 000
Durham	14 000	21 000	21 000
Northumberland	15 000	13 000	15 500
Shire counties	42 000	44 000	50 500

produced at the various stages in the process. Technically or politically it was not too difficult a process.

It does seem to have taken a long time to reach the stage of the guidance being issued by the Secretary of State. From an invitation in July 1989, it was four years before the guidance was finally published as RPG7, *Regional planning guidance for the northern region* in September 1993 (DoE 1993f). The main periods of delay were at the start and finish of the process. It did take several months for the three county councils and their partners to get organized. It also took the DoE some time to issue their consultation draft and final guidance, particularly as the main technical work was already undertaken by the County Officers' Working Group. Table 3.3 illustrates the timetable for each stage of the process for the northern region..

Table 3.3   Procedure for preparing Regional Planning Guidance for the North

Invitation to prepare advice	July 1989
Working Group commenced	June 1990
Consultation draft issued	April 1991
Draft advice submitted	December 1991
DoE consultation draft	February 1993
SoS issues guidance	September 1993

A successful strategy?

For several years Northumberland County Council has been endeavouring to extend the green belt to the north of Newcastle upon Tyne and North Tyneside. This has featured in structure plan alterations and local plans, but was ruled out on technicalities by the DoE. The regional planning guidance proposes that the county council considers the extension compatible with the advice in revised PPG2, *Green belts* (DoE 1995), and this now features in the structure plan that was put on deposit last year.

This guidance has been likened to a polo mint, since "the gap in the middle", Tyne & Wear, is not included. The strategic guidance for the metropolitan area was issued in June 1989 as RPG1 (DoE 1989d). This provides guidance to 2001, whereas the surrounding regional guidance is for the period to 2006. Monitoring and review of guidance should in the future cover the whole region and it is proposed that this should cover the period to 2011.

At present the metropolitan authorities are busy producing their Unitary

Development Plans and do not want to be diverted from that task. In fact there are important issues at stake, including the old problems of housing provision, employment sites, and the future boundaries of the green belt. The last thing they want at the time of writing is to review regional guidance, particularly as it may reduce their scope for growth on the periphery of the built-up areas.

The responsibility for monitoring has been taken on by the North of England Assembly (which includes Cumbria). A standing conference is to be formed to consider monitoring, joint arrangements and the future review. It will comprise the three county councils, the metropolitan districts, and a district council from each of the three counties. For the present, the initiative to achieve progress still rests with the county councils. However, local government review beckons, with proposals announced for both Cleveland and Durham. Whatever happens, the number of strategic planning authorities is likely to increase and, at best, this will delay the integration of the regional guidance. There is a possibility of a situation arising where several of the smaller unitary authorities in the region will be dominated by the larger metropolitan districts to the detriment of an even distribution of resource allocation, and this is already happening to some extent with the government's City Challenge schemes and the Single Regeneration Budget, both of which have some winners but many losers.

Conclusions

The role of regional planning guidance has clearly developed in a significant way within the overall statutory policy framework in the 1990s. However, some concerns still need to be addressed. For example, PPG12 stresses that guidance is to be limited to matters that are relevant to the preparation of development plans. The Assembly of Welsh Counties, in their 1993 *Overview report on strategic planning guidance in Wales* (AWC 1993), also noted that strategic guidance is seen by the Secretary of State as being confined to those matters necessary to enable local planning authorities to prepare their structure plans and local plans: the Secretary of State "is not looking for a regional plan" (para. 1.4). Whereas the founders of town planning did not have a narrow focus of the role of land-use planning, but rather a wider concern for improving social, economic and environmental conditions, in the 1990s regional planning guidance has sought to limit its role. It is not easy, however, to see how the role of land-use planning can be separated from policies closely tied to achieving some vision of societal objectives. Although regional planning guidance cannot cover every economic and social issue, and must necessarily focus on those major issues that have land-use implications for development, some confusion persists as to what is expected in terms of end product. Within Wales, strategic–regional planning guidance has inevitably become linked to the current proposals for local government reform and discussion of a Welsh Assembly.

41

It remains to be seen, therefore, whether regional planning guidance develops into something more than land-use planning. Whatever the eventual outcome, the 1990s have witnessed a remarkable revival of interest in regional planning, with local authorities taking the initiative. Given both the European and national context of the statutory planning policy framework, it seems almost inevitable that the momentum built up so far will be maintained, and further enhanced in the years ahead. With local government reorganization being implemented in the later 1990s, for many areas there will be added pressure for some strategic level of planning to assist the operation of the newly established unitary local authorities. Regional planning guidance is here to stay; much has been achieved during the past ten years, but much remains to be resolved.

CHAPTER 4

Structure planning policy and strategic planning guidance in Wales

Richard Jarvis

Introduction

In the mid-1980s, structure planning as undertaken by county councils looked set to be relegated in status to an "advisory role" in the form of "statements of the County Planning Policy". However, the publication of the Green Paper *The future of development plans* in 1986 (DOE/WO 1986) generated wide debate among not only planning professionals but also many of those affected by the planning system. In spite of this the government still seemed convinced that structure plans should be replaced by "statements of County Planning Policies". In the space of a year, between the publication of the White Paper *The future of development plans* (HM Government 1989), and PPG15, *Regional planning guidance, structure plans, and the content of development plans* (DOE 1990) in May 1990, structure plans were rehabilitated and the 1991 Planning and Compensation Act further strengthened the status of both structure plans and local plans in consideration of applications for planning permission.

By the mid-1980s England and Wales had achieved complete coverage with structure plans, and many counties had begun working on structure plan "replacements" and "alterations". In contrast, local plan coverage was very sparse. Criticisms have been made of structure plans for being too detailed and procedurally cumbersome; nevertheless, structure plans have provided the only development plan coverage in many areas. Structure plans are valuable as both a process and product, and this chapter will illustrate the importance of both, by reference to the development of economic and environmental initiatives that have taken place in Clwyd.

In July 1994, the Local Government (Wales) Bill received Royal Assent. The structure of local government in Wales will change with the abolition of the county and district councils and their replacement with 22 unitary (all purpose) authorities. Wales will have unitary development plans – a system of planning that will be different from development planning in non-metropolitan England and Scotland. Furthermore, the Strategic Planning Guidance exercise in Wales is different from regional planning guidance in England and National Planning Policy Guidelines issued in Scotland. There is a prospect of a patchwork of different planning systems developing in this country. It is right to pause to assess the implications of these changes for the future of structure plans and strategic planning guidance in Wales.

Structure planning in the 1980s

Government economic policy in the 1980s centred around monetary and, to a lesser extent, fiscal policies that were primarily aimed at reducing inflation, reducing public expenditure and offering incentives to enterprise. Deregulation was seen as an important element in the strategy to free enterprise from unnecessary burdens. In 1985 the government published a White Paper entitled *Lifting the burden* (HM Government 1985) that set out a whole host of measures aimed at removing what the government saw as encumbrances on the development of enterprise.

Lifting the burden promised changes in the planning system, including the setting up of special development zones and changes to the General Development Order and Use Classes Order. The White Paper also indicated changes to development plans – structure and local plans – which the government felt had become procedurally too slow and cumbersome and, in the case of structure plans, had tended to go into far too much detail. The government seemed to be warning that further consideration would be given to ". . . changes in the content and procedures of development plans and in the relationship between development plans and development control" (ibid. 3.13).

The White Paper *Building business . . . not barriers* (HM Government 1986), again heralded changes that would be designed to simplify and improve the development plan system and indicated that a consultation paper would be published later that year.

In September 1986, the Secretaries of State for the Environment and for Wales jointly issued the consultation paper entitled *The future of development plans*. That consultation paper set out measures aimed at improving land-use planning at regional, county and district levels. The Green Paper proposed measures, including voluntary groupings of counties, to advise the Secretary of State on the regional planning guidance to be published; abolition of county structure plans and the introduction of statements of county planning policies that would not be part of the development plan; district-wide development plans containing all land-use policies with the exception of minerals; and removal of the need for district councils to obtain a certification of conformity with county policies. Interestingly, the Green Paper proposed the introduction of "rural conservation areas" to replace the variety of locally defined areas shown in development plans and the transfer of some additional development control powers to the county councils concerning major applications (e.g. for retailing and major housing developments).

The publication of the consultation paper initiated a wide-ranging debate. The County Planning Officers' Society and the Association of County Councils made strong representations to government in support of structure plans and measures that could be taken to improve strategic planning (CPOS 1986/1988). In Wales, the County Planning Officers' Society for Wales made its own submission to the Secretary of State for Wales (CPOSW 1987). However, it was the debate by organizations such as the Council for the Protection of Rural England over the future of surplus agricultural land and the pressures of some Members of Parliament with constituencies in southern England that perhaps had some of the most influence on government policy towards structure plans.

In January 1989 the government issued the White Paper entitled *The future of development plans* that indicated the intention to "simplify the planning process and improve its efficiency so as to serve the needs of development and the interests of conservation thus protecting and enhancing the environment in town and country". The White Paper brought forward many of the measures outlined in the Consultation Paper issued three years earlier, although it dropped the proposals for rural conservation areas and changes to development control responsibilities.

Planners in Wales noted with interest paragraph 2.9, which pointed to the need for a "distinctive approach to the development of regional planning guidance". In particular, they noted that the Welsh Office intended to produce a series of guideline documents for consultation with local authorities and other bodies in Wales.

The renaissance of strategic planning

The government appeared to have had a change of heart in seeking to retain structure plans between the publication of the White Paper in 1989 and the publication of DOE PPG15 in May 1990 and the publication in October 1990 of PPG15 (Wales) (WO 1990b). There were perhaps three reasons for this. First, the government was experiencing considerable pressure arising from public concern about the demands for development in certain areas, notably the South East and South West. Secondly, there was a growing concern about environmental matters arising from the public endorsement for "green issues". The Prime Minister – Margaret Thatcher – in her now famous "green speech" to the Royal Society in September 1988 led the way in putting the environment on the political

45

agenda. Thirdly, there was considerable concern about the future use of surplus agricultural land, and organizations such as the Council for the Protection of Rural England were expressing the need for responsive strategic planning to safeguard areas from development.

In September 1990 the government published its much heralded White Paper on the environment, *This common inheritance* (HM Government 1990). This White Paper gave land-use planning an important role in measures that were being formulated to protect and enhance the environment. The 1991 Planning and Compensation Act enhanced the status of the development plan. In particular, it required (through Section 54A) that planning applications be determined in accordance with the development plan unless material considerations indicate otherwise. This was heralded as moving to a "plan-led" system.

The government had, therefore, drawn back from relegating the status of structure plans in the development plan system to providing a much stronger framework for the development of strategic and local planning policies in England and Wales. Perhaps this was a recognition by the government of the important role that development planning can play in the move towards sustainable development policies. The 1991 Act maintained the legal basis of structure plans but allowed county councils to approve their own structure plans without having to refer them to the Secretary of State for approval. Although the Secretary of State still has the reserve powers to intervene if he is not happy, the main consequence of the change in arrangements so far has been to allow county planners potentially much more freedom to determine the content and style of their development plans although in practice the Welsh Office still examines draft plans in considerable detail. The local planning system remained unchanged with the exception of a promise in the 1989 White Paper that local plans were now to be district-wide. This was given legislative force in the 1991 Planning and Compensation Act.

Structure planning in Clwyd: process and product

The development of structure planning in Clwyd

Structure plans create the planning framework for the development of local planning policies and planning decisions. They have to strike a balance between development and the protection and enhancement of the environment. Structure plans also have the key role in the development plan hierarchy by providing the essential link between national and regional guidance on the one hand and local planning policies on the other.

The product of the continuous structure planning process, which incorporates the essential elements of monitoring and review, is a plan that relates in general terms to the county's area. However, the process of structure planning has positive benefits that county councils have employed to develop a wide range of initiatives, many of which relate to securing resources (e.g. from Europe) and specific economic development initiatives.

Clwyd's first structure plan was submitted to the Secretary of State in May 1979. The plan, comprising 119 policies, was based on four key objectives intended to achieve:

- moderate growth
- improved economic strength
- an efficient transport system, and
- safeguarding the environment and local communities.

Although the plan failed to anticipate in 1980 the closure of steel-making at Shotton, with the direct loss of over 8000 jobs, it was remarkably prescient in its approach to resource utilization and the environment.

Even before the closure of steel-making at Shotton, Clwyd had the enviable honour of having the highest rate of unemployment of all the Welsh counties and one of the worst unemployment rates in this country. In the late 1970s it was recognized that Clwyd had a "brittle economy" (Clwyd County Council 1976) rising from the dominance of the steel, textile and aerospace industries. The late 1970s saw the beginning of the decline in the county's basic industry with the closure of Courtaulds textile plant in Flint. The process of closure accelerated in the late 1970s and early 1980s, with the result that unemployment peaked at 19.2 per cent in January 1986. The structure plan therefore adopted as one of its key objectives the need "to secure a high level and variety of employment throughout Clwyd".

The plan also aimed "to minimize the environmental loss arising from development pressures and to restore lost amenities". It has to recognize that Clwyd is a border county set between the populous northwest region of England and the remote and less populous splendours of Snowdonia, and that the county had experienced pressures from housing development arising from in-migration in the 1960s and early 1970s, and from industries such as quarrying and tourism. The plan therefore sought to provide a more coherent and cohesive form of development and it prevented the sprawl of housing and other developments in the countryside. Policies aimed to secure new housing in towns and urban areas, and to reduce travel through the location of employment sites in main centres.

Emphasis was also placed on "making the best use of existing facilities and minimize new investment to essential needs only". This objective was again consistent with the approach to review land commitments (of the former planning authorities in Flintshire and Denbighshire) and consolidate growth in major centres.

The major trunk road improvement programme to the A55 and A483 was just beginning in the late 1970s, but the thrust of transport policies was to improve the county's main distributor routes carrying a substantial element of freight traffic, enhance environmental conditions in town centres and villages, and relieve the most highly congested sections of the main distributor routes. The emphasis

47

was to be on selective road improvements and traffic management rather than costly schemes.

The plan recognized the need "to have special regard to the aspirations of local communities and local needs". This objective recognized the pressures that Clwyd had faced in the 1960s and 1970s from rapid growth and change. There was concern about Clwyd's identity in view of its proximity to the Merseyside and Manchester conurbations, and it was recognized that there was a need to safeguard Welsh-speaking communities. Rural economic initiatives were seen as important in maintaining viable communities and "Clwydfro", an organization possessing the specific brief to help sustain rural enterprise, was established.

The plan sought to protect the built and natural environment. The county signalled its intention to prepare a Special Landscape Area Local Plan, in which conservation and enhancement was to be a priority and new development was required to conform to higher standards. The county council also worked actively to secure the Clwydian Range Area of Outstanding Natural Beauty.

Work began on the Clwyd Structure Plan First Alteration in the late 1980s and the plan was eventually submitted to the Secretary of State in January 1990. The broad objectives of the first alteration were similar to those of the original structure plan, although the emphasis changed in some important respects.

The first alteration emphasized the need to restructure the county's economy and reduce unemployment. The aim was to make policies more positive in setting out a need for specific land requirements to meet the differing needs of industry, to remove unnecessary restrictions and to reflect current issues such as rural diversification and the need to attract prestige employment developments.

The assessment of housing need moved from the more mechanistic approach adopted in the earlier plan to one based on a recognition of housing demand and an attempt to accommodate this where it would not prejudice important planning policies on agricultural land, green barriers and the environment. The plan again put forward policies to concentrate most development in main settlements, give an indication of the scale of growth expected and allow a small amount of development in main villages.

The first alteration introduced a new section on shopping policies and set out criteria for the consideration of developments outside existing shopping centres. The plan also put forward a comprehensive set of policies for the consideration of minerals development, setting up a series of criteria policies that would apply to all minerals applications, and specific policies for the various types of minerals found in the county.

The Structure Plan Second Alteration, looking at development strategy beyond 1996 and into the first decade of the next century, reflects the current concerns for the environment. It has four key objectives that underpin the policy proposals in the plan:

- *Using existing resources*: direct development to existing settlements, recognizing the importance of town centres for social, economic and community reasons.

- *Optimizing the location of development and reducing the need to travel*:
  seeking to protect the best agricultural land, areas of sensitive environment, and locating developments where it can support alternatives to the
  use of private transport.
- *Containing the scale of development in sensitive environmental areas*: the
  structure plan has always sought to restrict development for environmental
  reasons. However, the approach is now being taken on a wider scale to
  restrain development on the coast where a combination of attractive landscape, the need to protect underdeveloped areas of the coastline, and the
  need to protect high-quality farmland mean that past housebuilding rates
  cannot continue.
- *Protecting and improving the built and natural environment*: the strengthening of open countryside and policies to protect historic parks and gar-
  dens, and the development of a forestry strategy. The strategy continues
  the aims of the original structure plan and the first alteration but seeks to
  secure a closer integration of land-use and transportation policies.

The Second Alteration has responded to the increased public concern for
environmental issues. It has sought to introduce the principles of sustainable
development into the plan. There are policies that seek to do this, but three new
interrelated policies have been introduced to achieve high quality of design in
development balance in the best use of resources, in their widest sense, and new
development located where it will minimize travel demand and facilitate the use
of public transport.

The influence of the Secretary of State

The Secretary of State influences the planning process in several ways, through,
for example, Planning Policy Guidance Notes and Circulars, ministerial statements and specific changes to planning policies. Before the 1991 Planning and
Compensation Act, the Secretary of State had a more direct involvement in
approving structure plans. In Clwyd's case the Secretary of State has generally
confined himself to minor modifications. For instance, in the structure plan submitted in 1979, the Secretary of State made minor modifications of wording,
accepted revised population projections put forward at the Examination in Public, and revised minerals policies put forward at a reconvened Examination in
Public.

The Structure Plan First Alteration, submitted in January 1990, was again
modified only in a relatively minor way. The Secretary of State introduced new
policies on housing for senior management and affordable housing, and modified two policies on minerals that were considered to go beyond national policy
guidelines. In approving the first alteration, the minister identified two tasks for
the second alteration: the county council was required to undertake a comprehensive review of options and priorities for highway improvements, and to

review the possibility of green belt designations as issues in the next structure plan.

Despite relinquishing direct approval of the submitted structure plan, the Secretary of State still has reserve powers to change policies that may be at variance to national policies. The Welsh Office can still have considerable influence in policy formulation through monitoring the progress of the emerging plan.

Strategic planning guidance in Wales will be an important issue to be addressed with local government reorganization and the abolition of county structure plans. The ability of Part 1 of the Unitary Development Plan to fill the gap is discussed later.

Relationship with the district councils

Structure plans have a key role in guiding the district councils in the preparation of local plans. Until the 1991 Act, district councils had to obtain a Certificate of General Conformity. After 1991, this was replaced by the Statement of Conformity, and the county council now has to express its objections to the local plan alongside other objectors at the Local Plan Inquiry.

The extent of local plan coverage in Clwyd was probably no worse or better than in other parts of the country. When the first structure plan was approved in 1982, there were no adopted local plans in the county. Work had begun on several local plans for certain key settlements, but in general it was the county structure plan that provided the only up-to-date development plan coverage for the county as a whole. Criticisms have been made of structure plans for being too detailed, but perhaps this was understandable given the dearth of detailed local plans.

By 1985, when work was beginning on the Structure Plan First Alteration, Clwyd had two adopted local plans. Delyn Borough Council had adopted the Mold Local Plan and the county council had prepared and adopted the Special Landscape Area Local Plan. Draft local plans had been prepared and considered by three districts, and work was known to have started on local plans in the other districts.

By the time the Structure Plan Second Alteration was approved by the Secretary of State in October 1991, local plan coverage had begun to improve. Two of the districts had adopted local plans, one covering the whole of the authority area and the other for the more populated coastal belt, and draft plans had been prepared and considered by the county council for the others.

The process of certification has played an important role, not only in ensuring that the local plans are in general conformity with the structure plan but also in improving the quality of the final product. Consideration of the draft stage of the local plan is important in rectifying potential problems that can give rise to non-certification at a later stage.

In Clwyd some of the issues meriting further consideration by the district councils following consideration of the draft plan by the county council have included:

- over-allocation of housing and employment land
- attempting to impose policies that are more restrictive than the equivalent in the structure plan and at variance with national planning policy guidelines
- settlement boundaries being drawn too tightly and, in one case a too restrictive policy being imposed on the number of dwellings that could be accommodated on one of these sites, and
- the introduction of new terminology that have not been explicitly defined, e.g. "opportunity sites" that could lead to a breach of several important structure plan policies.

In the main it has been constructive discussions with the districts that have resolved conflict between the county structure plan and the district local plans and, where matters cannot be resolved, objections have been lodged at the Local Plan Inquiry. The certification process has generally ensured conformity across the county and the process has improved the quality of the final local plan. The county council has been able to secure clarification of policy wording and interpretation, and to point the way in terms of recognizing important trends, e.g. high-quality employment sites and the need to address strategic global environmental issues.

Structure plan as a process rather than a product

The structure plan is clearly the end product of a process of research, plan formulation, consultation, monitoring and review. However, the process has proved to be of considerable value in developing new initiatives to tackle problems that perhaps lie outside the strict interpretation of the development plan.

Although the structure plan, submitted in May 1979, failed to anticipate fully the implications of the Shotton steel-making closure and the depth of the international recession that affected many advanced economies in the early 1980s, the strategic planning process has responded in several ways.

In 1982, the county council published its "programme plan" for regenerating North East Clwyd (Clwyd County Council 1982). This plan set out the development context for the re-use of the former steelworks site, the further development of Deeside Industrial Park and proposals for a third crossing of the River Dee. This was followed with new initiatives such as the Newtech Innovation Centre (Clwyd County Council 1983). The programme plan approach was extended to southeast Clwyd (principally around Wrexham) and specific measures for high-technology industries were considered for the area (Clwyd County Council 1984). Links were formed with the North East Wales Institute of Higher Education, Clwyd Area Health Authority and the county council to develop Wrexham Technology Park (Clwyd County Council 1985).

The programme plan approach was applied to coastal Clwyd but it was later abandoned in favour of a wider strategic approach arising from the need to produce regional economic development strategies to secure funds from the European Regional Development Fund.

It was during the mid-1980s that, in consultation with the district councils, Clwyd produced a tourism strategy (Clwyd County Council 1987) that set out a broad context for the development of tourism-related initiatives in the county. Reference was made to the need to balance the development of tourism in Clwyd (e.g. rural and special interest tourism) with the need to provide for the traditional market attracted to Clwyd's coastal resorts.

During the 1980s the A55 trunk road was improved throughout the county, effectively providing a fast dual-carriageway route from the northwest of England to northwest Wales. Clwyd wished to capitalize on this investment, but at the same time it recognized that the road was in effect its "shop window". County and district planners joined together and produced a report that identified areas for opportunity and for restraint, and effectively provided an important "informal plan" until such time as the Structure Plan First Alteration was approved and local plans had been adopted (Clwyd County Council 1987).

The development of strategic planning initiatives has continued into the 1990s with proposals for an indicative Forestry Strategy and a Nature Conservation Strategy.

The value of strategic planning

Producing structure plans is one aspect of a whole process founded upon a particular approach. The County Planning Officers' Society (1993) set out several examples of "strategic planning achievements". That paper gave several examples of what strategic planning has achieved, but perhaps its main conclusion is the catalytic role that county planning has in enabling other organizations to achieve particular goals.

The Clwyd structure plan has enabled the county to respond to particular opportunities and threats; it has provided a framework in which discussion can take place as witnessed by the development of local plans through the statutory consultative process.

Effective strategic planning has been necessary to prevent wasteful capital investment, as was evident in the debate over the provision of employment sites within individual districts and the need to ensure that not every interchange site is a location for high-quality employment. On housing, for example, the structure plan has had to ensure that individual districts meet their contribution to the overall housing requirement.

The structure plan has had to recognize that growth cannot continue indefinitely as witnessed by the need to restrain it in some areas for environmental policy reasons. Only strategic planning at an appropriate scale can direct development elsewhere.

The structure plan has had to address several cross-boundary issues such as the implications of the Secretary of State's decision to maintain the existing green belt boundaries around the City of Chester and, in Gwynedd, restrictive housing policies. Other cross-boundary matters such as estuaries, the coast, Areas of Outstanding Natural Beauty and Sites of Special Scientific Interest, need a coherent and consistent policy context.

The structure plan can therefore be seen as both a process and a product. Its importance lies in the fact that it provides a framework for addressing issues which:

- cross boundaries and have long term implications
- embrace areas large enough to deal with areas of growth as well as areas of restraint, (e.g. town and country)
- enable a balance to be struck between development and conservation
- provide an interpretation of national and regional policies across broad areas
- counterbalance the undue influence of parochial interests on issues of wide community importance, and
- provide an essential balanced policy context for the work of the many single-purpose government agencies and other bodies whose work involves the use of land.

The next section looks at the development of strategic planning in an all-Wales context.

Strategic planning guidance in Wales

In the White Paper on *The future of development plans* (HM Government 1989), it was stated that

the particular administrative and planning circumstances in the Principality, especially the multi-functional role of the Welsh Office, required a distinctive approach to the development of regional planning guidance.

The Secretary of State for Wales proposed, therefore that a series of guideline documents should be produced by the Welsh Office for consultation with local authorities and other bodies.

There are two important features about strategic planning guidance in Wales. First, it is seen by the Welsh Office as essentially all-Wales aspatial guidance, whereas regional planning guidance in England has a strong spatial element. Secondly, the county councils (through the Assembly of Welsh Counties) were given the task of taking the lead of reviewing, in collaboration with the Council of Welsh Districts, the National Parks and other interested bodies, the strategic planning guidance relevant to structure planning and local planning in Wales. The initial brief requested that the review should cover:

- a broad assessment of the existing planning guidance that provides the framework for the preparation of development plans
- an identification of the main strategic planning issues likely to affect Wales in the next 10–15 years, with proposals for any changes to the strategic framework
- the Secretary of State also invited the Assembly of Welsh Counties to address the green belt question as part of the review of strategic guidance; Wales, unlike England, has no statutory green belts but rather policies such as "green barriers" and "green wedges" defined in structure and local plans.

As part of the process of reviewing strategic planning guidance, the Welsh Office issued a range of factual "sectional papers" and policy "summary guideline reports" to explain the strategic framework built up over many years by central government and its agencies. In all, the Welsh Office produced 13 sectional reports (these contain mainly factual data on the Principality) and nine policy guideline reports.

The Secretary of State for Wales saw strategic planning guidance as being confined to those matters necessary to enable local planning authorities to prepare their structure plans and local plans. It was made clear that the Welsh Office were definitely not looking for an updated version of *Wales: the way ahead* (HM Government 1967). Strategic planning guidance in Wales was to be different from regional planning guidance in England and was certainly to be nothing like the "all singing and all dancing" regional plans of the 1960s and 1970s. In developing the work programme, the Assembly of Welsh Counties established 14 topic groups to cover a wide range of planning matters ranging from waste management to transport and telecommunications. In essence they reacted to the topic approach adopted by the Welsh Office in the publication of their sectional and policy guideline reports. The methodology is set out in a report entitled *Strategic planning guidance in Wales – process and procedures* (AWC 1990).

The relationship between the objectives and the development of strategic planning guidance for structure and local plans is illustrated in Figure 4.1.

It was felt that strategic planning guidance for Wales needed to be developed within seven broad objectives. The prime objective is "to ensure that Wales can enjoy a quality of life at levels comparable with the best in the European Community". This objective is supported by several other objectives that are concerned with:

- developing land-use planning policies that reflect the principle of sustainable development
- protecting and enhancing the natural and built environment
- recognizing the distinctive language and culture
- improving the economic health of the Principality
- improving access to housing

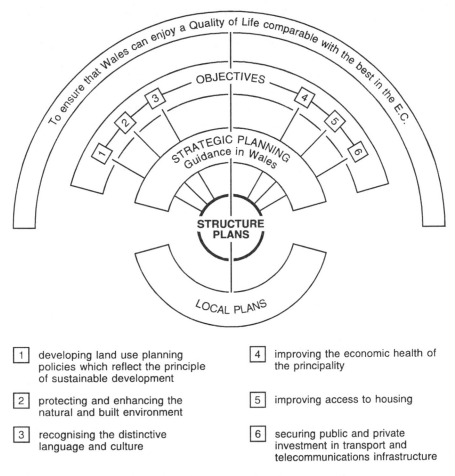

1. developing land use planning policies which reflect the principle of sustainable development

2. protecting and enhancing the natural and built environment

3. recognising the distinctive language and culture

4. improving the economic health of the principality

5. improving access to housing

6. securing public and private investment in transport and telecommunications infrastructure

Figure 4.1 Strategic planning guidance in Wales: the process.

- securing public and private investment in transport and telecommunications infrastructure.

In the model each planning role is clearly defined and relates to a level of government: strategic planning guidance to the Welsh Office, structure plans to the county councils, local plans to the district councils. The model seeks to set objectives as the basis for developing strategic planning guidance in Wales, while acknowledging that there are uncertainties involved in looking to the future, and acknowledging the need continually to adapt in the light of changing circumstances. In essence these principles and objectives have to be applied across the discrete topic areas.

The final report, submitted to the Secretary of State (AWC 1993), set out four "key action points" as a means of guiding the Welsh Office in the priorities that needed to be addressed in developing strategic planning guidance for Wales. The report called for the development of a comprehensive policy strategy for Wales covering the details set out in the transportation, rural, coastal and urban topic reports. It was felt that the issues raised in these topic reports needed to be dealt with in a more integrated way. It was also suggested that the concept of sustainable development needed to be investigated further, recognizing that sustainable development has long-term implications and that moving to sustainable land-use policies requires much more detailed consideration. The report felt that new policy guidance was required for waste management and energy. In relation to the Welsh language, it was noted that town & country planning guidance had enhanced its status in Circular 53/88 (WO 1988), but that there were several issues that needed to be addressed and, in particular, guidance was required on assessing the significance of the impact of a proposed development on a Welsh linguistic community. The Welsh Office was asked, among other things, to look at the prospect of developing linguistic audit and community impact assessment methodologies.

In the light of the environment White Paper, *This common inheritance* (HM Government 1990) and the government's concern with the concept of sustainable development, it was suggested that early consideration should be given to reviewing and amending several guidance notes relating to minerals. There were also several issues relating to retailing, employment, housing and tourism, recreation and sport that needed to be addressed.

The AWC was concerned, however, that strategic planning guidance should have a subregional focus within an all-Wales context. This conclusion was based on the fact that differences in the character of the constituent parts of the Principality needed to be reflected in the development of strategic planning guidance. It was felt that the subregional framework should be concerned with:

- formulating policies and proposals at a strategic level for major land-use and transportation changes and the protection of the physical environment
- providing a framework for local authority planning policies
- providing the basis for policies, plans and programmes being developed, for example, by the Welsh Development Agency, the Wales Tourist Board, the Countryside Council for Wales, the Sports Council for Wales and the private utilities
- providing an indication to the private sector of the strategic intentions for development and conservation in Wales
- providing an input to regional planning guidance being developed by adjacent regions, i.e. the North West, the West Midlands and the South West
- providing the forum for translating the concept of sustainable development into meaningful land-use policies.

Local government reorganization in Wales and the implications for strategic planning

PPG12 (Wales) is very clear that the primary function of strategic planning guidance in Wales is to provide the necessary framework for the preparation of structure plans (WO 1992a). In *Strategic planning guidance in Wales general paper* (WO 1990a), the Welsh Office states that

> at the All Wales level, therefore, planning is necessarily in many ways a flexible and multi-faceted response to changing circumstances, but containing major elements that have imparted a structural stability to land use across the Principality. The first level at which a comprehensive, integrated, strategic land-use planning document is statutorily required is the county structure plan. The sequential approval of county structure plans by the Secretary of State provides, in turn, subregional frameworks for local plan-making and decision-taking.

The same document states later

> the main co-ordinated level is that of the Secretary of State for Wales and the Welsh Office, but the integration of spatial planning at subnational levels is largely the responsibility of the County Councils in making, monitoring and implementing their structure plans and the district council, in respect of local plans. Ad hoc co-ordination and integration is undertaken when special circumstances require it as in the Secretary of State's programme for the valleys.

Structure plans, therefore, have a key role in translating national and regional policies (Welsh Office policies) to a more tightly defined spatial area. In the Welsh Office's words, they provide subregional frameworks for local plan-making and decision-taking. The Local Government (Wales) Act proposes to replace structure and local plans with unitary development plans. The strategic element is based on guidance from the Secretary of State and there is also concern about the possibility of strategic planning being lost in the drive towards the new unitary authorities. The Welsh Office view is that Part 1 of the UDP – that is the element that would deal with strategic issues – could be achieved by voluntary co-operation between the new unitary authorities.

In its progress report *Reviewing local government in the English shires* (LGC 1993b) the Local Government Commission made several relevant points that are equally applicable to the delivery of a strategic planning service in Wales. In particular, the Commission accepted that ". . . a unitary development plan system would make for greater speed and efficiency in plan-making, but it is not convinced that it would provide an adequate means of resolving strategic conflicts in all cases". The Commission also doubted whether joint preparation of Unitary Development Plans would be a workable option in most areas, given the wide territory that would have to be covered, noting, in particular that "there is a risk that Unitary Development Plans may become a recipe for Balkanization of development strategy of the area as a whole".

The Commission made several other points that supported the need for effective strategic planning:

- the higher level of interdependence between larger urban areas and their surrounding areas
- the close links between land-use and transportation planning
- the tendency (noted from the abolition of the metropolitan counties) for guidance to cling to the lowest common denominator and failure to resolve inter-urban and inter-rural conflicts, and
- the doubt about the ability of regional planning guidance to resolve interterritorial conflicts.

The Commission supported strategic planning being delivered through the structure plan over wide areas, but felt that minerals and waste should generally be the responsibility of individual unitary authorities irrespective of the size. Overall, the Commission has paid regard to the need to safeguard strategic planning, but this concern has not dictated the shape of its eventual proposals.

In Scotland, the strategic planning function is being safeguarded by the inclusion in the Local Government (Scotland) Act of provisions to retain the structure plan. These will be prepared either by an individual local authority or by a group of local authorities, depending on circumstances. The Act also provides a mechanism for the Secretary of State to intervene, if necessary, to determine appropriate structure plan areas. None of this is present in the Local Government (Wales) Act. Reliance on voluntary arrangements for joint working to provide the subregional strategic framework for land-use and transportation planning has all the dangers recognized by the Local Government Commission in England, although some commentators remain optimistic of the new unitary authorities being able to work together (Harris & Tewdwr-Jones 1995). Without statutory backing, there is nevertheless a danger that strategic planning in Wales may be eclipsed and that a strategic policy vacuum will exist. This danger is compounded by the fact that strategic planning guidance currently lacks a subregional or spatial element.

Implications for the future

Professional planners in Wales will seek to make the new system of planning work. However, the Welsh Office will be required to fulfil their brief in providing effective strategic planning guidance to enable the gap left by structure plans to be filled in an effective manner. In many ways, Wales has never needed strategic guidance more than at the present time. The growing concern for environmental matters has not abated with the economic recession. People are more than ever concerned about the use of resources and the implications for future generations. There are conflicts – witness the debate over wind farms in Wales – that have major land-use implications and need to be resolved.

There is without doubt a need for effective strategic planning as local authorities try to come to terms with the wider global environmental issues. Strategic issues need strategic responses. As we have seen in the case of Clwyd and in other counties, the process is just as important as the product. It would be dangerous to jettison strategic planning as we try to grapple with wider environmental concerns.

In the government's environment White Paper, *This common inheritance*, the point is made that

> if greater prosperity is making people more interested in the quality of their lives, it is proper to look at how public policy and administration attempt to reflect this. The Government needs to ensure that its policies fit together in every sector, and that we are not undoing, in one area, what we are trying to do in another; and that policies are based on a harmonious set of principles rather than a clutter of expedience (ibid.: para. 1.6).

Without structure plans there is a danger of having strategic planning by ad hoc decisions made through planning inquiries and appeals. Major infrastructure projects such as barrages and roads have important implications for the areas in which they are located. There is a need for a framework in which to place these projects so that their impacts can be fully understood. The Confederation of British Industry and the Royal Institute of Chartered Surveyors have made calls for effective strategic planning in their joint report, *Shaping the nation* (CBI/RICS 1992). The report recognized that strategic guidance had to be developed at national and regional level to provide a framework for land-use and infrastructure planning; it saw the planning system operating in a way that enhanced the co-ordination of decision-making between government departments and between local authorities. Interestingly, the report called, among other things, for ". . . strengthened regional planning guidance" and ". . . the retention of those authorities that can take a strategic approach to their work".

Interest in structure planning has waxed and waned over time. The 1986 Green Paper on *The future of development plans* seemed to spell the end of structure plans. However, with the publication of PPG15 in May 1990, structure plans were again back on the agenda. The institutional change taking place with local government reorganization in Great Britain is creating a period of further uncertainty for strategic planning.

Developments in Europe, particularly with prospects of an enlarged European Union, are going to result in calls for regional plans. Policies aimed at reducing regional disparities are an important element of EU policy. The Commission has stressed the need to present coherent regional strategies as part of any bid for European assistance. The move to smaller unitary authorities with the loss of wider strategic planning considerations could place local authorities in Wales at a disadvantage vis-a-vis other regions in Europe.

59

Strategic planning guidance in Wales will, inevitably, have to assume a spatial dimension. It may be that the Welsh Office will have to move closer to regional planning guidance along the lines of the English model in order to maintain effective strategic planning in the Principality. 1995 marks the 30th anniversary of the Planning Advisory Group seminal report, *The future of development plans* (PAG 1965). That report provided the foundations for the 1968 Town and Country Planning Act, which formed the basis of our present development plan system. It may be that we should pause and revisit that report before we move to embrace a new planning system based on Unitary Development Plans. Looking towards the third millennium, strategic land-use planning must be an important part of Wales the way ahead.

CHAPTER 5

Local planning policy – the Newbury approach

Alan Jones

This chapter is not about a "how we did it approach" to local planning policy. It will, however, say something about the Newbury experience. It will use this experience as a way of linking the theory and practice of plan-making with some of the issues concerning the changing organizational relationships that affect the cascade of policies from national to local level.

Introduction

Newbury district is typical of many others in terms of its policy development. In the early 1980s it was a totally unreconstructed shire district settling down after the previous reorganization. A plan adopted in 1981 (NDC 1981) replaced the former Newbury and Thatcham Town Map, and another adopted in 1982 (ibid. 1982) dealt with the rural areas in west Berkshire. Together they gave almost complete district coverage. The statutory planning background remained largely unchanged up to the beginning of 1988. A new structure plan had gone through a lengthy and tortuous preparation and was awaiting approval in that year. It was evident that, for two years or more, planning control had operated without a clear and firm policy base. This was having an effect on appeal success rates. Housing land supply and major allocations were hostages to fortune. The local plans section was depleted and demotivated, with a virtually non-existent work programme. No preparation had been made for a new local plan and no survey base existed.

Within a few weeks of arriving at the council in January 1988 as planning director, I was called to a Conservative group meeting to advise on difficulties being experienced with development pressures. The advice, which the group accepted, was that their three most important priorities were: first, policy;

secondly, policy; and thirdly, policy. The approach the council adopted – and which will be dealt with in more general terms later – was this. Make it simple. Keep it local. Involve the public. Above all, get it in place quickly.

Although the modifications to the structure plan had been published in January 1988, the plan was not approved by the Secretary of State until November that year (BCC 1988). By building up and motivating the team, dishing out the work as a sixth-form project and learning not to be too precious about detail, the planning department had its first district-wide local plan out to public consultation in September 1989 (NDC 1989). Its impact on the development control process was immediate. Public consultation, editing and refinement were carried on side by side and the deposit version was published exactly a year later (ibid. 1990).

There was of course still much to be done: appraisal and negotiation in respect of objections; preparation for and handling of the local plan inquiry; consideration of the Inspector's recommendations; the publication of modifications (ibid. 1993b); running the gauntlet of Department of the Environment scrutiny (of which there will be more later); and final adoption. The plan was not adopted until December 1993 (ibid. 1993a).

A local plan is like a butterfly or a daffodil: it is at its highest power when it first spreads its wings or comes into bloom. This happens around about the time of the deposit copy and everything that happens thereafter is about preparing the way for its replacement. In this way Newbury saw the public inquiry process, the modifications and so on, not so much as a legitimation of the policies forged through public consultation, but as the basis for the next round, namely, the preparation of a better and more intelligible plan. The review of the plan, which got off the ground before the original one was adopted, was a return to our original values with attitude: make it simple, keep it local, involve the public, but above all, do it quickly.

This chapter will return to these principles, but first it will offer some comments about the nature of the plan-led system.

Life in the plan-led system

So we now have a plan-led system. But what do we mean by that and is it any different to the way things were before?

Many have argued that Section 54A of the Town and Country Planning Act 1990 brought about a radical change in the planning system. To remind you, Section 54A provides that:

> Where, in making a determination under the planning Acts, regard is to be had to the development plan, the determination shall be made in accordance with the plan unless material considerations indicate otherwise.

There are two views of the significance of this change. The first is that it is the most fundamental shift in emphasis in the government's approach to planning since 1948. The second is that it makes no real difference. It has been argued elsewhere (Jones 1991a,b,c) that Section 54A was the culmination of a change from the period of "lifting the burden" and general overhaul of the planning system towards modernization and "spring cleaning", all of which was connected to the "turquoising" of the Conservative Party. The weight that local planning authorities give to the plan clearly depends upon its relationship with the other material considerations and the presumption in favour of granting permission. The relativities of these factors have changed over time in response to political change, DOE advice and the decisions of courts. Section 54A is but another adjustment in response to national priorities. Although it introduces a significant change in emphasis in the spirit of the system, there has been no practical change in law and procedure, as Ian Gatenby and Christopher Williams explain in Chapter 9.

From 1948 to the present day, local planning authorities have been required to deal with planning activities by having "regard to the provisions of the development plan, so far as material to the application, and to any other material consideration" (Section 70(2) of the 1990 Act). However, over the same period there has been a presumption, albeit of varying strengths, in favour of the applicant and/or development. This so-called "first presumption" is supplemented by others applying in particular circumstances, for example, the presumption in favour of development in cases where there is less than a five-year supply of land. As a corollary, it has become established that, where permission is to be withheld, the "burden of proof" lies with the local planning authority to demonstrate that the development is unacceptable and that there are sound and clear cut reasons for refusal. However, up to the mid-1980s the assumption underlying such principles was that the development plan was the most important of the material considerations. In discharging the "burden of proof" the planning authority was likely to turn first to the development plan for support and guidance. The dominance of the development plan was secured through the development plan directions, regulations, attendant advice and the appeals system. It was reinforced by the requirement that, where an authority was minded to grant permission for a proposal that would, in their opinion, conflict with or prejudice the objectives of the plan, they should first advertise it and take into account any objections. Some of these proposals must also be notified to the Secretary of State, and the general principle is underpinned by the call-in procedure. The advice of Sweet & Maxwell's *Encyclopaedia of planning law* is that since the provisions of the statutory development plan may be material to the application, and since the validity of the plan's policies and proposals cannot be challenged by legal proceedings after adoption/approval, the plan has a "deemed materiality".

The courts have held many times, however, that there is no obligation on a local planning authority to adhere slavishly to the plan. Furthermore, where planning authorities wish to refuse permission it is not sufficient to argue that proposals are contrary to the plan. It is necessary to demonstrate that the proposal would frustrate the objectives that the relevant policy was designed to promote. This is a recognition of the presumption in favour of the applicant. However, that presumption is not overriding and its weight may change relative to the plan and other considerations, over time. The advice of the *Encyclopædia of planning law* is that:

> . . .it was not a statutory rule and did not have the force of law; nor did it simply reflect the statutory or legal position. It was a policy presumption for planning administration, and as such it could be changed: the Secretary of State may qualify, or even reverse the presumption without a change in law (EPL, also Graham 1990).

It appears, for example, that the presumption has been changed over the years both in formulation and in terms of its relativity to the development plan and other considerations.

In the 1947 system, according to the Ministry of Housing and Local Government, it was limited to "cases where there is no serious issue involved and where the authority can produce no sufficient reason for refusal". In such cases, the applicant was to be given the benefit of the doubt, and development was to be encouraged unless it caused "demonstrable harm to interests of acknowledged importance". This phrase, introduced in 1953, was to fall out of common usage until the mid-1980s. Meanwhile, there are difficulties in reconciling the "first presumption" with other presumptions against development, such as those applying in green belt and other areas of special protection.

It was Circular 14/85 (DoE 1985) that introduced the most important variation on the balance between the presumption in favour of the applicant and the weight accorded to the development plan. It reintroduced the concepts of demonstrable harm and interests of acknowledged importance, and a new interpretation that the development plan was but one of the material considerations. Circular 14/85 thereby strengthened the presumption in favour of allowing applications, and its main principles were repeated in the then current PPG1 (DoE/WO 1988), where the old principle was restated that: "if the planning authority consider it necessary to refuse permission, the onus is upon them to demonstrate clearly why the development cannot be permitted". This advice challenged the weight to be given to development plans and was a reflection of the political change in attitude, borne out of the emphasis on employment creation. In terms of law and procedure, however, little had changed. PPG1 pointed out that development plans are not prescriptive, that they do not offer more than a broad framework, that they do not show exactly what will or will not be allowed, and that the plan is only one of the considerations that must be taken into account. There were, however, reciprocal points: that where the plan is up to date it will be given considerable weight; and, more importantly, that: "strong contrary planning grounds will have to be *demonstrated* to *justify* a proposal which conflicts with it" [author's emphasis] (ibid.: para. 14).

This last statement was perhaps an indication of things to come. That where the plan is in highest currency, and other considerations do not override it, there may be a burden of proof on the applicant or even a presumption in favour of the plan. In any event, the message in relation to development plans was clear: they should confine their scope to land-use planning matters (i.e. those relating directly to the physical development or the use of land), construct policies having regard to all known considerations material to such matters, and keep them relevant to today's conditions. If plans are kept up to date, base their policies on an analysis of the importance of acknowledged interests, and set their objectives as a means of avoiding harm to such interests, having regard to other considerations, they are not simply one consideration but the embodiment of many, if not all, considerations pertinent at the time.

This is not the place to review in detail the circumstances in which the 1990 Act was amended with the new Section 54A. Suffice it to say that the statements made at the time by the minister, Sir George Young, and the guidance that has emerged since, make it clear that the plan is the starting point or the first consideration when one looks at planning applications. The force of this section is that it alters the balance between the plan and the presumption in favour of the applicant as set out in the then current [1988] version of PPG1. The *Encyclopædia of planning law* gives the following advice:

> the presumption in that (1988) form was irreconcilable with the new S.54A
> . . . which weights the balance in favour of the development plan . . .
> Thus the presumption is now, if anything, in favour of the development
> plan . . . (*EPL*).

Regrettably, the presumption in favour of the plan is not reflected very clearly in the replacement PPG1 (DoE/WO 1992a). The plan prevails where the development is in accordance with it, but where there is a conflict the usual tests apply.

The phrasing of Section 54A is important in this respect. At first glance it appears to be a significant shift in favour of the plan from the "have regard to" statement in Section 70(2) to the "determination shall be made in accordance with" of Section 54A. However, a moment's serious consideration suggests that the balance has not shifted very far. District plan policies are hardly ever so clear cut that a determination could be made in accordance with them without regard to detailed evaluation. The question of whether a proposal is in accordance with the plan will remain a matter of local professional and political judgement against a set of policy criteria and other considerations. Since Section 54A was not augmented with advice that the onus is now upon the applicant to prove that the development is in accordance with the plan, the burden still remains on the local planning authority to provide reasons for refusal, linking policy objectives to tangible harm.

The reasoning used by both the applicant and local planning authority in this respect is therefore no more than a recasting of the long-established process of examining the proposal against material considerations within and beyond the plan. What is also clear is that material considerations are an ever-expanding concept (Purdue 1989). The courts have been prepared to approve an ever-increasing range of factors within the legitimate range of planning issues. Most of them cover some 21 pages of the *Encyclopaedia of planning law*. The spectrum is so broad that even limitations confining the relevance of material considerations to planning matters fairly and reasonably related to the application produces a discussion far beyond the compass of any development plan. Furthermore, if a particular factor is a material consideration within or beyond the scope of the plan, the key issue is what weight it should have in the balance.

There is an important message here for the process of local policy-making. The plan is more than one material consideration because it is the means by which most of the relevant considerations affecting the planning of a locality are generalized and exposed to public debate. But the plan is only a snap-shot of the locality and the considerations that make up the "decision environment". No plan, however up to date, can be the embodiment of all considerations relevant to the decision-making process. The implications for local policy-making is clear: however good it might be, the local plan is far from perfect and can never be comprehensively rational or long lasting. Of course the plan must be professionally respectable, representative of the concerns of the local community and competently written. It is however, always partial, transitory and at best a guide.

Simply planning

"The local plan has become the poor planner's substitute for the novel" (with apologies to Ruth Glass, re Community Studies).

The main message in Newbury's experience is that local plans should be simple. They should be simply concerned with planning and they should be simply written and presented. This has advantages in terms of speed of preparation, shortening the process between deposit and adoption, and strengthening the possibility of the plan retaining its relevance to current issues after it is adopted. It will also make the plan easier to review and improve its shelf life while that review is taking place.

Indeed, a simple and concise approach is recommended by PPG12:

... authorities should bear in mind that the more detailed the plan, the longer it is likely to take to adopt, and the greater the chance that it will not be up to date when it is adopted. (DOE 1992b)

PPG12 provides a great deal of advice about the scope, content and form of local plans: what to include and to leave out, the duration of the plan, the level of detail appropriate to the plan and so on. It also deals with the role that local plans play in the hierarchy of land-use planning policy. This is not the place to repeat the detail of this guidance. However, the main message is that "Plans should be clear, succinct and easily understood by all who need to know about the planning policies and proposals in the area." (ibid.: para. 5.3).

There are also some key principles:

- the plan should include the planning authority's policies and proposals for the development and use of land
- it should also refer, by way of background, to the overall strategy and other policies and proposals of other authorities and government departments
- it should include policies on particular topics (conservation of natural beauty and amenity, improvement of the physical environment and traffic management) and other matters prescribed by other PPGs.

Some of this guidance runs contrary to the requirement for clarity and succinctness.

The plan must, as PPG12 suggests, deal with the planning authority's policies and proposal in the context of overall strategy. Furthermore, it must deal with the full range of economic, social and environmental considerations and in particular the impact of change. However, the planning authority must also communicate with people about the key local planning issues, in particular new or emerging issues; and it must do this within a timescale and a budget. There was a lawnmower repair man who had a board outside his workshop saying that there were three types of job: quick, cheap and good. A quick job would not be cheap, a cheap job would not be quick, and a quick cheap job would not be any good. The trick is how to make the local plan, quick, cheap and good.

First, the plan must stick to land-use planning issues. The local plan is not a local authority corporate strategy. Essentially it is a plan about land use and development – an obvious point perhaps, but one that seems to cause endless problems for some authorities. Most district planning authorities will have a range of strategies dealing with other matters: economic development, housing, community development, leisure, the environment, car parking, transportation and so on. They may even be published in different forms. The local plan is by its very nature more synoptic and will touch upon and overlap several of these other strategies, informing, developing and perhaps implementing their objectives in various ways. But the local plan is not the hub of this wheel. This is the role of corporate strategy, whether or not it is formalized in terms of a corporate or community plan.

The plan can also be simplified by cutting out descriptive material – its purpose is not to provide a district guide. Similarly, there are many virtuous issues that the council may be concerned with: control of pollution, promotion of a healthy lifestyle, reduction of greenhouse gas emissions, protection of endangered species, and so on. However, it is not the role of the local plan to save the whale or prevent the overheating of the planet. In so far as these issues have land-use implications, they may be addressed in passing and local plan policy may have some small part to play, but the labouring of these issues at every opportunity is no more than a matter of fashion.

67

Another way in which plans can be simplified and made more concise is by the removal of a great deal of repetition of national, regional and strategic policies. To an extent this contradicts the guidance in PPG12, which requires local plans to demonstrate that their policies are consistent with national policy. We must therefore find ways of cross referencing with and underlining national, regional and strategic policy, without repeating it at length. The purpose of the local plan is to give those policies local expression.

If we follow this approach, the plan is simplified, clarified and improved at each review. In accordance with the Development Plan Regulations 1991 it is then possible to rely upon an existing policy statement to list extant policies that are to be continued into the new plan. These policies need not then be considered at a local plan inquiry, unless objectors are able to show that there have been significant changes in circumstances. The review of the plan can then focus on those issues and policies that are now out of date and on the changes in circumstances, new material considerations and more current issues, that require the development of new policy.

There are of course, disadvantages to this approach. Simple and concise local plans may lack the comfort of repetitive policy statements cascading down from national to local level, the usual barrage of policies that overlap and reinforce one another, and the substantial amount of reasoned justification. Planners engaged in development control may feel that the plan does not adequately cover the key issues affecting the range of development opportunities in the district and may, indeed, encourage development to exploit the loopholes. The development industry, amenity societies and other groups interested in local planning may object to the gaps that appear to exist, and perhaps the development industry will feel that the plans offer less certainty than the more traditional tomes to which we have become accustomed. Perhaps the DOE should revisit the development plan regulations to allow plans to appear in two parts, both with statutory force: a core document of established national strategic and local policies and a review update dealing with new issues.

We shall have to wait and see how the simple and concise approach is received by the government, the development industry and the community at large. One clear opportunity that it does offer, however, is for making plans more readable and user-friendly. The transition from dry transfer lettering to desktop publishing and all the attendant improvements in presentation and graphics capability (including the use of geographical information systems) mean that plans could get the message over much more effectively. They can be tighter in style, making use of photographs and diagrams, and perhaps even loose-leaf. They can, of course, always be backed up by a series of pamphlets providing detailed information, policy criteria and supplementary guidance. Peter Suttie, the Director of Planning at Banff and Buchan District Council, has described how this approach is taking planning closer to the people:

Being able to break our Local Plan down to its component parts so as to minimize the scope for confusing the customer is but a very small step in the direction of providing a user-friendly planning system in northeast Scotland. (Suttie 1993)

We can all learn from their experience.

Keeping it local

Just as it is important that the local plan is not complicated and lengthened by the inclusion of unnecessary national, regional and strategic policies, so it is important that these levels of policy do not deal with inappropriate detail or interfere in matters that would best be determined locally. The most common area of concern is the point at which structure plans mesh with local plans. It is understandable that there should have been a degree of overlap and duplication in the early rounds of structure and local plan preparation. But these ought to have been filtered out in successive rounds. Structure plans, as well as local plans, benefit from editing and shortening, so as to concentrate on key issues, leaving the detail to the local plan. This follows the advice in PPG12 that where structure plans are reviewed:

It is important that they are made more concise, by concentration on key land-use issues, and by exclusion of detailed policies that are more appropriate to local plans. (DoE 1992b: para. 5.7)

It is perhaps a recognition that this advice is too often disregarded that PPG12 gives particular emphasis to the level of detail in structure plans. This reiterates the well worn phrase that the main function of the structure plan is to state in broad terms general policies and proposals of strategic importance, thus providing the framework for the detail of local plans. The structure plan may indicate the scale of provision to be made in the area as a whole, including, for example, figures for housing in each district and, where appropriate, the broad location of major growth areas. It may also indicate the general location of individual developments likely to have a significant effect on the plan area. However, we still see structure plans that provide detailed development control policies and site-specific allocations. The arguments that such detail is required to inform major infrastructure decisions, or to focus properly the public's attention in the run-up to the Examination in Public, do not stand up to closer examination. When in doubt it is worth returning to first principles. One of the first principles so often forgotten is that the structure and local plan together form the development plan. They are not competing for the same business.

The other main problem area is the intervention by the Secretary of State. The powers of the Secretary of State to issue a direction requiring the modification of a plan before its adoption or to call the plan in, are long established and part of the normal checks and balances that ensure development plans are consistent

69

with national and regional policies. We are told by PPG12 that the purpose of these powers is to deal with development plan policies that are at odds with national or regional policies or which are so technically defective that they could cause great difficulties to plan users. We are also told that the Secretary of State would expect to use these powers sparingly and as a last resort.

Imagine the surprise at Newbury, therefore, when after the normal period of public consultation, detailed and lengthy negotiations with objectors with a view to reaching agreement, an expensive local plan inquiry and the publication of modifications to meet, in every respect, the Inspector's requirements, the Secretary of State intervened on a matter of detailed wording.

The first approach from the Secretary of State informed the council that since re-establishing a plan-led system with Section 54A of the 1990 Act, the Department of the Environment now scrutinizes draft plans more closely than in the past (an interesting admission!). The Department's principal concern is to identify policies that appear to conflict with guidance in PPGs and that do not appear justified by unique local circumstances. Most of the Secretary of State's comments could be accommodated in the modifications. One phrase contained within the plan – that there was in certain circumstances "a presumption against development" – attracted particular attention. The Secretary of State wanted the phrase replaced. The council was not prepared to remove it and could see no reason why it should.

The DoE responded by reminding the council that the planning system should operate on the basis that applications "should be allowed, having regard to the development plan and all material considerations, unless the proposed development would cause demonstrable harm to interests of acknowledged importance". Apparently the Secretary of State now consistently intervenes whenever draft plans set out what he regards as inappropriate presumptions against development. However, his department did not explain how the "presumptions against" in the Newbury Plan were in conflict with government policy, particularly since some of the "presumptions against" were designed to prevent demonstrable harm to sites of special interest and to other matters of acknowledged importance. The best that the Department could do was to point the council to part of an after-dinner speech given by Sir George Young to the Oxford Planning Conference in September 1992. The council was somewhat surprised that the content of an after-dinner speech should appear to be the justification for the Secretary of State's intervention, particularly as it had not been published as Planning Policy Guidance or in the form of any circular or other direction.

The council refused to alter the wording and the Secretary of State subsequently issued a direction requiring the modification to be made and preventing the plan being adopted in the interim. The Secretary of State wished to see the reference to "presumption against" replaced with wording to the effect that development "will not normally be permitted". The council promptly applied for judicial review on the grounds that the Secretary of State's direction was unintelligible and irrational. The council's case was as follows.

First, the use of the words "presumption against" does not necessarily con-flict with the Department of the Environment's general line on the presumption in favour of the applicant. There is nothing in the latest version of PPG1, *General policy and principles* (DoE/WO 1992a), that is materially different from the orig-inal PPG1, Circular 22/80 that preceded it or any similar reference traced all the way back to 1948. Secondly, if the Secretary of State's intervention was because of the re-establishment of a plan-led system, it is clear from paragraph 25 of PPG1 that Section 54A does not affect the policies in the development plan itself, it affects the development-control decision-making process alone. In other words, the effect of Section 54A is to put added weight upon the policies con-tained in the plan, whatever their content may be. Thirdly, the council could not discern any conflict between the local plan policies and national or regional pol-icy guidelines. Fourthly, the council could not comprehend, and the Secretary of State was unable to explain, what benefit would result from changing the wording as suggested. Fifthly, the Secretary of State could not point to any national, regional or strategic guidance that justified this change in wording. In the council's view, the change in wording would lead to confusion, debate and extra expense at planning inquiries.

Lastly, the Secretary of State had failed to recognize that the local plan must be in general conformity with the structure plan, and that plan, approved by him, included several references to "presumption against". The Secretary of State's response was that the plan was approved before Section 54A and the new PPG1 came into being, and appeared to be saying that if the local plan did not fit the structure plan, then never mind, there will be another one along later.

Unfortunately, the case never reached the courts. In a letter that confirmed that the council's modifications conformed with the earlier direction, the Secre-tary of State withdrew from the case, studiously avoiding the whole debate about "presumptions against".

Involving the public

We all know about public consultation. The process has been around a long time and we are all practised in it. The one-sentence short course on public consulta-tion is that, although we all consult, some of the time we are notifying and informing, and at other times we are inviting comments and debate, but we are not always genuinely willing to be persuaded by the results. The one issue that appears to cause greatest frustration to consultees, and that decides the success or failure of public consultation exercises, is that councils do not always make it clear when they are notifying and informing and when they are inviting com-ments or involvement about issues on which they are genuinely undecided. This harks back to Sherry Arnstein's "ladder of participation", which takes us from placating the public at the lowest level to power-sharing at the highest level

(Arnstein 1969; see also Ch. 11). A further problem is that public consultation, at whatever level, involves only parts of the community and benefits some groups more than others.

During the preparation of the Newbury district local plan, control of the council passed from Conservatives to Liberal Democrats and there was a subsequent strategic shift towards greater public involvement and partnership with the community. The introduction of public speaking rights at the Area Planning Subcommittees was one way in which the planning service was taken closer to the community and made more open. The review of the local plan offered a major opportunity to show how the strategy could be further developed.

In particular, there was a concern that local plans are produced in camera without regard to the fact that all sections of the community have aspirations about the district and some, particularly those involved in the development process, have very real influence. The more traditional approach to plan review would suggest a certain amount of technical work to produce options for policies and proposals that would then be exposed to political debate and filtering before finally going out to public consultation. Typically, what happens is that those parts of the community – particularly the development industry and the amenity groups – that are dissatisfied with the policies and proposals object, and a debate ensues that is supposed to inform the council's decision-making process. The process benefits the articulated and well represented more than the rest. Furthermore, since the emphasis is on objections to the plan, it is inherently negative, with little opportunity to promote policies and proposals. In this review the council decided to reverse the process and begin with an open debate.

In June 1993 the council invited submissions from landowners, developers, agencies and amenity/interest/resident groups to make submissions on the future scale, type, form and distribution of development in the district for the period 1996–2006. To make the process manageable the submissions were limited to proposals for ten or more houses, or for industrial, commercial or retail development of $1000\,m^2$ or more. The intention was to consider these proposals at a series of hearings presided over by a panel comprising members of council, a representative from the local branch of CPRE and a representative of the local business community.

The closing date for submissions was the end of September 1993. In mid-October, copies of the submissions were sent to the county council and the relevant parish councils. Where appropriate, consultations took place with a variety of agencies. In early November, guidance notes were sent to all prospective participants in the panel hearings, together with a timetable. A brief report was prepared by council officers on each of the proposals against a simple evaluation matrix. Copies of these reports, together with responses from the consultees, were sent to the relevant proposer, parish council and ward members.

All of the sessions went smoothly and to time, thanks to the co-operation of all participants. The process yielded much useful information, particularly in informing the council of land available for development, the aspirations of the development industry and particular interest groups, what was on offer to the community by way of benefits, and the public perception of environmental constraints. The process also facilitated a much wider public debate than is usual at this stage in the process. In some parts of the district the debate was even more extensive, with parish councils holding public meetings attended by the council's officers and other interested parties.

Not surprisingly, this process included a great deal of work in considering and appraising the submissions in the light of the hearings. The issues were debated by the political groups and the decisions used to shape the main policies and proposals in the draft plan. The main elements of the plan informed by the debate on the submissions were then drafted and considered by the review panel that had conducted the hearings.

The most formative local planning issue in Newbury district and the one that had attracted greatest public interest, was the quantum and distribution of housing development. To take a theme of public involvement one step further, in June 1994 the council set up community working parties to consider specific allocations. Each community working party was authorized to appoint its own chairman and was serviced by the council's officers. The work of the community working parties informed and in many cases modified the draft policies and proposals to be put before the review panel and the council's service committees.

In December 1994 the council formally published its Draft Local Plan Review for public consultation (NDC 1994). (This plan conforms to the Berkshire Structure Plan which was published in deposit draft form in November 1992, subjected to an EIP in June/July 1993 and is currently being modified by the county council.) The next stage in the local plan process will be to publish the deposit plan, which, subject to the resolution of the structure plan housing allocation dispute between the county and the Secretary of State, will be in spring 1996. That plan will include design statements on housing allocations prepared by the community working parties.

Effectiveness in local policy-making

So far this chapter has concentrated on the technical aspects of the plan-making process. From the point of view of the management of that process, there are three main issues to be considered. First, how do we manage performance in policy-making? Secondly, how do we approach the assessment of policy effectiveness? Lastly, how do we know that it is all good value for money?

Turning to the first question of performance management. All local plans sections have work programmes. However, it would be interesting to know how many of them have developed service plans, applying planning techniques to the provision of the service. The service plan can be used as an internal management document setting out objectives, priorities and targets. Through the use of time

73

recording, it can be used to assign resources to particular tasks and to link the work plan with the projected budget. The potential of this approach is that it can be taken well beyond an internal management tool and can be used to generate options for service development, whereby different service levels and their resource implications are exposed to political choice. The service plan can be set up in a way that breaks down the activities into their component parts and identifies their priority on a scale ranging from inescapable through to dispensable. Since each activity is capable of operating at different levels of service, these can then be offered as choices. The resource implications of each service level can be charted. Members of council are thereby able to select a basket of service activities that matches their aspirations with the available budget. The resource implications, both up and down, of service changes are more easily understood.

The most difficult part of any service plan relating to policy-making is how to construct performance indicators. The service planning exercise, with its identification of objectives and targets and the production of service level options, goes a long way towards assessing performance in relation to inputs and intermediate outputs. However, it does nothing in relation to the assessment of policy effectiveness or final outputs. A great deal of work has been carried out on performance measurement and indication in the public sector. The main conclusion would appear to be that there are few simple and robust proxies that describe performance in the round. Although comprehensive and multi-criteria systems can be created to assess issues such as policy effectiveness, their applicability on a day-to-day basis may not be manageable.

Under the Planning Research Programme the DoE commissioned PIEDA plc (planning, economic and development consultants) to carry out a study of the evaluation of the effectiveness of land-use planning. Their report was published in 1992 (DoE 1992d). The study used an adapted version of Lichfield's Planning Balance Sheet. Working on a central proposition that the function of planning is to balance economic and environmental costs and benefits in the public interest, it used the balance sheet to test the effectiveness of policies in achieving their objectives against a model statement of planning objectives and a scale of costs and benefits. It applied this methodology to several case studies, one of which was Newbury. Although the methodology is relatively simple, the complexity of the exercise increases in its application and it is highly questionable whether it would be adopted by planning authorities as a regular exercise. However, its use as an occasional check on individual and group perceptions in the office is valuable. In respect of Newbury, however, the study bears out what was known intuitively and by experience among the officers and members, and it underlines the success of the overall strategy and particular policy objectives. What is most valuable is that it provides a means by which these perceptions can be made more structured, if not more objective.

Finally, let us consider the issue of value of money. The government's view is that consumers receive value for money when they are satisfied with the provision of a service about which they have a real choice of supplier. Local authorities know only too well the ways in which this philosophy has affected services through compulsory competitive tendering (CCT). Whatever one thinks about CCT from an ideological standpoint, few would doubt that it has had a radical and in many respects beneficial effect on the management of local authority services. Most of us also know that many of these improvements may never have been addressed had we not been compelled to compete. The disadvantages of CCT are also known to us. Principal among them are that the local authority is not always allowed to compete on an equal basis, that the authority and the community at large can lose control over the choice of supplier, and that the process may not be value for money in the long run.

Although there is not the slightest hint at the present time that CCT will be extended to planning services, the experience of CCT in other areas is encouraging many authorities to look at out-sourcing, voluntary contracting out and externalization. The use of consultants for specialist activities such as landscape appraisal, economic analysis and more recently environmental audits is common place. It is unlikely that many authorities will follow the example of Berkshire County Council and externalize the whole of the planning service, in their case to Babtie Public Services Division. However, more councils are likely to look to the private sector for the preparation of the whole local plan. It would also not be surprising if the government provided some encouragement in the form of legislation setting performance targets for plan-making. Local authorities wishing to retain their in-house team should be putting systems in place for performance management, the evaluation of policy effectiveness and for the assessment of value for money.

These issues are even more important now that we have a plan-led system in which it is a statutory requirement to produce district-wide local plans. There have been many criticisms of the local plan system over the years, the most common of which being that the process is slow and cumbersome, gives little certainty to the development industry, is capable of arbitrary decisions with serious economic consequences, does not genuinely negotiate away objections, and can grind to a halt in the lengthy inquiry and modification stages. These objections will be sharpened by the duty introduced in the 1990 Act to produce district-wide local plans and to keep them under review. The DOE will wish to keep an eye on the ways in which local planning authorities manage their performance and will want to develop ways of assessing effectiveness and value for money. In the early drafts of the Planning and Compensation Bill, reference was made to the possibility of the Secretary of State introducing regulations requiring local plans to be produced to a particular timescale. At that time, it appears that this might be followed in the policy-making arena by the introduction of league tables based on development plans. There was also speculation that local planning might be put on trial. If plan-making authorities did not perform as required, the government might be tempted to introduce legislation requiring this work to be subjected to competition.

The DOE consultation paper on fee setting (DOE 1994e) may provide a more recent clue to current government thinking. Should the proposals go ahead, local authorities defined as good performers (in terms of development control and local planning) would be allowed to recoup their full costs (as prescribed by DOE policy) by setting their own planning fees. Poor performers would be obliged to use national fee rates and would be unable to recoup any deficit between prescribed costs and fee income by adjustments to their standard spending assessment from the DOE. In this scenario, poor performers are bound to get worse. It is only a small step from here to the introduction of approved consultation regulations as a means of introducing a default system. All of this is speculation of course, but the scenario has its precedents, even to the point of suggesting that consultants engaged in default would perhaps be allowed to set their own fees.

Conclusions

Local planning policy exists at the interface between the political and economic forces for change in society – operating for the most part at the international and interregional levels – and the mediation of interests that affect the most salient aspects of people lives. It allows difficult distributional (political) choices to be made on a pseudo-technical basis (Reade 1987). More cynically, in recent times, "rebuilding" of the system replaced its "demolition" as the Conservative Party recognized that the growth versus environment debate was brought into sharpest focus in those areas where the greatest concentrations of Tory voters live (Ehrman 1988). It is not surprising, therefore, that the weight given to planning policy relative to other considerations, and fashions and trends in local policy-making, follow the ebb and flow of changing political priorities. Similarly, the issues dealt with by local policy will to a large extent be a response to the rapid and fundamental changes in British and European society. Restructuring of the UK economy, internationalization, technological convergence, and the consequent opportunities for growth and environmental change, are reinforced by significant demographic and social restructuring, shifts in ideology and a recasting of social processes into spatial forms.

However, local planning policy remains in essence a means of reconciling economic and environmental costs and benefits at a local level. It gives local emphasis and expression to national and strategic issues. It would of course be nice if there were a set of explicitly stated and politically agreed criteria providing a consistent and stable framework for national and regional land-use policy. However, we know from experience that on such matters governments prefer flexibility to strong political direction. Therefore, we simply have to accept that local planning policy will continue to be produced in the context of the even-handed and sometimes duplicitous nature of central government guidance on land-use issues. No local planning authority, having produced a local plan during the changes in government attitude to out-of-town retailing marked by the new PPG6 (DOE/WO 1993), could fail to recognize the realities of this situation.

In conclusion, therefore, local planning policy must do its best to deal with the uncertainties brought about by constant change in the economic and social conditions of the national and the political responses that cascade through a variety of regional and local institutions, often with conflicting interests. A local planning document can never deal with all of these matters adequately. It will never be comprehensively rational or timeless. Indeed, to award the plan a weight and status that suggests otherwise would be bad planning. These documents are a way of communicating to the general public a set of democratically agreed principles about local land-use issues for a short period in the history of the community. At their best, they do this plainly; adding local knowledge and understanding to the more abstract concepts of strategic policy, and by genuinely involving local people. These documents are most effective when both the policy choices and the management of the process have been subjected to democratic control. The debate about internal management, performance, review and the strengths and weaknesses of competition in the delivery of such services is interesting, but in another sense a distraction. The unique and irreplaceable principle of local policy-making is that it is democratic. Local planning authorities creak with the difficulties of recognizing and accommodating the vast range of planning "customers" and their conflicting expectations. Local democracy is not a perfect response to this problem, but the counter-factual – a system of planning decisions without democratic involvement – is unthinkable.

CHAPTER 6
Planning policy in Scotland

Keith Hayton

Introduction

The legislation governing Scottish planning is similar to that of England and Wales. However, the local government structure and the national guidance provided by the Scottish Office gives a far sounder foundation for the preparation and implementation of development plans. Despite this, plan production has been slow and the plans themselves have often been less than ideal. Outside of the development plans framework Scotland is distinctive in that a variety of central government bodies, especially the Scottish Development Agency, have played a key role in physical regeneration. However, the relationship of their activities to development planning has often been obscure. Scottish planning is now facing a variety of challenges. The reform of local government may undermine the effectiveness of strategic planning and increase the role of the non-elected Local Enterprise Companies in determining strategic priorities.

Although there has been considerable direction of the planning system, it has been claimed that this has reflected a consensus between central and local government. An alternative view is that development planning had been ineffective in dealing with some of the major issues, and direction and intervention had therefore become irrelevancies. The challenges that planning now faces mean that if it is to survive it must become more pro-active and place more emphasis upon implementation within the development plans framework, thereby showing that it has something to offer.

The legislative framework

Scotland is not a northern extension of England. Although constitutionally part of the UK, it has a similar but subtly different planning system. Although it has been considerably amended over the years, the key statute governing Scottish planning is still the 1972 Town and Country Planning (Scotland) Act, rather than Town and Country Planning Act 1990. However, a consolidating act is apparently being prepared (Scottish Office 1994a: 7). The 1972 Act sets out the framework for the preparation of structure and local plans and the administration of the development control system.

Until the 1991 Planning and Compensation Act was introduced, one of the main things that distinguished Scottish planning was the requirement for complete local plan coverage, although this has still not been attained. This requirement was introduced in the 1973 Local Government (Scotland) Act that allocated planning responsibilities to the district, islands and regional authorities. Parts of the 1991 Planning and Compensation Act apply to Scotland, for example the status of development plans in determining planning decisions is governed by Section 58, that is identical to Section 26, which is applicable in England and Wales. However, other parts of the 1991 Act do not apply. For example, in Scotland authorities are not allowed to approve their own structure plans. This remains the responsibility of the Secretary of State, who can approve them with or without modifications and, therefore, can have a significant impact upon planning policy at the local level. This impact can also be exercised through the Secretary of State's ability to call in and determine planning applications. The Scottish Office states that this has "been seldom used", with only 57 applications having been determined between 1989 and 1992, most of which dealt with trunk roads (Scottish Office 1994a: 18). However, this power has been used to deal with contentious applications that were arousing considerable debate at the local level, as seen most recently with the call in of the application for a super-quarry in the Western Isles. The regional councils also have the power to call in applications that are contrary to the structure plan or raise issues of general significance to the region. This power again has apparently been used "sparingly" (Scottish Office 1994a: 18).

There are many other relatively minor differences. For example, there is different legislation for the Scottish use classes and general development orders, and planning terminology is also often different. For example, listed buildings are categorized as Grades A to C rather than I and II. However, the main initiatives that were at one time seen as challenging the integrity of the planning system, for example enterprise and simplified planning zones, exist in Scotland. A general overview of the Scottish planning system is given in *The planning system* (Scottish Office 1994a) and more detail of the legislation is provided by Collar (1994).

Overall there are undoubtedly more similarities than differences between planning legislation north and south of the border. However, planning practice, especially at the strategic level, is arguably more distinctive. There are several reasons for this, but the basic one is the local government structure that came into being in 1974.

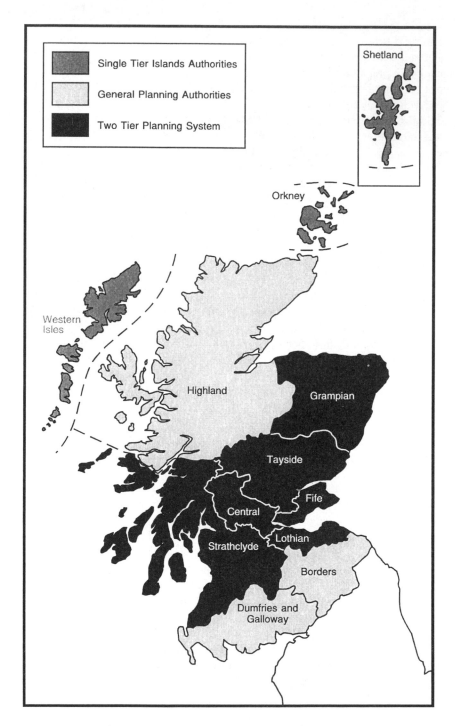

Figure 6.1 Local government reform in Scotland 1974.

Local government structure

The 1974 reform of Scottish local government introduced a two-tier system of 9 regions and 53 districts in mainland Scotland, and three unitary authorities were set up to cover the island areas of Orkney, Shetland and the Western Isles. Not all of the new authorities were given planning powers, so that at the moment there are three combinations of local authority structure and planning service delivery (Fig. 6.1):

- Within six of the regions, planning is a service provided by both region and district, with the region being responsible for strategic planning, in particular the preparation of the structure plan, whereas the districts prepare local plans in conformity with this and are mainly responsible for development control.
- Within the rural regions of Borders, Dumfries and Galloway and Highland, although there are district councils, they have no planning responsibilities. These "general planning authorities" are therefore responsible for all development plan preparation and the development control service.
- The three islands authorities are again responsible for all planning functions within their areas.

These differences essentially reflect geography and population density, with the general and islands authorities covering remote and sparsely populated areas which, although they account for 57 per cent of Scotland's land mass, contain only 10 per cent of its population.

The original proposals for reorganization (Wheatley 1969), were firmly based upon the principles of regionalism. Thus, Wheatley argued that the proposed Highland and Islands Region was a cultural region in that, despite its large size, it had a unity based upon topography, climate and shared experiences. Similarly, the West Region, which essentially became Strathclyde, was claimed to be a nodal region in that Glasgow's dominance gave it cohesion. The proposed regions therefore were based not upon urban/rural differences but upon cohesion of which nodality was the key factor. Unfortunately Wheatley's recommendations were altered considerably, especially on the east coast, where regions were created that were more akin to English counties (Keating & Boyle 1986: 25). The regions that exist today therefore represent a compromise between regional principles and political reality. Although they may not be ideal from a regional planning point of view, and their boundaries can be argued about, most do allow strategic planning to occur over areas that have some meaning in functional terms, encompassing travel-to-work areas and housing markets. These structural benefits to planning practice were further assisted by the services that the regions were to provide, with the regions being given responsibility for major infrastructure services such as water, sewerage and highways. Thus, the regions are not only able to prepare strategic plans for areas that are "regions" in many senses, but they are also responsible for some of the key infrastructure services that have a crucial role to play in implementation. This effectiveness has probably been

81

helped by the role that the Scottish Office, initially through the Scottish Development Department (SDD) and now the Environment Department, has taken in providing guidance.

The National Planning Guidelines

The National Planning Guidelines (NPGs) were introduced by the Scottish Office in 1974 to give guidance to local authorities on how to deal with development issues that were of national significance. Their background has been outlined elsewhere (Rowan-Robinson et al. 1987: 371–3). The first NPG, dealing with coastal planning for the oil and gas industries, indicated those locations where development should be encouraged and those where, because of factors such as environmental quality, it should be resisted (Scottish Development Department 1974). By the time their replacement by National Planning Policy Guidelines (NPPGs) was announced in 1991, seven NPGs were still either wholly or partly operational (Table 6.1).

Table 6.1 National Planning Guidelines in Scotland effective in 1991 and their current status

Guideline	Date	Status1
Coastal planning	1974	Current in part
Aggregate working	1977	Replaced by NPPG 4
Priorities for development planning	1981	Parts replaced by NPPGs 2, 3 and 4
Skiing developments	1984	Current
High technology: individual high-amenity sites	1985	Replaced by NPPG 2
Location of major retail developments	1986	Current
Agricultural land	1987	Current

1. For the titles of the NPPGs, see Table 6.2.

The NPGs were accompanied by a series of Land Use Summary Sheets (LUSSs) and Planning Information Notes (PINs). The former summarized the current situation for, and considered the implications for planning of, particular land use activities. There were 17 of these by 1986. Not all were related to NPGs. For example, ones on water supply (1978) and groundwater (1981) had no direct relationship. Apparently NPGs only followed from a LUSS where changes were thought likely to have national significance (Lloyd & Rowan-Robinson 1992: 95). The PINs, which had no direct relationship to the NPGs, gave planning authorities information on the land-use implications of particular activities, for example telecommunications, to help them in their discussions with developers.

The NPGs have been categorized by Rowan-Robinson et al. (1987) as falling into two groups:

- The locationally specific, which dealt with nationally significant land resources. In some instances these were defined by an Ordnance Survey map (e.g. sites for large industry and petrochemical development in the Priorities for Development Planning NPG (Scottish Development Department 1981)).

- Those not locationally specific but which dealt in more general terms with a resource, for example agricultural land (Scottish Development Department 1987). In these cases the NPGs were providing general policy advice for structure and local plans. For example, a presumption against the development of prime agricultural land and the requirement to give a reasoned justification when such land is proposed for development.

It is claimed that the nature of the NPGs changed in 1981 (Raemaekers et al. 1994). Before then they were seen as advisory. Following the publication of the *Priorities for development planning* NPG in 1981 (Scottish Development Department 1981) they began to become more prescriptive as they began to deal with non-site-specific policy. In its turn, this began to cause confusion as to their status and relationship to other documents such as Circulars.

The impact of the NPGs

It has been claimed that the NPGs gained "a considerable measure of acceptability by those involved in the land development process" (Lloyd & Rowan-Robinson 1992: 97). They have also been praised by those responsible for drawing them up (Lyddon 1985: 29) and by a wide range of commentators (for example Cullingworth & Nadin 1994: 63; and perhaps most influentially by the Nuffield Foundation 1986: 104, 183). Although this praise may be deserved, it is based on limited evidence as to the NPGs' impact on the planning process. The danger is that the praise results in some of the more critical comments about them being overlooked. The criticisms can be summarized as follows:

- Topic coverage has been rather idiosyncratic. For example, transport infrastructure has not been covered. If it had been, then what Coon (1989: 84) identified as one of the "greatest disappointments of Scottish development plan practice", the failure to integrate land-use and transport planning, might have been partially overcome. Even more strangely, urban renewal, which was identified by the SDD's Chief Planner as one of the major changes in planning (Lyddon 1985: 29), was never dealt with.
- The guidelines have been reactive rather than pro-active. For example, the 1974 Coastal Planning Guideline was introduced following the Drumbuie public inquiry, whereas the 1984 Skiing Guideline followed the public inquiry into the expansion of the skiing area in the Cairngorms (Rowan-Robinson et al. 1987). The retrospective nature of much of the earlier guidance makes claims about the guidelines' potential for anticipating conflict (Rowan-Robinson & Lloyd 1991) rather difficult to accept, as does the fact that some guidelines were summarizing what was already happening

rather than providing any new policy direction (Rowan-Robinson et al. 1987: 376).

- They have been breached, as when there were oil developments outside of the Coastal Guideline's preferred development areas (Gillet, quoted in Rowan-Robinson et al. 1987: 376).
- They have had a rural bias (Raemaekers et al. 1994: 8). However, one reason for this may have been that other government bodies such as the Scottish Development Agency (SDA) were heavily involved in urban regeneration. This may also be a partial explanation for the lack of coverage of such issues as urban regeneration.
- They have not been subject to any systematic review. Although some were replaced (e.g. the 1977 guidance on petrochemical development and 1978 guidance on major shopping centres), like the production of the guidelines this review and replacement process seems to have been rather idiosyncratic.
- Finally, their status became unclear: were they advisory or had they to be conformed to? As has been pointed out, a key problem was that they became both, with some guidelines offering authorities a large element of discretion, whereas others contained elements that were mandatory. Unfortunately, not all authorities apparently recognized this (Rowan-Robinson & Lloyd 1991: 17). The outcome was that the distinction between NPGs and Circulars became blurred (Raemaekers et al. 1994: 4).

These criticisms indicate that the guidelines were not without their problems. However, the key factor resulting in their replacement by the NPPGs was ambiguity over their status and purpose.

The National Planning Policy Guidelines

In the late 1980s the Scottish Office commissioned The Planning Exchange to review its planning publications. The unpublished report apparently claimed that the purpose of the NPGs and their relationship to other types of guidance was unclear (Lloyd & Rowan-Robinson 1992: 98). The outcome was the publication of a consultation paper in 1991 (Scottish Office 1991) that proposed to replace the NPGs with a new series of NPPGs. The White Paper *This common inheritance* was also influential in that it contained a commitment to review NPGs to ensure that they took full account of environmental considerations (HM Government 1990: para. 20.10).

The outcome was the introduction of the NPPGs to replace the NPGs, the discontinuing of the LUSSs and the PINs, and greater clarity over the content and purpose of the various planning guidance documents. Guidance now comes through three types of publication from the Scottish Office's Environment Department (Scottish Office 1994a: 8):

- NPPGs that state government policy on land use and other planning matters that are judged to be of national importance. When appropriate, these will be supported by a "locational framework". They are also to be regularly reviewed. The English and Welsh equivalents are the Planning Policy Guidance (PPG) notes.
- Circulars that will now concentrate upon the explanation of legislation and associated procedural matters. Again there is a close parallel here with English and Welsh practice.
- PANs that will identify and disseminate advice on good practice on such things as plan preparation and how to deal with specific issues through the planning system, such as farm and forestry buildings and wind energy. By mid-1994, 44 had been issued of which the 15 published since 1984 are arguably the most relevant. There is no English or Welsh counterpart to these, given their theoretical advisory status.

The statements of government policy in NPPGs and Circulars are now to be material considerations that are to be taken into account in development plan preparation and development control, as are the English and Welsh PPGs. The changes were therefore intended to clarify the confusion that had arisen over the status of NPGs. At the present time (mid-1995) six NPPGs have been published, while a further five are in draft form. As new ones are published, then any relevant NPGs will be replaced (Table 6.2).

Table 6.2 National Planning Policy Guidelines in Scotland as at August 1995.

	Date issued	
Guideline title	Draft	Final version
1. The planning system	December 1992	January 1994
2. Business and industry	October 1991	October 1993
3. Land for housing	August 1991	July 1993
4. Land for mineral working	July 1992	April 1994
5. Archaeology and planning	August 1992	January 1994
6. Renewable energy	June 1993	August 1994
Land for waste disposal	October 1994	
Roadside facilities	November 1994	
Retailing	February 1995	
Planning and flooding	May 1995	
Sport and physical recreation	August 1995	

It is clearly too early to review the impact of the NPPGs. However, drawing upon an analysis of the documents and the Raemaekers et al. work (1994) for the Scottish Branch of the Royal Town Planning Institute (RTPI), several comments can be made:

- The policy/advice distinction is not always clear. For example, it is claimed that PAN 38 (Structure Plans: Housing Land Requirements) (Scottish Office 1993b) is far more prescriptive than advisory (Raemaekers et al.: 7–8), whereas NPPG4 advises local authorities to identify areas of local environmental significance in their development plans (Scottish Office 1994c).

- In part this overlap is probably a consequence of the increased size of the NPPGs over the NPGs. For example, NPPG4 contains 24 pages of relevant text, whereas the NPG and LUSS that it replaced came to 10 pages. The increased size may give greater scope for interpretation by both planners and developers. Given that the NPPGs are now explicitly "material considerations", one outcome may be more challenges to the planning system;

- There are frequent mentions of sustainability. However, it is often difficult to avoid the conclusion that this is tokenism. When sustainable principles conflict with government ideology, then ideology wins. Perhaps the most obvious example of this occurs in NPPG4 where there is talk of recycling and re-using waste (Scottish Office 1994c). However, the document then goes on to support in principle the development of up to four coastal exporting super-quarries. This reflects the government view of the primacy of the market. Yet, as long as the market can obtain the resources it needs at an acceptable price from super-quarries, there will be little need for it to look to other ways of meeting demand such as by recycling. If sustainability is to be taken seriously, then one would expect the government to give a lead that extends beyond words.

- Like the NPGs, the production of NPPGs seems rather idiosyncratic. For example, alongside of the public debate about transport infrastructure in Scotland (e.g. the Skye bridge, the proposed second Forth road bridge and the continuing debate about the rail crossing of the Dornoch Firth), the production of guidance on archaeology seems a rather strange priority (Scottish Office 1994b).

- Despite a commitment to reviewing guidance "regularly" (Scottish Office 1994a: 8), no indication has been given as to how frequently this will be done, nor what the review strategy will be (Raemaekers et al. 1994: 13).

- There still seems to be a strong rural emphasis and no guidance is apparently planned on urban renewal, according to the latest Planning Bulletin. This is surprising, given that it is now apparently the intention to extend the regeneration principles underlying the Urban Partnerships more widely throughout Scotland (Scottish Office 1993a), which will have major implications for the physical environment.

Only time will tell if the NPPGs are to be an improvement over the widely praised NPGs. However, in the short term the main concern may be the sheer volume of guidance, with the current six NPPGs totalling over 125 pages. Admittedly, much of this is background information. However, it does seem rather ironic that the amount of guidance is growing at the same time as the plans themselves are becoming smaller and more concise. Indeed, the situation already exists where the guidance is lengthier than some plans. Will this lead to "better" plans? Arguably the NPGs and PANs did not seem to have a major impact on some elements of development planning, in particular the speed of preparation and coverage. Only time will tell if the NPPGs can overcome these problems, which have affected development planning since 1974.

Development plan coverage

The 1972 Planning Act had not been implemented prior to local government reorganization in 1974 (Lyddon 1980: 66). This arguably benefited the new authorities, as they could start structure and local plan preparation with a clean sheet. Yet this advantage may have been partly negated by the absence, on any large scale, of the subregional planning studies that dominated planning in England and Wales in the 1960s. Although they may have had a limited impact upon planning, they did allow staff to gain experience of a range of quantitative techniques that were then used in the first-generation structure plans.

The first structure plans to be approved in Scotland were for Lothian and Orkney in late 1979. By mid-1983, 10 of the 16 plans that it was proposed to prepare had been approved. However, complete coverage had to wait until 1989 (Fig. 6.2), that was far slower than the Scottish Office had hoped (Coon 1989: 79). The three Islands authorities and six of the Regions (Borders, Dumfries and Galloway, Highland, Lothian, Strathclyde and Tayside) aimed to cover their areas with one plan. The other three split their areas with Central aiming for three plans, Grampian two and Fife two. Since then Central and Fife have produced region-wide replacements, and Grampian has almost completed theirs.

Generally, Scottish structure planning has been characterized by a process of continuing replacement and modification. Although commendable, this caused

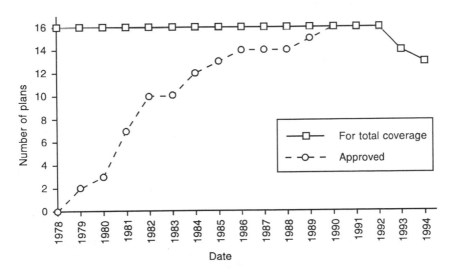

Figure 6.2   Structure plan coverage in Scotland.

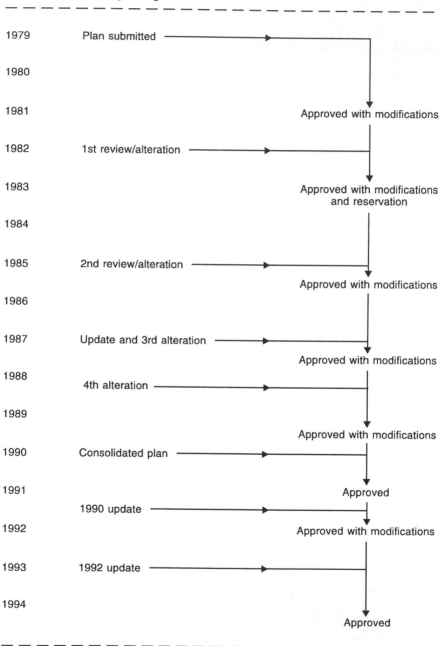

THE PLAN APPROVER
The Scottish Office

THE PLAN PRODUCER
Strathclyde Regional Council

1979   Plan submitted

1980

1981   Approved with modifications

1982   1st review/alteration

1983   Approved with modifications
and reservation

1984

1985   2nd review/alteration

                                   Approved with modifications

1986

1987   Update and 3rd alteration

                                   Approved with modifications

1988   4th alteration

1989

                                   Approved with modifications

1990   Consolidated plan

1991   Approved

   1990 update

1992   Approved with modifications

1993   1992 update

1994

                                   Approved

Figure 6.3   Structure plan process in Strathclyde.

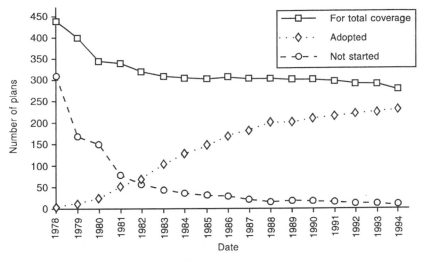

Figure 6.4 Local plan coverage in Scotland.

confusion because of the proliferation of plans, alterations and updates in some regions. Figure 6.3 illustrates the complexity of the structure plan in Strathclyde. Before the approval of the consolidated plan in June 1991, "the" structure plan consisted of as many as eight separate documents. Although there were good reasons for these updates and alterations, at times it is difficult not to agree with Lyddon's comment that "a strategic plan that is subject to kaleidoscopic change every two or three years is a contradiction in terms; it is neither strategic nor a plan" (Lyddon 1985: 29).

Complete coverage of Scotland by local plans was required from 1973 (Coon 1989: 78). Perhaps unsurprisingly, local plan preparation has been both slower and has not been characterized by the regular updating that has been a feature of some structure plans. In part this reflects the unrealistic number of plans that were to be prepared. Originally it was estimated that 424 plans were needed to give Scotland-wide coverage (Coon 1989: 79). Since then there has been a gradual decrease in the number, so that by April 1994 complete coverage would be given by 277, 35 per cent fewer (Fig. 6.4).

This has been mainly caused by a move towards the production of district-wide plans. Thus, at April 1994, 24 of the 37 districts with planning powers either had such plans adopted or were in the process of preparing them. However, the Scottish Office is still concerned about progress for three main reasons (Scottish Office 1993c: 10):

- There is no local plan coverage for some areas after 20 years, with no progress having been made on seven plans by April 1994. Although these cover remote rural areas where there are likely to be limited development pressures, in particular large parts of the Western Isles and Orkney, this must still be a cause of concern.
- The time taken to prepare plans is very long, with the Scottish Office

89

claiming that many take more than ten years to produce, whereas even replacement plans have taken an average of four years.

* Many adopted plans are now quite old. For example, of the 226 plans that had been adopted by February 1993, four date from 1978 and 80 per cent were adopted over five years ago. The concern is that such plans may not reflect current conditions and as such may fall foul of Section 58 of the Planning and Compensation Act.

These problems of the age and relevance of local plans also have implications for public involvement in the planning process and the consistency of planning decisions. This comes about as, in those areas where the planning framework is out-of-date, planning policy may be determined through planning appeal decisions. The Reporters (the Scottish term for planning inspectors) make such decisions without any public involvement. As they also have delegated authority to determine almost all appeals, this means that there is an absence of any policy overview from the Scottish Office. Decisions may therefore be inconsistent not only between authorities but also within the same authority.

Unfortunately, the problems identified by the Scottish Office are very similar to those highlighted by Coon five years earlier (Coon 1989). In part they no doubt reflect staffing and management problems and the ambitious nature of the early plan targets, with for example Glasgow District originally intending to produce 47 plans. They also reflect the nature of the plans. These tended to be overlong, with too much emphasis given to the reports of survey, whereas policy coverage tended to deal with things that were often peripheral to land-use planning and was "complex and long-winded" (Scottish Office 1992: 10).

The Scottish Office has attempted to deal with these problems by producing advice that has stressed the advantage of rapid and attractive plan production and the need for plans to concentrate more upon land-use issues (Scottish Development Department 1984, 1988, 1989). Although this has begun to have an impact, it is paradoxical that the implementation of Section 58 of the 1991 Planning and Compensation Act may lengthen the time local plan inquiries take, thereby undermining these attempts to speed up plan production. This comes about as the increased status given to local plans may mean that developers, and others with an interest in land use, are now more interested in influencing the content of the plans with a view to ensuring that they contain policies that will favour their interests. If this is not done before the plan is adopted, then it may be far more difficult to make changes at a later date. Section 58 may therefore be undermining these attempts to speed up plan production. However, the problems with local plans may also reflect a feeling in some authorities, from both officers and members, that the development plan system may be irrelevant in coping with their problems, especially if these are ones of economic decline. This has undoubtedly resulted in a reliance in some areas on non-statutory plans and alliances with public bodies such as the Scottish Development Agency (SDA) and Local Enterprise Companies (LECs), which have the resources to not only plan but to implement these plans.

The Scottish Development Agency

One of the distinctive features of planning in Scotland was the SDA. Although it had planning powers, these were hardly ever used (Lloyd 1990). Instead the Agency was able to work in partnership with local authorities throughout the country to formulate and implement several urban renewal projects. It has been argued that the reason for the relative harmony that characterized SDA-local government relations was a coincidence of interests: the SDA, either on its own initiative or as a result of pressure from the Scottish Office, was setting up area renewal projects in areas where local government was keen to see action (Hayton 1992). The SDA had the advantage over local government in that it had the resources to implement plans. In this way it acted as a buffer between the local authorities, which were largely run by the Labour Party, and the Scottish Office, which was under Conservative control for the majority of the Agency's life. It allowed the Scottish Office to intervene at arm's length and allocate resources to Labour controlled authorities in a way that did not cause political unrest at either national or local level, as the SDA, although "a central government agency, is not a central department" (Keating & Boyle 1986: 106). In effect the SDA behaved in a very similar way to many of the Urban Development Corporations (UDCs) in England and Wales, yet was able to do this with the collusion of local government and without the adverse criticisms that many UDCs have attracted. It is therefore untrue to claim that there was a reluctance to designate UDCs in Scotland (Cullingworth & Nadin 1994: 33). There was no need. The SDA did an almost identical job, promoting property-led regeneration, yet in a way that was acceptable both at the local and national political level.

The very active role of the Agency in urban regeneration and its influence may also have been responsible for the lack of NPGs dealing with urban renewal. At its crudest this may have reflected a view that there was little that the Scottish Office planners could teach the Agency about urban regeneration. Production of such guidance may also have caused internal problems within the Scottish Office, given the SDA's heavy involvement in urban regeneration. The department with responsibility for planning, then the SDD, might have been seen as trying to interfere with activities of the SDA that were the responsibility of another department, then the Scottish Economic Planning Department.

Scottish Enterprise

In 1991 the SDA was merged with the Training Agency in Scotland to form Scottish Enterprise. The new body inherited the powers of its parent organizations. However, its impact upon land-use planning is likely to be far greater. This is as Scottish Enterprise has delegated the majority of its responsibilities to a network of LECs with which it contracts annually to deliver a range of services. The LECs are non-statutory bodies: companies limited by guarantee, run by boards of directors, at least two thirds of whom are senior private sector managers. However, their structure as private companies is belied to some extent by the status they are to be given in the planning system. Thus, NPPG2, while stating that structure and local plans will set the context for the LECs' plans, also states that planning authorities may wish to consider whether their existing plans need alteration, particularly if they were prepared before the LEC was operational. In this case the LEC is to be consulted so that it can contribute to the plan (Scottish Office 1993f: para. 52). The danger is that, when taken with the various recommendations in the NPPG relating to such things as making available an adequate amount of "marketable land for business and industry", safeguarding high-amenity single-user sites and creating a framework whereby industrial and business development applications can be approved, the LECs come to exercise an undue influence upon the content of development plans. Their unelected nature and the secrecy with which they have conducted their activities could therefore mean that the planning system becomes used to serve the interests of a secretive minority rather than the wider community. This possibility may be hastened by local government reorganization.

The future of Scottish planning

The Scottish planning system, especially its strategic dimension, has been widely praised, not only by independent commentators but also by central government (HM Government 1990: para. 20.9). Despite this it seems as if its effectiveness will be dramatically reduced by the impending reform of local government. The White Paper detailing the new structure stated that the essential features of the planning system would be retained (Scottish Office 1993e: 8). Although this may be true, there can be little doubt that the system's effectiveness will be severely tested by the move to replace the existing two-tier structure of districts and regions by a unitary system. There may be nothing inherently wrong with a unitary planning system. Indeed, one has operated in the islands and three rural regions since 1974. What is a major cause for concern are the boundaries of the 28 proposed authorities. These are shown in Figure 6.5.

The Wheatley Commission based its local authority boundaries on the recognition of the functional interaction between urban and rural areas. The present proposals ignore such interaction, as can be seen from the boundaries of the four cities of Aberdeen, Dundee, Edinburgh and Glasgow, which are essentially those of the present district councils. Effectively, a line has been drawn around the urban areas cutting them off from their rural and functional hinterlands. This currently applies to the districts, but it is in the context of a two-tier system. The regions can produce strategic plans that attempt to strike a balance between the needs of the urban, suburban and the rural areas. This may be more difficult to

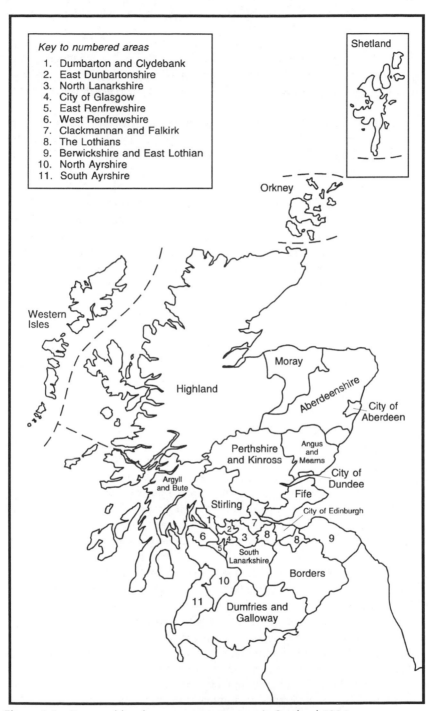

Key to numbered areas

1. Dumbarton and Clydebank
2. East Dunbartonshire
3. North Lanarkshire
4. City of Glasgow
5. East Renfrewshire
6. West Renfrewshire
7. Clackmannan and Falkirk
8. The Lothians
9. Berwickshire and East Lothian
10. North Ayrshire
11. South Ayrshire

Shetland

Orkney

Western Isles

Moray

Highland

Aberdeenshire

City of Aberdeen

Perthshire and Kinross

Angus and Mearns

City of Dundee

Argyll and Bute

Fife

Stirling

City of Edinburgh

1 2 7
6 4 3 8 8 9
5
South Lanarkshire

Borders

10

11 Dumfries and Galloway

Figure 6.5   Proposed local government structure in Scotland 1994.

do under the proposed new arrangements, under which structure plans will be prepared in two ways (Scottish Office 1993e):

- Those authorities that are "natural area (s) for a structure plan" will continue to produce them on their own. These authorities are not defined, but it seems probable that they will be the region and island authorities that are retained (Dumfries and Galloway, Highland, Fife, Orkney, Shetland and the Western Isles).
- Elsewhere, adjacent authorities will be expected to work together to produce strategic plans, although neither the White Paper nor the Reform Act defines these authorities. This will be done later through secondary legislation. The emphasis is upon voluntary joint working, although the Secretary of State will have reserve powers to set up statutory joint boards, and such boards can also be established if requested by the authorities concerned.

Strategic planning around the cities and in heavily urbanized central Scotland therefore will revert to the type of voluntary arrangements and joint committees whose deficiencies were in part responsible for the 1974 reform (Hague 1994: 14). Joint committees will have no powers to employ staff and will be dependent upon secondees from their constituent authorities. The resultant divided loyalties may not only make the formulation of an effective plan difficult but its implementation may be even more problematical. One example of these difficulties can be seen from the experience of the Clyde Valley Planning Advisory Committee which, before local government reorganization in the 1970s, tried with limited resources to define and police a green belt around the Clydeside conurbation.

There are also likely to be political problems with these non-statutory arrangements, as any strategic overview is lost as individual authorities try to maximize their own development opportunities. Alternatively, authorities may try to resist development if it is felt that this will have a detrimental impact upon them, regardless of any strategic justification for it. The consequences may be a surplus of sites, too few sites, or sites allocated in areas that are unlikely to be attractive to developers. The new authorities will also no longer be directly responsible for water and sewerage, thereby breaking the direct link between plan preparation and infrastructure provision. The effectiveness of strategic planning will be seriously undermined as a consequence. The outcome in urban Scotland will be the replacement of the two-tier planning system by a new two-tier system. The lower tier will consist of elected "unitary" authorities with responsibility for local planning and development control. The upper tier, of unelected bodies, will have notional responsibility for strategic planning. In practice their abilities to formulate and implement effective strategic plans may be very limited.

To overcome these problems, if only in part, several options have been suggested. For example, the Scottish branch of the RTPI has tabled amendments to the reform Bill that would require that structure plans be prepared by statutory joint boards in areas where joint working is required. The boards, unlike joint committees, would be able to employ their own staff and would have a degree of independence that would make plan preparation and implementation far more effective. It is argued that such boards would be able to stand above the more parochial interests of individual unitary authorities, so that a strategic planning dimension could emerge (Royal Town Planning Institute in Scotland 1994). Alternatively, it has been suggested that regional planning guidance be prepared by the Scottish Office for central Scotland to overcome the dangers of a lack of any strategic focus (Raemaekers et al. 1994: 15). Either option seems suboptimal when compared to the present system, but the RTPI's suggestion probably has the most to commend it. Superimposing regional guidance on top of the existing NPPGs could see the new authorities left with very little discretion in their ability to respond to local circumstances.

The loss of a strong strategic voice may also result in the influence of the LECs growing (Hayton 1992). In some areas they may be the only single body able to take if not a regional then at least a subregional overview. They could therefore become the de facto unelected and unrepresentative strategic planners. This danger is increased by the resentment felt by some district councils, especially within Strathclyde, that strategic planning has favoured Glasgow at their expense. They may as a result form alliances with the LECs with a view to attracting more development to their area. The need to achieve consensus through the preferred strategic planning option of voluntary joint working may see other authorities unwilling to challenge the resultant over-allocation of sites.

The future of the Scottish planning service was thrown into further confusion in March 1994 when it was announced that the planning system was to be reviewed. The resultant consultation paper, published in July (Scottish Office 1994d), indicated that it was not the intention to change the basic system but to look for ways by which it could be made more efficient and effective. Despite this, the range of issues suggested for consideration is very wide, covering almost all aspects of the system from its purposes through to the detailed workings of the development control service. The danger is that too much "administrative" change may undermine the integrity of the planning system. The example of the consultations over local government reform, where commentators have suggested that the Scottish Office misinterpreted the responses (McCrone et al. 1993), also needs to be borne in mind before anyone becomes too complacent about the Scottish Office's intentions. Planning will also be affected by the wind-up of the new towns, while the financial calculations upon which the case for local government reform rests may pose a significant threat to planning employment (Hayton 1994). All these factors mean that public sector planning in Scotland approaches the second millennium against a background of considerable change and uncertainty.

Conclusions

The legislative basis for Scottish planning is broadly identical to that in England and Wales. The main differences in practice arise from the local government structure, which allows for more effective strategic planning, and the longstanding and widely praised provision of national advice and guidance by the Scottish Office. However, these factors do not seem to have had much impact upon the speed of plan production nor upon the quality of some of the plans. They may also prove to be shortlived advantages as local government reform undermines strategic planning while the guidance given through the PPGs in England and Wales may be proving to be clearer, more comprehensive and consistent than that provided by the NPPGs.

Outside of the statutory planning framework, Scotland is distinctive in that central government agencies have played a major role in urban regeneration. This has usually been in close partnership with local government, although the relevance of the development plan framework in this process, especially at the local level, has often been difficult to identify.

Central government, working through the Scottish Office and bodies such as the SDA, has therefore had a significant impact upon planning. However, in population terms, Scotland is a small place. It could therefore be argued that it suffers from a surfeit of advice, instruction and intervention which must stifle local initiative and frustrate the legitimate aspirations of elected members and local communities. However, several commentators have argued that this is not the case. Two main reasons are put forward:

- Scotland's size means that it is relatively easy for close informal and formal relationships to develop between central and local government (Lyddon 1980: 67; Rowan-Robinson et al. 1987: 376); and
- the involvement of local authorities in the formulation of such measures as the NPGs and NPPGs, so that the final outcome represents consensus rather than top-down direction (Rowan-Robinson et al. 1987: 379; Rowan-Robinson & Lloyd 1991: 18).

These factors led the Chief Planner in the SDD to claim that the NPGs were "not a national policy, (but) part of the 'centre–periphery dialogue'" (Lyddon 1985: 29). Unfortunately, like many other claims about the effectiveness and impact of NPGs, evidence to substantiate these claims is hard to come by. One of the few pieces of research that has looked at the extent to which the Scottish Office has responded to users' priorities in producing NPPGs contradicts this rather cosy view of consensus (Raemaekers et al. 1994: 13). Thus, of the eight priorities for NPPGs identified by users in 1991, one had been produced by late 1993, four were planned (although no date had been set when they would appear) and three were apparently not listed. Clearly, despite claims to the contrary, the priorities of the Scottish Office do not always appear to reflect those of users. However, the claims about the restrictive nature of central government guidance in England and Wales (Tewdwr-Jones 1994b) have not been repeated in Scotland. One explanation might be that planners and politicians in Scotland are more complacent and therefore more willing to accept central government direction without complaint. Alternatively, it might be that much of the direction and guidance aimed at the development plans system has been seen as irrelevant, simply as the plans themselves were often seen as an inappropriate mechanism for dealing with the most pressing economic, environmental and social problems. Thus, writing in 1981, Wannop argued that development planning was of limited importance alongside of a host of economic and social regeneration initiatives that were being promoted by local government and other agencies (Wannop 1981). In 1994 the names of the initiatives may have changed, but it is difficult to avoid a similar conclusion, especially about local planning. Strategic planning may have offered more, particularly in areas such as Strathclyde, where it undoubtedly had a major impact on directing development into brownfield sites in the Clydeside conurbation. Yet its success undoubtedly owed much to the Scottish Office's willingness to see agencies such as the SDA devote resources to overcoming problems in these areas rather than exploiting opportunities elsewhere. It remains to be seen if it can be as effective under the new arrangements where the LECs have more autonomy and undoubtedly want to focus more upon areas of opportunity, rather than get sidetracked into dealing with what are essentially social problems.

This is not to say that planners do not have a significant role. Indeed, one of the interesting things about the LEC network is the number of senior staff who trained as planners. That they are no longer working in local authority planning may say something about its frustrations. If, therefore, the statutory planning system of development plans and development control is to survive in anything like its present form, it may need to place far more emphasis upon implementation and developing creative partnerships with those who have the resources to implement. However, this survival may depend upon this change of emphasis taking place within the framework of the development plans system. Accordingly, this needs to become more pro-active and to convince the wider development community of its relevance. A step in this direction will be to improve the quality of plans, so that it will no longer be possible for commentators to describe them as "ambiguous, illogical, contradictory, unsubstantiated, inapposite, tendentious, obscure and poorly presented" (Coon 1989: 82). These criticisms were made in the context of considerable advice from the Scottish Office on the plans' form and content. If this had not been provided, it is frightening to think what the plans would have been like.

The Scottish planning system undoubtedly faces many threats and challenges in the mid-1990s. Yet its survival may rest not with central government or bodies such as the LECs changing their plans, but with the system itself and those who operate it proving that it has something to offer.

Acknowledgement

The author is grateful to Brian Parnell, Visiting Professor in the Centre for Planning, University of Strathclyde, for his comments on the first draft of this chapter.

PART TWO

Changing institutional and legal frameworks

CHAPTER 7

Planning policy implications of local government reorganization

John Clotworthy & Neil Harris

Introduction

The emphasis of this book is to document and explore the changing nature of planning policy within the British planning system. Many of the preceding chapters emphasize the rapidity with which the framework that guides the formulation of policy has changed. But, a much more fundamental change is taking place that will have a direct bearing on planning policy – the very "institutional framework" through which planning policy is both formulated and implemented is being radically changed through a process of the review of local government. It can be argued that the proposals for the reorganization of local government are more radical than recent changes in the planning policy framework itself, as defined by central government legislation, policy statements and guidance. The relationship between the "institutional framework" and the "policy framework" is an intimate and interdependent one. Both impose constraints upon and open up possibilities for one other. This chapter is therefore central to all of the other issues addressed in the book, as it considers changes in the planning system "hardware", on which the effectiveness of all "software" depends. Because of the fact that the implications of reorganizing local government extend to each and every aspect of local planning policy, no single study could hope to address all of the relevant issues. Consequently, we focus on those issues that we consider most relevant to both the formulation and implementation of policy at the local level. It is inevitable that certain issues will be omitted, but such is the nature of the topic.

In the following pages, we aim first to provide the background to the present review of local government in terms of the process of the review and the reasoning given for reorganization. We then identify the principal issues arising from reorganization as they relate to planning policy, and we go on to develop the potential implications for the planning system. A case study of the present and future planning system in the southwest of England is then given to elaborate upon and exemplify what can otherwise seem abstract issues. Finally, we consider in broad terms what the future may hold for planning policy and service delivery, and whether the inevitable upheaval that reorganization necessarily involves signifies a genuine threat to effective planning, or whether it indeed opens up opportunities that would not otherwise have arisen.

The initiation of the review

The present reorganization of local government in England, Scotland and Wales was first formally announced in December 1990 by the former Secretary of State for the Environment, Michael Heseltine, in a statement to the House of Commons, accompanied by statements for Scotland and Wales by the respective Secretaries of State. The announcement of a review of local government represented a general dissatisfaction with the pattern of local government established by the Local Government Act 1972. It was claimed that the present system, conceived and established less than 20 years previously, was inefficient, bureaucratic and unresponsive to the public it should serve.

The Department of the Environment clearly stated in its consultation paper of April 1991 that "In the Shire Counties, certain aspects of the two-tier system are unsatisfactory" (DoE 1991b: 5). The first of these unsatisfactory characteristics was that "Some authorities which emerged from the 1974 reorganization are still not wholly accepted by all the local communities which they serve" (para. 22). Furthermore, the consultation paper went on to state that "The very existence of two tiers can also cause confusion over which tier is responsible for which service" (para. 23), with the resultant loss of accountability. Unitary authorities would also enable greater co-ordination of functions (para. 24), and the planning function was used to exemplify this claim: "In some areas where the two tiers need to work together, such as planning, there may sometimes be conflict and tension between the policies of county and district councils". The advocacy of the government for a structure of unitary authorities rested upon these simple arguments concerning the deficiencies of the two-tier system. This essentially comprised the justification for the review. However, the same consultation paper states that "In some areas there could be a case for two tiers. The aim will be to achieve the structure which best matches the particular circumstances of each area" (para. 27). Therefore, implicit in these statements is the marginality of the government's case for reorganization, in that it may be outweighed by the "particular circumstances" of areas. One would expect that an activity as fundamental as a national review and reorganization of local government would be supported by much greater substantiated reasoning. This incoherence of argument has caused delay

101

and difficulties in progressing the review in England, and in addition begs the question whether the whole process of reorganization can be justified.

The consultation paper issued by the Secretary of State for Wales rested on similar arguments for abandoning the present two-tier system of local government in favour of unitary authorities. References to friction and confusion, clouded accountability, lack of effective co-ordination between tiers, and expensive duplication of effort, amounted to an equally vague and fragile argument. This is particularly so in that the consultation paper stated that, in arriving at the present two-tier system:

> It was considered also that there were merits in principle in dividing local government functions for an area between two authorities, so that one could provide a check and counter-balance to the other and competing interests and considerations could be adequately voiced. (WO 1991a: para. 21)

No reason was forthcoming to explain why this should no longer be the case in any future local government structure.

The deficiencies of the existing structure of local government are nevertheless a central component in explaining why local government is presently being reorganized. There has been both academic and professional debate over the past 20 years that would support the government's view on dismantling the present system (Leach & Moore 1979, Alexander 1982, ADC 1990). Nevertheless, debate has also produced arguments for the retention of the present two-tier system (Norton 1986, Boyne et al. 1991, Council for the Protection of Rural England 1991). In particular, it has been noted that the many deficiencies of the present two-tier system could be resolved by a reconsidered and clearer allocation of functions and duties between the two tiers (Assembly of Welsh Counties 1991).

In the absence of a coherent and comprehensive justification for undertaking a review of local government, there has been speculation of a "hidden agenda", in that reorganization is only being undertaken in the political self-interest of central government. The detailed interest and involvement of the government in the activities of the Local Government Commission affords some weight to the claims of political intent. Although it is acknowledged that "government make few friends out of local government reform" (Redcliffe-Maud & Wood 1974: 5), it would be naïve to believe that any government would initiate a review of local government in which it would diminish its political position, or at least by intent. Similar claims were made in the early 1970s in the build-up to the previous reorganization:

> It was inevitable that reorganization was to be a game of political tactics as it was effectively the rebuilding of the arena in which all future electoral battles would be fought. (Ritchie 1979: 31)

Leach (1992a: 47), however, claims that the idea of a hidden agenda for local government, obscured by the process of reorganization, is "too conspiracy-theory orientated", and therefore remains an incredible, but nonetheless popular, prospect.

The government's criticisms of the present system of local government are particularly valid in relation to planning, and the planning function has never been at its most efficient, resting uneasily and being constrained with the present structure of local government. The reason for this is historical. The fundamental structure of the present planning system was initially conceived by the Planning Advisory Group, set up in May 1964 to conduct a "general review of the planning system" (Planning Advisory Group 1965: 1). The Planning Advisory Group proposed a planning system "which would distinguish between the policy or strategic decisions on the one hand, and the detailed or tactical dimensions on the other". This was conceived to be a dual system of plans, to be prepared by a single local planning authority. The recommendations of the Planning Advisory Group were accepted in principle by the government of that time and subsequently legislation was introduced in the form of the Town and Country Planning Act 1968. The proposals of the Planning Advisory Group and the 1968 Act were both based upon the expectation that local government would undergo reorganization into unitary authorities, as later recommended for the non-metropolitan areas of England by The Commission for Local Government in England in 1969 (The Redcliffe-Maud Commission). However, the incoming Conservative government of 1970 rejected the recommendations of the Redcliffe-Maud Commission and gave effect to a two-tier structure of local government with the introduction of the Local Government Act 1972. It was necessary to introduce further primary planning legislation to reconcile the provisions of the Town and Country Planning Act 1968 with those of the Local Government Act 1972, and this was done by the introduction of the Town and Country Planning Act 1971. Norton (1986: para. 2.5) states that in introducing the 1972 Act, "The seeds of instability had been sown". The 1972 Act undermined the very principles upon which the Town and Country Planning Act 1968 was based (Alexander 1982: 55; Brazier & Harris 1975: 255). As Buxton (1974: 61) notes:

> The division into two of what was originally conceived as a unified activity is not, however, likely to work out easily in practice. Confusion rather than illumination is more likely to follow when one authority attempts to amplify and particularise another's plans.

Therefore, concerns over the present system were expressed from the outset and for many the present reorganization has arrived twenty years too late.

Progressing the review

The process of reorganization has been progressed separately in England, Scotland and Wales. This is markedly different from the previous reorganization, where the review was combined for England and Wales. The process of review in England is described in detail below and this is followed by a briefer description of the process of review as it has been undertaken in Wales, highlighting the principal differences with England. The reorganization process in Scotland is described in detail in Chapter 6.

England

In England, the Local Government Commission was appointed by the government under the provisions of the Local Government Act 1992. The Local Government Commission began its considerable task of reviewing English local government in July 1992, under the chairmanship of Sir John Banham. The Commission was to conduct a review of such areas as may be specified by the Secretary of State for the Environment, and to recommend structural, electoral and boundary changes as it thought desirable. The Local Government Commission was required by Section 13(5) of the Local Government Act 1992 to have regard to the need to reflect the identities and interests of local communities, and to secure effective and convenient local government.

The essence of the approach in England (and, it might be argued with hindsight, the thinking which led in due course to such a confused outcome to the review) is captured in the following extract from the Secretary of State's address to the House of Commons in 1991:

> There is therefore now an opportunity to think afresh about the structure of local authorities. But the Government does not see this as an opportunity to impose a new pattern of local authorities according to a national prescription. Nor do we believe that it is necessary to have a uniform pattern of authorities in every part of the country. Local people should have an important role in determining what structure of local government best reflects their community loyalties. This does not mean therefore the wholesale abolition of either county councils or district councils, nor even unitary authorities everywhere. It means arriving at the right solution for each community. We intend to adopt a practical approach in response to local views and local conditions. But it seems likely that we should move to a larger number of unitary authorities.

Under the terms of the Act, the Secretary of State directed the Local Government Commission to have regard to both procedural and policy guidance issued by him in the exercise of its functions. The policy guidance was issued in July 1992 and later revised in 1993.

The Local Government Commission was originally instructed to review the English Shires in five successive tranches, the first of which included the supposedly unpopular 1974 "new" counties of Avon, Humberside and Cleveland. The recommendations of the Local Government Commission on the first tranche of local authorities were submitted to the Secretary of State for the Environment by late 1993. The Secretary of State accepted recommendations for unitary authorities in two of the areas, referred back to the Commission proposals to retain the status quo, wholly or partly, in three areas, and deferred a decision in three more. The actions of the Secretary of State at that time continued to show a clear preference for unitary authorities, although this position was to change as the review proceeded.

This is not the place to dwell on the inadequacies of the work of the Local Government Commission or the brief it was given, although there was widespread criticism of both. In August 1993, the President of the Royal Town Planning Institute, following discussions with the County and District Planning Officers' Societies, wrote to the Secretary of State for the Environment expressing serious concern about the pattern that was emerging and its implications for the planning system. He said

> What we have got so far from the Commission are proposals where in some cases structure planning will be weakened by having to depend on voluntary joint arrangements, whereas in others, the provision of responsible local planning will be equally doubtful.

There was "wide concern among those who will have to operate the proposed systems and that their variety will create even greater confusion than is alleged already to exist" and "there is a need to be certain that by changing the present system, we are making things better and not worse. I do not believe this can yet be demonstrated".

The proposals of the Local Government Commission that emerged appeared fraught with inconsistency and lack of rationale. It was all too evident that the fundamental reasons for the review had not been thought through at the outset, and that the elongated timescale would compound problems. The Local Government Commission produced an analysis of its progress in December 1993 – *Reviewing local government in the English shires – a progress report* – although this in itself was not sufficient to prevent further detailed criticism.

In an attempt to assert greater control over the process of review, the government revised its policy guidance in November 1993, and accelerated the timescale for the remainder of the review, which was to be completed during 1994. The new authorities were intended to come into effect in 1996 and 1997. The changes effectively placed a greater emphasis on the establishment of unitary authorities, on a scale larger than existing districts and smaller than existing counties. Locally agreed solutions would carry weight and would be influential in the recommendations of the Local Government Commission. Most of the guidelines, relating, for example, to community identity, cost effectiveness, public preference and accountability, remained unchanged. This attempt by the government to redirect an independent commission in the course of its work must be seen as highly unusual and indicative of their serious concern emerging at the progress of the review.

In January 1994, the revised policy guidance was challenged in a judicial review by Lancashire and Derbyshire County Councils on the grounds that it was incompatible with the terms of the Local Government Act 1992. The newly inserted presumption in favour of unitary authorities was subsequently required to be deleted. Both the government and the commission asserted that the review would carry on as intended. With hindsight, however, this ruling may be seen as a turning point: it removed any inhibition the Commission may have felt about recommending retention of the status quo, and subsequently led to greater divergence of the Local Government Commission's recommendations and the government's agenda.

The process survived a series of further judicial reviews, and districts and counties endeavoured to work more closely together, both with each other and with the Local Government Commission, to produce agreed options to be put before the public. A more comprehensive consultation process was carried out for the later tranches, with leaflets being sent to every household. The Commission produced sets of options, expressed as ordered preferences, through the spring and summer of 1994.

When most of their final recommendations appeared, late in 1994, it became clear that there had been a sea-change in the Commission's thinking, with the existing two-tier system recommended for retention over a majority of the English Shire counties.

It is a matter for speculation whether the High Court's decision in January 1994 played a role in the Commission's shift of emphasis, although public opinion certainly did. In many areas, support was lukewarm for change and strong for retention of the present system. This was, of course, always likely to be the case in rural England. The government's determination that "local people should have an important role in determining what structure of local government best reflects their community loyalties" (Heseltine 1991) ultimately undermined their original quest for a mainly unitary structure.

At the same time, the government's preference for unitary authorities waned during 1994, in the face of opposition from many Conservative Members of Parliament in the Shires and the concerted efforts of Conservative peers in the House of Lords to retain county councils. The turning point was in October 1994 when John Gummer, Secretary of State for the Environment, announced that he did not propose to accept the Commission's final recommendations for unitary authorities in Somerset and North Yorkshire, given the strength of local opposition.

In February 1995, the Secretary of State rejected wholly unitary recommendations by the Commission for Bedfordshire and Buckinghamshire, allegedly bowing to political pressures again. There are to be unitary councils for major urban areas at Milton Keynes and Luton, with the surrounding county areas remaining two tier. This "hybrid" solution has become the most common outcome where change is proposed.

In March 1995, Sir John Banham was sacked as Chairman of the Local Government Commission, having failed to toe the government's line for too long. A new Chairman and new members are to be appointed to carry out a further, limited review of selected urban areas with a view to conferring unitary status on them. It looks as if the main outcome of the review in England will be a partial return to the pre-1974 pattern of county boroughs.

The state of play for the whole of England as at March 1995 is summarized in Table 7.1. Twelve counties will retain two-tier local government in their entirety, and only 14 will be abolished entirely. The remainder areas will have a "hybrid" system of local government. The proposed unitary authorities are mainly urban and include large regional cities such as Bristol, Nottingham and Plymouth, but also rural areas such as Herefordshire and Rutland.

Table 7.1   Proposed local government reorganization in England, January 1995.

County	Final recommendation	Govt. decision	
Avon	4 UAs	Accepted	
Bedfordshire	3 UAs	1 UA/2 tier	
Berkshire	5 UAs	6 UAs	
Bucks	4 UAs	1 UA/2 tier	*
Cambridgeshire	No change	Accepted	*
Cheshire	No change	Accepted	*
Cleveland	4 UAs	Accepted	
Cornwall	No change	Accepted	
Cumbria	No change	Accepted	
Derbyshire	1 UA/2 tier	Accepted	
Devon	2 UAs/2 tier	2 UAs/2 tier	*
Dorset	4 UAs	2 UAs/2 tier	
Durham	1 UA/2 tier	Accepted	
East Sussex	1 UA/2 tier	1 UA/2 tier	
Essex	1 UA/2 tier	1 UA/2 tier	*
Gloucestershire	No change	Accepted	*
Hampshire	3 UAs/2 tier	2 UA/2 tier	*
Hereford & Worcester	1 UA/2 tier	1 UA/2 tier	
Hertfordshire	No change	Accepted	
Humberside	4 UAs	Accepted	
Isle of Wight	1 UA	Accepted	
Kent	No change	Accepted	*
Lancashire	No change	Accepted	*
Leicestershire	2 UAs/2 tier	2 UA/2 tier	
Lincolnshire	No change	Accepted	
Norfolk	No change	Accepted	*
Northants	No change	Accepted	*
Northumberland	No change	Accepted	
North Yorkshire	3 UAs	1 UA/2 tier	
Nottinghamshire	1 UA/2 tier	1 UA/2 tier	*
Oxfordshire	No change	Accepted	
Shropshire	No change	Accepted	*
Somerset	3 UAs	No change	
Staffordshire	1UA/2 tier	Accepted	
Suffolk	No change	Accepted	
Surrey	No change	Accepted	
Warwickshire	No change	Accepted	
West Sussex	No change	Accepted	
Wiltshire	1UA/2	1UA/2 tier	

* Further reviews of selected towns to take place

Wales

The present reorganization of local government in Wales is the first in which the distinctive differences between England and Wales have been recognized through to implementation, for it represents the first reorganization of modern Welsh local government in its own right, separate from England (previously, Wales had been reviewed separately but never proceeded to the stage that the present reorganization has reached). Although the essential structure of local government in Wales is the same as for non-metropolitan England, there are certain characteristics that clearly set them apart (Boyne et al. 1991, Council of Welsh Districts 1991, Hambleton & Mills 1993). It is therefore only appropriate that local government in Wales has been considered separately.

In Wales, the Welsh Office has conducted what may be considered a more prescriptive and authoritative review compared with that in England. The Secretary of State for Wales issued a consultation paper in June 1991, titled *The structure of local government in Wales*. The paper presented three options for discussion, all of which portrayed a pattern of a different number of unitary authorities. Patterns of 13, 20 and 24 unitary authorities were depicted and the consultation paper reported that "The Secretary of State considers that the structure of 20 unitary authorities . . . has significant attractions and appears to offer the best basis for further discussion." (WO 1991a). However, comments on the other models and any alternative suggestions were invited, although the preference of the Secretary of State for Wales was to prove of considerable weight in the final structure of 22 unitary authorities (see Fig. 7.1), as now defined in the Local Government (Wales) Act 1994.

As Harris (1994: 19) states, "there is concern that the consultation paper issued by the Secretary of State for Wales has not been so much a genuine exercise in consultation as the prescription of the agenda for reorganization". The agenda had been defined and the Secretary of State for Wales was considered to have pre-empted genuine debate and discussion on the relevant issues, first by presenting specific options, all of which were based on unitary authorities, and secondly by stating a preference for one of them. As Boyne & Law (1993) identify, local authorities were in effect invited to "bid for the local government franchise" as unitary authorities. Similar accusations have been levelled at the consultation procedures in Scotland (McCrone et al. 1993: 14) and in England, on which Leach (1992b: 3) comments that it was "a consultation paper in name only. The overall thrust of the Government's plans was by then already settled".

Prior to the publication of the Welsh Office's White Paper (WO 1993b), the Welsh Office issued two other consultation papers, *The role of community and town councils in Wales* (WO 1992a) and *The internal management of local authorities in Wales* (WO 1991b). The first of these papers aimed to encourage debate on the possibility of strengthening and enhancing the role of community and town councils in Wales under a unitary local government structure. In the subsequent White Paper, only an enhanced representational role was proposed for the com-

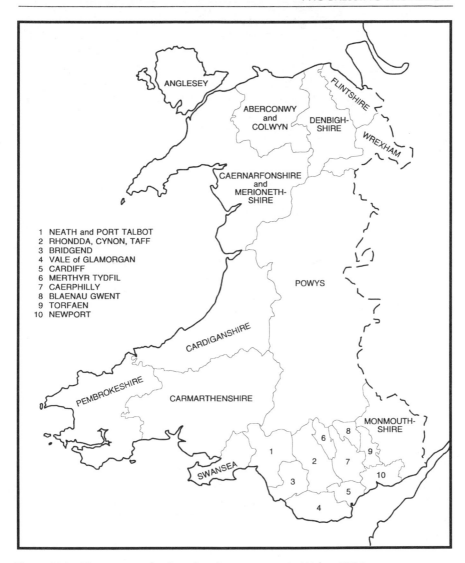

Figure 7.1 The pattern of unitary local government in Wales, 1994.

munity and town councils of Wales. The second of these consultation papers concerned itself with the potential for new and innovative forms of internal management within local authorities. The Local Government Management Board is assisting in securing this by publishing its document *Fitness for purpose* (1993), which provides a flexible and constructive framework within which choices can be made on the organizational structures that would best suit each local authority.

There has been widespread criticism within Wales of the prescriptive nature of the reorganization process, the lack of opportunity for informed and open

109

debate, and the relatively undemocratic nature of the review. Nevertheless, because the direction taken by the Welsh Office has been much more authoritative, it has thereby avoided the extent of policy drift that has plagued the process in England (Leach 1994a). Therefore, whatever the merits or otherwise of the manner in which the Welsh Office has proceeded with its review of local government, it has been much more successful in achieving its intentions than its English counterpart. There is a much clearer sense of direction within Wales than in England, and consequently practical debate has progressed more rapidly towards post-reorganization issues.

Implications for the planning system

The prospect of local government reorganization has raised many issues, many of which have been thoroughly debated. In the following paragraphs, we identify and discuss the most salient issues that have arisen. The detailed implications of reorganization can only be genuinely assessed through direct experience and involvement at the local level, and our experience of this is given in the following section. Nevertheless, certain key issues relating to planning have dominated the discussion, including the appropriate size and shape of the new authorities, the reliance on joint arrangements to secure effective strategic planning, the future form of development plans, and the opportunity for decentralized service delivery.

The size and shape of the new authorities

The need for effective strategic planning has not been a primary determinant in drawing up the boundaries of the new authorities. Once it became clear that the existing counties (regions in Scotland) were generally to be removed in favour of smaller authorities, it was obvious that strategic planning policies would either have to be prepared locally by joint arrangements or imposed by central government.

The principal feature of this process of reorganization has been the backing given by the government to unitary local government. As stated above, the essential features of the development plan system were based upon the assumption that local government would be reorganized into unitary authorities and, therefore, a return to unitary local government should be welcomed in principle. Throughout the process of reorganization, the Royal Town Planning Institute has advocated unitary local government, although it draws attention "to the fact that planning is exceptional amongst local government services in the range of scales at which it operates" (Royal Town Planning Institute 1991b: 3). The Institute, however, qualifies its statement, claiming that it "has always supported the principle of unitary authorities – though with the important caveat that an effective system of strategic planning, at regional level and subregional, is essential" (ibid.: 1). This is the classic dilemma in considering the structural and organizational requirements of the planning function and is essentially one that can be properly addressed only in the light of local circumstances. There is no generally accepted optimum size of local authority, and even though it may be possible to define such an authority in financial terms, such as taxation cost per person for a specified range of services, it becomes increasingly difficult with the introduction of concepts of effectiveness and democratic representation. The introduction of unitary authorities at too small a scale and in too great a number has the potential for parochialism in policy-making and lack of a strategic perspective. Policy-making can become too fragmented and lack consistency between areas. On the other hand, the creation of local authorities that are too large and few in number can result in insensitivity to local requirements, a feeling of under-representation on the part of local communities and a loss of diversity. Planning, and planning policy in particular, depends as much as any other function on achieving the correct balance between these competing factors as a result of its explicitly spatial characteristics.

It seems that the government is unwilling, where there is local opposition, to recognize the close links between cities and large towns and their hinterlands by redrawing boundaries accordingly. If further review results in more "unitary islands" within two-tier counties (e.g. Northampton, Peterborough, Blackburn or Exeter), this problem will become more widespread (it is, of course, already inherent in the structure of the metropolitan areas.) Many planners see this as a lost opportunity, but it serves to emphasize the importance of ensuring that joint arrangements are as effective as possible.

The effectiveness of joint working arrangements

One of the principal points of concern that has been continuously expressed by members of the planning and related professions throughout the process of reorganization, is the provisions or, more accurately, the lack thereof for securing effective strategic planning arrangements. The need for some element of strategic planning is in recognition of the fact that the issues planning policy tackles have relevance beyond the immediate area of administration in which they are explicitly dealt with. The government's response to date has relied on the effectiveness of voluntary joint arrangements to satisfy the requirements of dealing with cross-boundary issues. There have been calls for the government to establish a statutory basis for joint working requirements to ensure that strategic issues are properly addressed (Royal Town Planning Institute 1993: 2). The government has so far declined to do this, on the understanding that joint working arrangements tend to be most successful when they are entered into voluntarily, and it is in the interests of those authorities to achieve this. This may be the case, although initiating voluntary arrangements is not often achieved in practice.

Boyne & Law (1993) highlight a further potential disadvantage in the formation of joint boards, in that decisions are often taken at the level of the lowest common denominator, if they are not shelved entirely. The overall effectiveness of joint arrangements is dependent on circumstances and variables that can dramatically alter the quality of results (Leach 1994b: 89). Leach (1994b) identifies both policy-making and plan preparation as circumstances where a low degree of effect can be achieved. However, Harris & Tewdwr-Jones (1995: 60) suggest that there is already considerable experience within the planning profession of successful voluntary joint working, and that the profession may be underestimating its capabilities in being able to establish effective joint arrangements.

In England, the Local Government Commission declared that it "harbours no illusions about the inherent problems in establishing workable arrangements, capable of taking hard decisions which transcend the immediate interests of the area as a whole" (LGC 1993b). The real risk of course is that authorities will not be able to agree and that the effectiveness of policies will be reduced by the "lowest common denominator" factor. To some extent this will depend upon the number of authorities involved, the geography of the area in question and its planning problems. For example, the present County of Avon which is almost ideal for strategic planning purposes, will be replaced by four unitary authorities, all of which are within or immediately adjoining Greater Bristol. There will be considerable difficulties in coming to agreement, for example, about urban growth issues. Paradoxically, in counties such as Somerset which are predominantly rural and have no single urban focus, three unitary authorities would have had a better chance of agreeing with each other, had the proposals been implemented.

It is interesting that, in Wales, the government is content to rely on "co-operation" on "certain strategic issues", whereas, in Scotland, structure planning areas will be specified and, perhaps, joint boards established – a much more "hands on" approach. England may turn out to be somewhere in between, although the Commission commented that it would like to see "a statutory duty on authorities to work together".

Various models evolved as part of the continuing debate in England. The South West Branch of the Royal Town Planning Institute in March 1994 recommended to the Commission as follows:

- The new authorities should be required by statute to set up joint committees to oversee the preparation of joint structure plans and to deal with other appropriate strategic issues.
- The relationship between authorities, in particular their commitment to the adoption and implementation of the structure plan, should be governed by a formal agreement (perhaps along the lines of the "Political Protocol" prepared by the District Planning Officers' Society).
- Joint committees should be carefully constituted so that the interests of small authorities are not dominated by large ones.
- Joint technical units should be formed to provide professional, technical and administrative support to the joint committees. These should be jointly

funded by the authorities, but have managerial accountability to joint committees. (RTPI South West Branch 1994)

The recommendation for legislation to require statutory joint committees was subsequently endorsed by the Institute nationally. The District Planning Officers' Society, on the other hand, shares the Commission's view that the threat of the Secretary of State's reserve powers would be enough to make authorities resolve their differences rather than surrender control of key aspects of the plans (DPOS 1994).

There is, additionally, power under the Town and Country Planning Act 1990 (Section 2) for the Secretary of State to establish a joint planning board. The policy guidance to the Commission discourages such joint bodies as lacking direct accountability. There must also be a fear that these would, if established, be filled by appointees. A joint committee drawn from locally elected councillors is much to be preferred in accountability terms.

The future form of development plans

The 1986 abolition of the English metropolitan counties was soon followed by primary legislation introducing Unitary Development Plans that combine the function of structure and local plans and are prepared within a framework of strategic guidance approved by the Secretary of State. Many wondered if the same approach would accompany the introduction of unitary authorities this time, but government ministers have stated that no fresh development plan legislation is expected to be introduced to accompany the proposed structural changes.

In Wales, the new unitary authorities will prepare Unitary Development Plans, comprising both strategic and detailed land-use policies.

Certain strategic issues . . . will require co-operation between groups of authorities . . . The Secretary of State will use his powers to intervene if he considers that strategic issues have not been adequately covered . . . (WO 1993b: para. 4.23).

The subject merits only two short paragraphs in the White Paper, one of which deals with the position of National Parks. There is no discussion of the likely effectiveness of either the new authority areas or the form of "co-operation" to achieve satisfactory strategic planning.

In contrast, in Scotland, the government has decided to retain structure plans and local plans, although in many cases it expects that the two will be prepared by the same unitary authority. The Secretary of State will take powers to specify those areas where joint preparation will be necessary and is willing to use his existing powers to intervene to take over the process himself or to establish a more formal joint planning board (Scottish Office 1993: para. 3.18).

In England, the Local Government Commission is specifically invited by the Local Government Act 1992 (Section 14(5)[d]) to recommend whether unitary

113

authorities should be required to prepare unitary development plans, or whether the present two-tier structure should remain. The policy guidance outlined three models:

- a unitary authority prepares a structure plan for the whole of its area and separate local plans for sub-areas
- a unitary authority prepares both a structure plan and a local plan for the whole of its area (one aim of this approach could be to enable groups of neighbouring unitary authorities to prepare structure plans jointly)
- unitary authorities prepare unitary development plans jointly or separately.

The Commission's "Progress Report" (paras 55–69 – the Land Use and Transportation Planning Functions) contains a good account of the problems that surround this issue.

The Local Government Commission accepts that a UDP system would make for greater speed and efficiency in plan-making, but it is not convinced that it would provide an adequate means of resolving strategic conflicts in all cases; there is a risk that UDPs may become a recipe for "Balkanization" of development strategy for an area as a whole.

The Local Government Commission did not believe that unitary authorities should prepare plans within a framework of subregional strategic planning guidance, either prepared by groups of authorities themselves or issues by the Secretary of State. Such a system of non-statutory procedures, with no rights of participation, is "unlikely to provide the clear lead required". The Commission therefore generally recommended that the existing two-tier planning arrangements should be retained with new councils becoming joint structure planning authorities. This would provide statutory procedures to enable the public and others to participate. The necessary legal framework is provided by Section 50 of the 1990 Town and Country Planning Act and the Secretary of State can make representations on draft plans and even intervene in the decision-making process, if he is of the view that strategic issues are not being properly addressed.

The Commission's Progress Report and its final recommendations for unitary authorities seem, despite its assertions to the contrary, to suggest a "model" for strategic planning with the following characteristics:

- the retention of structure plans for present county areas (in the first instance)
- unitary authorities too small to prepare structure plans on their own – therefore necessitating joint responsibility
- locally agreed (i.e. "voluntary") arrangements for joint working
- reliance on the "threat" of intervention by the Secretary of State under Section 21 of the Local Government Act 1992 to secure satisfactory joint working arrangements
- strategic minerals and waste policies should be included in the joint structure plans.

For the proposed Berkshire and North Kent unitary authorities, the Commission has recommended UDPs. Elsewhere it has recommended the model described above. For the Isle of Wight, the Commission's recommendation was reversed by the government in favour of a UDP. Elsewhere, it has so far accepted the Commission's model.

There is a real risk that the process of reorganization will, in itself, jeopardize the preparation and implementation of sound planning policies. Uncertainty over the future leads to short-term thinking. Management time that was being diverted into justifying preferred structures is now in some cases fully occupied preparing for the real thing. Morale remains low in many planning policy teams. The result is a loss of impetus in the preparation of structure and local plans.

This situation holds considerable dangers for the planning system over the rest of the decade and beyond. The leading issue for many will be housing. For example, a failure to deliver a rolled forward structure plan on time will delay district plans, which could lead to a shortfall in the five-year supply of housing land that will leave planning authorities vulnerable on appeal. Staff time may have to be diverted to appeals, further slowing down policy preparation. For managers of the planning process, adherence to structure and local plan programmes must be kept at the forefront of their priorities, whatever chaos is going on around them. The resources available for most of the new unitary authorities will be fewer than for county councils, and in any case, local authority finances are currently being restricted. Will the new councils be able to provide the specialist input required to provide high-quality planning services? Conservation, landscape, archaeological and minerals expertise are obvious examples. Will they manage by sharing or purchasing advice from consultants? Can existing specialist teams be kept together? Experience in the metropolitan districts has shown that such teams are difficult to sustain when budgets are under pressure. On the positive side, change provides a golden opportunity for innovation and improvement, once the disturbance has settled. There are undoubtedly advantages to be derived from strategic and local planning policy preparation being conducted together, particularly alongside the range of other local authority services.

Reorganization and the planning system in Avon, Gloucestershire and Somerset

The Local Government Commission started to review Avon, Gloucestershire and Somerset, as part of the first tranche of local authorities, in September 1992. Most of the existing councils made representations justifying unitary status on their existing boundaries. At this early stage, it was clear that two sides were emerging on the planning aspects of the debate. County councils advocated the benefits of scale in strategic planning and retention of specialist expertise. District councils claimed they would be more responsive to local needs and could co-operate with other districts to prepare strategic plans.

The South West Branch of the Royal Town Planning Institute was particularly keen to see effective strategic planning arrangements maintained in the Greater

115

Bristol area, bearing in mind that the County of Avon was targeted for abolition from the outset of this exercise. It commented that in defining unitary authorities, the Local Government Commission, in paying regard to the "identity of interest" of areas, should focus not on "nostalgia" but on such socio-economic criteria as journey-to-work areas.

In February 1993, the Local Government Commission unexpectedly floated a series of "subcounty" options, involving districts, or combinations of them, for comment by the affected councils. The objective was to test the scope for locally agreed solutions, in the context of the unacceptability, in the main, of solutions based on individual districts.

The draft recommendations of the Local Government Commission were published for comment by organizations and individuals in June 1993 (see Table 7.2).

The recommendations proposed the abolition of the County of Avon and the establishment of eight unitary authorities, representing a reversion to former historic counties. This particular theme of reversion to former patterns of local government has evolved to be a key feature of the government's proposals as the process of reorganization has progressed.

Table 7.2 Local Government Commission's draft recommendations for Avon, Gloucestershire and Somerset, June 1993

In Avon	Population	
Bristol	37000	as existing
North-West Somerset	177000	Woodspring as existing
North-East Somerset	192000	Bath, Wansdyke and part Mendip
South Gloucestershire	220000	Kingswood and Northavon
In Gloucestershire	Population	
Forest of Dean	76000	as existing
Mid-Gloucestershire	205000	Gloucester and Stroud
East Gloucestershire	247000	Cheltenham, Cotswold and Tewkesbury
In Somerset	Population	
South & West Somerset	422000	as existing, less part Mendip

In publishing its draft recommendations, the Local Government Commission concluded that:

> In planning terms, there is a good case for maintaining a strategic planning framework for the area of Avon in any successor structure. The Commission is not satisfied that informal working arrangements or co-ordination between new authorities in the present Avon and Gloucestershire areas would ensure that strategic issues were properly dealt with if there were a move to unitary development plans.
>
> It therefore proposes to recommend that the new authorities should assume joint responsibility for structure planning and for waste and mineral plans, initially on the basis of the existing structure plan areas. There may be advantages in a more flexible approach over time, which would involve areas in neighbouring counties with closely related interests. Local

plans would then be the responsibility of each new authority independently but within the structure plan framework.

The Local Government Commission evaluated a series of alternatives in its report and invited comment upon them. These involved, in Avon, a unitary authority for Bristol on extended boundaries and, in Gloucestershire and Somerset, retention of the two-tier system with a lesser or greater number of unitary authorities respectively.

A period of internal campaigning ensued, during which the positions of various councils were widely regarded as partisan. Once again, the planning debate revolved around the problems of reconciling the strategic and the local aspects of service delivery within a unitary context. At one extreme, the very large "South and West Somerset" prompted the Local Government Commission itself to comment that, in support of its recommendation, "there could be a danger of the Council becoming remote from local needs . . .". These potential problems could be addressed by devolved management and decision-making, improved access to residents and more delegation to town and parish councils. The Commission has based its proposals on the assumption that such devolved management would take place.

At the other extreme, the proposed Forest of Dean unitary authority could only be justified in terms of very strong local identity, and the reliance on co-operative arrangements with larger neighbours was readily acknowledged by the Commission.

In Avon, the "Greater Bristol" issue remained dominant, with some local bodies seeing the planning benefits of including at least the immediate hinterland of the city in the same authority. For example, Bristol Chamber of Commerce and the Institute of Directors proposed a unitary council based on "travel-to-work" areas and Bristol Civic Society sought expanded boundaries. Predictably, the adjoining areas affected, particularly Northavon and Kingswood were opposed to such a prospect. The South West Branch of the RTPI pointed out that, for effective strategic planning, a much larger Bristol hinterland would have to be taken into account.

More widely, the Institute made sweeping criticisms of the Local Government Commission's proposals (RTPI South West Branch 1993). The Branch concluded:

> that no case has been made for the reorganization in the form now proposed. It would therefore argue that rather than pursue proposals lacking any rationale, it would be preferable to retain the present system, which does at least enable local and strategic planning to be delivered in a structured way and within a statutory rather than a voluntary framework.

Public opinion was intended to be influential in the Commission's final recommendations, although establishing precisely what it was proved less than straightforward, from a combination of opinion polling, leaflets, letters and public meetings. Avon's public was generally in favour of the recommendations,

117

with strong opposition from adjoining areas to any expansion of Bristol's boundaries. In Gloucestershire, there were stronger feelings than elsewhere against change and a preference for retention of the present system. In Somerset, there were mixed messages, but a preference was evident for several smaller unitary authorities, rather than one large one.

When the Local Government Commission's final recommendations were presented to the government and published in December 1993 (LGC 1993a), they followed these trends in public opinion (Table 7.3). The Avon proposals were unchanged, including the arrangements for strategic planning. In Gloucestershire, it was proposed to retain a two-tier system of local government. In Somerset, three unitary authorities were now proposed:

Table 7.3 Local Government Commission's final recommendations for Somerset, December 1993

	Population	
South Somerset	195000	South Somerset, part Mendip
Mid-Somerset	140000	Sedgemoor, part Mendip
West Somerset	125000	Taunton Deane, West Somerset

As with Avon, there would be joint responsibility for strategic planning, with locally agreed arrangements. In Somerset, a campaign aimed at retaining the status quo ensued, which attracted the strong support of the four Conservative Members of Parliament in the county.

In March 1994, the Local Government Commission were asked by the Secretary of State for the Environment to undertake a further review of Gloucestershire to see if satisfactory unitary proposals could be established.

In October 1994, the Secretary of State for the Environment confirmed his acceptance of the Commission's proposals for the County of Avon; he concluded that "establishing four unitary authorities for the area would best reflect local identities and interests and achieve effective and convenient local government". The parliamentary orders creating four unitary authorities in Avon were approved in March 1995. However, for Somerset, "after taking account of the number and strength of the representations which I received opposing the recommendations", he decided that the two-tier system should be retained (see Fig. 7.2).

In January 1995, the Commission recommended for the second time that there should be no change in Gloucestershire. However, consideration is now being given by the Secretary of State to including the city of Gloucester in his fresh round of reviews (March 1995).

Implications for planning in Avon

The area of the County of Avon has more socio-economic coherence than most

Figure 7.2 Map of Avon, Gloucestershire and Somerset, showing council boundaries and recommended new structure of local government.

county areas. It is focused on the regional capital, Bristol, and its smaller neighbour, Bath, some 12 miles to the east. There are strong linkages between the two, and their joint spheres of influence encompass the whole county. It is also very self-contained, in the sense that 90 per cent of the people who live in Avon also work there – probably higher than any other structure plan area.

The urban area of Greater Bristol extends substantially into the proposed South Gloucestershire on its northern and eastern sides, and there are closely related settlements in all the authorities bordering Bristol. South Gloucestershire

119

contains a series of disparate communities whose main common feature is their relationship with Bristol. Northeast Somerset makes more geographical sense, combining Bath with much of its hinterland.

It is essential that, if the major planning issues such as accommodation of housing growth pressures, meeting employment needs and traffic congestion, are to be tackled effectively, strategic policies are prepared and implemented successfully across the whole Avon area.

The Avon example illustrates well our earlier doubts about the appropriateness of Unitary Development Plans for the new authorities. Unlike the metropolitan areas, where the strategic guidance is at least more localized, under present circumstances, reliance would be placed on strategic guidance for the whole of the southwest region. This would prove wholly inadequate as a co-ordinating framework for strategic planning – the difference in scale is simply too large.

In all its submissions to the Local Government Commission, Avon County Council made a strong case for the retention of the county council because of the need to prepare strategic planning and transportation policies over the area covered by the county. The Commission, in its final report, made the following two comments:

> The Commission is concerned to ensure the strategic land-use planning for Avon should not be undermined by the introduction of Unitary Authorities. For Strategic Planning the new Unitary Authorities in the present Avon should assume joint responsibility for structure planning in the whole of their combined area in each County retaining the present Structure Plan area.

In October 1994 the Secretary of State, in announcing his endorsement of the recommendations of the Local Government Commission in relation to Avon, stated "I propose to accept the Commission's recommendations on Strategic Planning as submitted". Both the Commission and the Secretary of State acknowledged the importance of continuing future strategic planning for the Avon area.

Following considerable discussion, all the local authorities in Avon concluded that strategic planning and transportation issues for the Avon area would be best served by the introduction into the Orders for the abolition of Avon of a statutory requirement for the four unitary authorities to work together to prepare, adopt and implement strategic planning and transportation policies for the area. Given the past and likely future animosity between local authorities on several issues, this unanimous agreement in this area was perhaps surprising but, nevertheless, all parties felt this was the best course of action.

The authorities campaigned at the DOE, at both officer and ministerial level, to achieve this statutory requirement. However, the Orders, when published, did not incorporate a requirement for the four unitary authorities to work together, but instead referred to Section 50 of the Town and Country Planning Act 1990 which allows local authorities to work together on a voluntary basis in relation to joint structure and local plans.

The authorities continued to press the case for a statutory requirement in the

Orders. At meetings the DOE officers fully understood the points being made by the authorities, but indicated that it was extremely unlikely that the Secretary of State would accede to the request. First, they did not accept that the Secretary of State had legal power to do what the Avon authorities were seeking and, secondly, they considered that, even if such powers existed, it was very unlikely it would be exercised. The Secretary of State's view was that arrangements for strategic planning should be left on a voluntary basis using the general provisions in legislation to facilitate this and a statutory obligation on authorities to work together would be inconsistent with the government's approach to deregulation. They also acknowledged that the Secretary of State had reserve powers if the arrangements did not succeed but, importantly, indicated that the DOE would be issuing guidance giving more details of how authorities would be expected to work together on strategic planning, and they considered this to be sufficient.

At a further meeting with Avon representatives, the Minister for Local Government explained that he did not wish to be over-prescriptive. He wanted to be sure that the new authorities had flexibility, and could not understand why, if all the current authorities were so committed to joint co-operative working, they felt it was so important to be bound by statute. He concluded with a statement that "the deputation had not convinced him on this matter".

The county council subsequently decided to seek judicial review of the Draft Orders but the subjects for this review did not include the strategic planning/transportation argument, as both Avon officers and members felt that was no legal case for pursuing the matter any further.

Meanwhile, county and district councils in Avon have addressed the draft terms of reference of a joint committee. The following set of duties has been suggested:

- a structure plan
- an integrated transportation plan
- an advisory role for transport policies and programmes
- an advisory role for waste management and minerals planning
- an advisory role for strategic environmental protection and enhancement
- an advisory role for economic development and related infrastructure planning
- an information, research and intelligence base related to the above tasks
- the provision of appropriate information to the constituent authorities and the general public relating to any or all of the above functions, as in the interests or promotion of the area as the committee shall see fit.

They have also considered a "protocol" to govern the likely voluntary relationship, which will, *inter alia*, carry a commitment to adopt joint strategic policies.

Discussion has also been proceeding about the nature of a "Joint Technical Unit" to service these functions. Preliminary indications are that a "core" staff of about 30 people will be required for strategic planning, information and research, strategic transportation and administrative support. These will be supplemented by staff seconded from the constituent authorities, and specialist advice will be "bought in".

The local plan process is not without difficulty during these changes. Procedurally, the Local Government Changes for England Regulations 1994 make general provision for the continuity of plans. These ensure that work already undertaken need not be repeated. They do not, however, provide for two separate plans, at different stages of the process, to be brought together. This is the situation which will apply to the district plans for Kingswood and Northavon (South Gloucestershire) and Bath and Wansdyke (North East Somerset).

More detailed provisions appear necessary, but the important practical issues are to ensure, first, that some flexibility is allowed about the timing of emerging plans being combined and, secondly, that part-district plans will not be treated as "non-compliant" and accorded less weight in the decision-making process.

In terms of local planning, reorganization presents an opportunity to put new, improved ways of delivery services in place; indeed, the geographical situation of some new authorities should at least put these on the agenda. The new South Gloucestershire, lacking a single focus, would seem a good candidate for a decentralized approach to both democratic decision-making and service delivery.

Conclusions

The present is an era of uncertainty in which only change is certain. For many, this has been unsettling and the review of local government has proven a distraction. There are also those who have seized the opportunities that a review of local government raises and have approached the issues with a degree of optimism. Where there is uncertainty, the opportunity exists to exert influence. It is dependent on the professional capabilities of those involved as to whether a period of uncertainty can be transformed into a period of opportunity. It is inevitable that practical difficulties will be experienced in implementing the proposals, but this should not be permitted to extinguish the few threads of optimism that exist. Flexibility, as well as optimism, is required if the government's proposals are to be successfully implemented.

The formulation and implementation of planning policy has not always featured centrally in the government's deliberations over the future shape and pattern of local government. We should, however, recognize that planning is only one of the very many functions in which local authorities are engaged. Local government does not exist only to satisfy the requirements of planning policy. This may appear an obvious point, although, on the basis of some of the comments expressed throughout the process of reorganization, it is one that unfortunately continues to need to be made. The future pattern of local government now proposed in Wales, Scotland and parts of England, represents the introduction of a system of local government on which the fundamental principles of present planning legislation are founded, in the form of unitary local government. This in itself should be welcomed.

The delivery and implementation of planning policy will inevitably be affected by the reorganization of local government. As stated, the nature of the institutional framework will have a direct influence on the policy framework. The explicit nature of this effect will be clear only following reorganization and only informed speculation can be made at the present time. There still remains more questions than answers and we pose several of these as a conclusion to this chapter.

First, will the lack of clarity of purpose in the initial period of the review undermine future achievements? Although progress has been made in many areas, there continues to be heated debate over the merits of undertaking reorganization, particularly so in England. The contention that local government reorganization may not yet take place cannot therefore be dismissed out of hand. This has been the fundamental flaw in the reorganization process, in that the inadequacy of the initial foundations has made for instability throughout the progress of the review. For reorganization not to go ahead would be unfortunate, for there is too much to lose and too many opportunities to allow to pass.

The reorganization of local government also raises questions as to the future nature and form of government policy guidance. The key concern in Wales is that the establishment of unitary authorities on the basis of the pattern proposed will enable the Welsh Office to strengthen its own policy position by assuming sole responsibility for strategic planning.

On the issue of strategic planning, the preferred form expressed by the government is voluntary joint working between authorities. There is concern that such arrangements will be ineffective in addressing strategic issues and it is accepted that the success of joint arrangements varies considerably. However, it is in the interests of local democracy that the new local authorities are seen to secure effective strategic planning voluntarily. However, the effectiveness of such arrangements on the scale proposed has yet to be proven, and if this continues to be the case, then the government may yet be required to add a statutory basis to inter-authority working arrangements.

As a final conclusion, it appears that there is genuine reason to believe that the present reorganization of local government offers opportunities for the planning policy framework. It is inevitable that adjustments will be required to be made to assimilate the new institutional framework with the policy framework, which has changed incrementally during the past 20 years. Local authorities and shadow local authorities should now have progressed to detailed consideration of how they each want to give these opportunities practical effect, and the developing policy framework should now proceed to assist in enabling them to do this.

CHAPTER 8

A future for strategic planning policy – a Manchester perspective

Ted Kitchen

Introduction

The broad thrust of my argument in this chapter is that strategic planning is not a planning activity that takes place at a particular spatial scale or as a particular topic alongside many others, but is rather a dimension of most planning activities even if it is not always separately recognized as such. Thus, central government planning policy, regional planning policy, structure planning policy and local planning policy all have strategic planning dimensions to them; no one of them, from this way of looking at the world, is inherently any more strategic than is any other, but neither is any one of them devoid of a strategic component.

To this end, 11 propositions are defined that to my mind are characteristic of this way of looking at strategic planning. They are, in other words, likely to be broadly common components of the strategic planning dimensions of whatever spatial scale or topic focus of planning activity is being attempted. They have been defined from trying to reflect on my own personal experiences in planning, which to varying degrees have involved most spatial scales and many topics, albeit sometimes tangentially, and they are illustrated from my experience of being fortunate enough to be involved in planning work in Manchester at a time when the city is rediscovering itself and making great strides forwards. The fact that this means that there is inevitably a spatial similarity about the examples chosen for illustrative purposes does not invalidate the claim that these are common components of strategic planning activities at various spatial scales. What it does not enable me to claim, however, is that all of these characteristics are to be found as part of all strategic planning activities, and indeed common sense would suggest that this would in any event be likely to be an exaggerated claim to make. It should be clear from all of this that I base what I say on what I have observed and participated in; these are not normative statements but are essentially descriptive ones. It is not part of the argument in this chapter that "good" strategic planning (whatever that may be) fits all these characteristics and, by extension, that the absence of some of these characteristics makes the activity somehow less good; I am merely trying to say what I think constitutes activity that I would recognize as strategic. Where experience suggests to me that there are statements about desirable or undesirable practice that can be made, however, I have made them in the elaborations of the 11 propositions that constitute the core of this chapter. But, as with all the other components of this line of argument, these are at the end of the day merely expressions of personal opinion.

The nature and characteristics of strategic planning

I do not have a definition of strategic planning that rolls off the tongue, save the entirely circular one that it is those planning activities that enable you to identify and give expression to your strategy. In a sense, however, I think this is probably about as good a definition as we need, because what matters here is not what we say but what we do. From this perspective, strategic planning activities are what we make them, and thus the problem of giving expression to them through the statutory planning process is put into its true perspective as a second-order problem. Put simply, it is not worth worrying all that much about how to give expression to strategic thinking if the strategic thinking is not very good in the first place. On the other hand, of course, it certainly is worth getting very annoyed with our strait-jacketed statutory planning processes if they limit or restrict perfectly sensible strategic thinking from being applied as fully or as effectively in our development plans as it could be. This might even raise the heretical thought that having development plans that all look identical on the Department of the Environment's bookshelves, or which all express policies in ways that use the same approved language, should not after all be the primary objective of central government planning policy, although from time to time people more cynical than myself who have also been on the receiving end of some of its more bizarre attempts at imposing uniformity have thought that it might be.

Leaving the knockabout elements of this aside, what I am proposing is really a set of 11 very simple propositions:
- Strategic planning is about being clear in what broad directions you want to go and about how you might get there.
- It is thus unique to each locality, and should be grounded in the history, aspirations, circumstances and people of that locality.
- It almost certainly is not limited to what is conventionally defined as "planning", but is about the place and its people on which all sorts of processes will impact in various ways.
- It will have messages for all sorts of "customers" of the service at different

125

levels of governments and in many walks of life.

- It really should not be all that susceptible to the latest national "good idea" that we are all supposed to chase like lemmings over the cliff until somebody else has thought of another one, and we then chase with equal vigour unless we are already broken on the rocks below.

- The basic principles will probably stand for quite some time, although they should be kept under constant review, but the detailed actions will change frequently according to opportunities and to people.

- It will probably be opportunity-led rather than problem-led, because, although it will be about using the former (among other things) to tackle the latter it will also be about lifting up aspirations and galvanizing people into action, which a problem-led approach is not often very good at.

- It will probably contain some long-term diagnoses where the action is very unclear, even if the direction that is desirable is much clearer.

- It needs to have a wide level of general support from the local community and as much specific support as possible from key actors who will actually have to do things to make it happen.

- It will be expressed in a variety of ways, only one of which (and arguably not often the most important) will be through the development plan.

- The only test that really matters is whether it works in its own terms and in its own area.

I should say, before going any further, that I am not attempting to demonstrate any universality of views about these propositions, merely that I am basing them on my experience and offering them as such to see whether they strike any chords with others. My experience is essentially in three of our great conurbations (Clydeside, Tyneside and Manchester), all of which are typified by long-term problems of industrial decline and of the need for a sound economic base to be re-created, by major physical and environmental problems often related to the process of industrial decline, by problems of lack of confidence that have sometimes produced ceilings on their aspirations set unnecessarily low, and all of which are populated by smashing people who could do far more to help the processes of regeneration if only we could find ways of enabling this to happen. None of these major concentrations of population is a "hospital case", although at times they have been treated as if they were and have perhaps at times also believed this themselves. Fundamentally, what they all need is to be seen for what they are: major locations of opportunity, able to contribute very significantly to the creation of the good life for all our citizens in the twenty-first century that I am sure we all aspire to, even it if seems a long way off at present. This is especially true to the near 20 per cent of their populations who are economically and socially deprived and for whom urban life offers very little. These beliefs and experiences will shape what I say, and so I set them out now for the avoidance of any ambiguity.

Clarity of broad direction

The distinction between strategy and tactics is well known. What is at the heart of it, when applied to planning, is the distinction between the broad direction you are seeking to move in and the frequent decisions that need to be made as part of this process over a sustained period of time. Sometimes, this broad direction may be a clear end, such as, for example, the desire to establish particular kinds of facilities in a particular locality. A good example of this is Manchester's decision to build a new concert hall worthy of the city's place in the country's musical life, and of the reputation the Hallé Orchestra had and is rebuilding, that preceded even a decision about a site (that within certain limits would not have mattered anyway) or about a possible funding package (where the only real questions were: could one be put together? and was the cost to the public purse likely to be acceptable?). Sometimes, the broad direction may be a series of objectives that are shared but where the action taken to achieve them may be less clear and may indeed change considerably, perhaps even to the surprise of most concerned. An example here is the Manchester Olympic bid, which was actually led by three objectives:

- to put the City more on the international map
- to obtain sporting infrastructure that would not otherwise have been achieved as part of urban regeneration, and
- to bring the Olympic Games back to Britain.

The output of the Olympic bidding process at two different points in time (bidding for the 1996 and the 2000 Games) was actually two different facilities packages, the first of which succeeded against the first of the above objectives only because none of it was built, whereas the second also succeeded against the second of the above objectives because the new velodrome has been opened and the new indoor arena is, at the time of writing, well under way towards completion. We have not yet succeeded against the third of these objectives, but perhaps winning the English nomination for the Commonwealth Games of 2002 may be a stepping stone towards this. In all of this, the objectives have been clear and common, but the detailed way forward has changed significantly.

Uniqueness of strategies

"Unique" is an over-used word, but my experience is that successful strategies are unique to localities, no matter how much they may have been influenced by other people's good ideas or successful experiences. This is because planning is about the interactions between places and people, which are subtle and ever-changing, rather than about the application of standard answers to common problems. In saying that, they need therefore to be grounded in the history, the aspirations, the circumstances and the people of a locality. I am picking out what are probably the four key elements of these interactions, although there may be others. The significance of these four is as follows:

- *History* – because this explains how and why we have got to where we are today, and probably enables both the main assets and the main problems of a place to be readily understood. Manchester is as it is, for example, because it was the world's first industrial city, at the heart of the transport revolution in the late eighteenth and early nineteenth centuries and of the industrial revolution that paralleled it, with a radical nineteenth-century tradition born out of both the desperate conditions of the industrial working classes (as studied by, among others, Engels in *The city*) and the self-important individualism of Manchester's industrial (principally cotton) magnates that helped them to conceive and then complete the construction of the Manchester Ship Canal in the 1890s.
- *Aspirations* – all communities are based upon the desires of their people to build a better life for themselves or to achieve some personal goals. Things do not get done without these essentially personal motivations, many of which of course are translated into practice through the political process.
- *Circumstances* – we always start from where we are, and a failure to understand contemporary circumstances and the factors affecting them can lead quickly to the failure of projects misconceived as a result. A classic example of this is the pressure in the 1960s to develop industrialized housing, which quite forgot the problems of manufacture and assembly and the irritating habit of rain to percolate every crack. Much of that housing has now been or is in the course of being demolished.
- *People* – a city's greatest asset is its people. They are the source of ideas, of contacts, of confidence, and ultimately it is their support for a strategy that will determine whether or not it has a chance of succeeding.

Planning strategies are not limited to "planning"

This is in a way a statement of the obvious. All the examples I am giving in this chapter are of strategies where there is an important town and country planning contribution to be made, but where they are not capable of being implemented solely (and often mainly) within the confines of contemporary town and country planning law. This is perhaps one of the most significant differences between the concept of a planning strategy as it is being outlined here and the formal concept of a development plan or of a planning document at a particular spatial scale. There is nothing new in this; Patrick Geddes and Lewis Mumford, for example, were very keen to write about planning as but one element in the general task of trying to improve the living circumstances of people. Their argument about the need for planning was based upon this proposition, and was grounded in an acute understanding from history of the living circumstances of ordinary people when gathered together in places where throughout most of their existence no such attempts had been made, rather than on any sort of tidy-minded argument for planning as an end in itself. I sometimes think we forget this today.

Messages for "customers"

Increasingly, I tend to think of planning processes as having all sorts of customers, with legitimate needs that we should seek to meet as best we can. Indeed, I would go further: our justification for our existence should be seen in these terms; we have no divine right to exist. Of course, in a pluralist society it is not going to be possible to meet all the legitimate needs of our customers, because many of these will be in conflict; and, in a society with limited resources and with imperfect mechanisms for allocating them, planning decisions will come up against "who gains and who loses" arguments all the time, often in ways that are not comfortable for planners themselves. Ultimately, the political process exists to deal with these matters, and in a democratic society it is right and proper that it should be. But there is a great deal that planners can do in these terms without having to resort to the political process to find ways of meeting legitimate needs that coincide, or that can be pursued without serious detriment to other customers, and this is in many ways a more appropriate model for planning activity than the "we know best" attitude that blighted so much planning activity, particularly in the 1960s and 1970s. The myriads of customer relations that exist in these terms in the planning field, many of which may not be consciously thought about by planners, form an important part of the backcloth for work on planning strategies, and equally such strategies should both influence and be tested by and through this network of relationships. Strategies cannot succeed without a good base of customer support, and this network of relationships can be used to judge whether this exists or can be created without having to go through the full panoply of strategy failure; but we still do not do this often enough.

Susceptibility to the latest "good idea"

The process of madly chasing the latest thing that we are all supposed to be concerned about is one that is well known to us all; indeed it could be said to have characterized urban policy in this country for some while now, especially when ministers have made flying visits to the USA. The real problem with this is that it is not always possible to discern from the outset whether the latest initiative is something that will be short-lived and soon forgotten, or whether it is something that will get absorbed into the panoply of practice and thereby improve it. The latest wheeze from government may often be regarded with a considerable degree of scepticism by practitioners, but if it is offered along with some real money that would not otherwise be available, it becomes very difficult for cash-strapped local authorities not to pursue it. The thing about all of this in relation to strategies, however, is (or should be) that it should not deflect us from our long-term goals, even if it does affect our short-term tactics. If it is a "good idea", the odds are that a successful strategy will incorporate it in some form or another at some time or another; and, if it disappears quickly, then we will have done our duty by our strategy in not allowing it to get deflected. Governments have a particular duty in this sense, it seems to me, to try to find ways of sustaining medium- and long-term initiatives designed to achieve major objectives, rather than constantly introducing and discarding initiatives like neophiliacs that have confusion as their main epitaph. Urban regeneration is a long-term business, and governments do seem to struggle with this idea, whereas, by definition, local authorities cannot walk way from the problems that characterize their patch.

Continuity of basic principles

In a way, this is the mirror image of the previous point. Soundly based strategies are likely to have broad goals or basic objectives that remain unchanged in their essence, although they may well be modified in their details as a result of the constant process of keeping them under review. It may well be the case, however, that the detailed actions taken in the name of these goals or objectives will change a great deal as circumstances change or as people come up with or discard ideas, and strategies ought to be robust enough to accommodate this without too much difficulty. For example, a desire to improve the living and working environment of East Manchester, the former "workshop of the world", where industrial disinvestment had just about been completed by the mid-1980s, is a task that in a sense will never be completed (because it is always capable of being improved), but the point will be reached where it can no longer be said that there is anything about that living and working environment that makes it worse than elsewhere in the city. The means of doing this may well change as circumstances and government programmes change, and this may well mean different things for the same sites at different points in time; and within certain limits; does this really matter? There are, in a mixed-use city, several things that many sites can perfectly sensibly be used for, and just because a map happens to have a particular colour on it this should not be worth a fight to the death to prevent other perfectly acceptable uses from becoming established and contributing to the overall objective. What is important here is the continuing validity of that objective, and not so much the choice between degrees of rightness in relation to individual sites.

Opportunities-led approaches

One of the things that does strike me as being quite different about much planning work now is the emphasis on opportunities as distinct from the emphasis on problem-solving that was typical, say, in the 1970s. Of course, one of the reasons for this is that we can no longer rely as we could then on apparently unending public sector investment programmes to tackle problems, even though at the time we often thought them inadequate for the job to be done. What we have to do today is to work with partners in an enabling way to get things done, with public expenditure playing a much more limited role, although still of value in doing some things that the market will not deal with effectively. I say all of this pragmatically; this is how it is; I make no comment on whether this is how it ought to be. One of the consequences of this approach, however, is that it forces you to evaluate your asset base, because it is out of this that opportunities get created. For example, Manchester in these terms probably has six primary assets:

- The Regional Centre, with its 120000 jobs mostly in higher-order services including higher education, in retailing, and in leisure and entertainment activities of various kinds. Having the largest single concentration of jobs in northern England at the heart of your city has to be a primary asset.
- The Higher Education Precinct, the largest single educational campus in western Europe with over 40000 students and tremendous potential (not always realized) for translating ideas into economic activity.
- Manchester's nodality in relation to transport networks, and particularly in this context Manchester Airport, which is now the seventeenth largest in the world when measured by international passenger movements.
- The city's base of existing high technology industry, which was strengthened in the late 1980s by the decision of Siemens to establish their Northern England headquarters in the city.
- The sporting, theatrical and musical life of the city, typified perhaps by the fact that Manchester United Football Club are the city's greatest international recognition point although their ground is not actually in the city.
- The city's people, constantly replenished over the years by waves of immigrants who come to the city and add their distinctive contribution to its life. Perhaps the most remarkable example in recent years has been the influx of Hong Kong Chinese money, making Manchester, after London, the greatest concentration of Chinese people in the country and creating a vibrant Chinatown in the city centre from an area that 15 years ago was very run down.

This sort of appraisal of an asset base readily facilitates large numbers of potential opportunities to be identified by seeking to build on these strengths. What it also does is to raise aspirations, to seek to build confidence, and to avoid placing unnecessary restraints on what a city might aspire to, as compared with an approach focusing on problems that may not always work well by these tests, no matter how admirable its understanding of the problems may be. Manchester's policies in the late 1970s and early 1980s tended to be of the latter kind, and as a consequence they put a low ceiling on what might be achieved; after all, if they gave the impression that we were not very confident in ourselves, how could we expect others to be confident in the city? The thing that actually began to turn this around was the feedback from the public on the city Centre Campaign of the early and mid-1980s, where the public actually told us that they had a better impression of the city centre than the Council itself appeared to have, at least when judged by its public statements. Of course, the really important thing to do with an opportunity-led approach is to try to make sure that opportunities are taken in such a way as to help to tackle the problems that exist. Probably the most severe problem facing our country's cities at present is the emergence over the past few years of growing numbers of people who are poor, unemployed or reliant on the black economy, and who are alienated from much of what cities have to offer. In some cities, this might today be as much as 15–20 per cent of the population, and it will grow and become a permanent phenomenon of urban life unless we do something about it. Urban regeneration based upon taking the very real opportunities that exist in our cities will fail unless it offers something tangible to these people, and perhaps particularly the young people among them, and this is arguably the greatest challenge facing our cities over the next decade.

Long-term diagnoses

There are many examples of strategic directions where the broad thrust is clear but the detailed action that is necessary is much less so. A good example of this is the need for our cities to progress towards sustainability, which virtually everyone would sign up for as a principle but that would then lead to major arguments about the next steps. An example of this is in the field of transport. I often say to our elected members that if we really do not do more to tackle the problems of traffic in the city centre, Central Manchester will be as bad (if not worse) by the year 2000 as Central London is today. This is not a precise forecast but an image, using an experience that people in the Council have frequently had (the need to go to London to see people in government, since they much less frequently come to us) to get across a point. At the same time, of course, traffic problems are to some extent the kinds of problems you want because they are a product of economic activity, and the difficulty is that this point is a very hard one to define and arguably (as Central London shows) you will not know that you have gone past it until you have. I believe that the solution to this problem is clear; we must re-invest in making urban public transport a quality product that people choose for positive reasons. We have begun this with Metro-link and the return of trams to the city's streets, but I worry that, unless we can add several extensions to it, the risk of it becoming an anachronism is very real; I do not want it in the future to be held up as an example of what urban public transport should have become but did not. The 1990s from this perspective should be the decade of public transport, although we are at the time of writing halfway through the decade, in these terms it has not yet begun. Perhaps the most important strategy in this situation is to keep on publicizing the need for action, because until this need is more widely acknowledged little will happen.

Broadly based support

Strategies need to be supported by the public if they are to have much chance of succeeding. This support can be active or passive, and may in many cases be little more than the absence of opposition, but the days when major strategies can be imposed upon a largely quiescent public have (hopefully) gone. One of the great things about the Manchester Olympic Bid, for example, was the very wide support it attracted from the community, and indeed it could not have gone as far as it did without that support, because a wide gap between the rhetoric of the campaign and the reality of public opinion would quickly have become obvious. Of course, it is also true that only a small fraction of people will be involved in major ways in implementing any strategy directly, and thus positive support among this group of key actors is absolutely essential to success. However, this group must never forget that it depends upon that wider public support. For example, the Olympic Bid's advertising would not have been effective if 450000 Mancunians in the many millions of contacts they make outside the city every year had been saying very different things as part of those contacts.

Limited role for development plans as a form of expression of strategies

Following on from what I have been saying, development plans will have a role in giving expression to strategies, but it will be a limited one given the time they take to go through the processes of gestation or change. Most development plans in my experience fail "Kitchen's Law", which is depicted in Figure 8.1.

Figure 8.1 "Kitchen's Law". $$\frac{\text{Time over which plan is useful}}{\text{Time taken to prepare plan}} > 1$$

This is simply saying that we should get at least as much value out of plans as the effort we put in, and since often plans do not pass this test we should not be surprised if doubts about their worth are expressed in some quarters. From this perspective, only limited reliance will be placed on such a document as a vehicle for expression, although this is not to say that plans do not have some uses that are valuable in the process of strategy expression. However, my experience is that this role is more likely to be a following one than a leading one.

Measures of success

If a strategy works in its own terms, in its own area, and to the satisfaction of the people involved, then it is a successful strategy. If it does not work then it is not successful. It does not seem to me that any other measures of success are worth serious consideration. This suggests that the number of external constraints imposed on processes of strategy-making should be kept to a minimum or (ideally) eliminated altogether, since these are likely to introduce tests outside those set out above. It also follows, if we would like statutory development planning to have a larger role in strategic planning than I have ascribed to it, that these same tests should be applied to statutory planning, rather than the emphasis on common types of plan and national uniformity that we have had ever since the 1947 Town and Country Planning Act. This emphasis on a high level of local discretion, a high level of public involvement and the ability to make quick changes where needed, would also of course improve conformity to Kitchen's Law, which I would argue is wholly desirable not just because I invented it (heaven forfend!) but because on strict value-for-money principles we ought to get at least as much value out of our plans as the effort we put into them.

Conclusions

The above propositions have been characteristics of my experience of strategic planning activities in Manchester. As I said at the outset, I make no claim as to their universality, or even as to their completeness; it may well be the case that others reflecting on their experiences in other locations would produce different propositions or characteristics. What they do suggest, however, is that strategic planning activities form an important part of continuous planning processes, providing a context for other activities and filling in the bits that those other activities may not do so well or even at all. In particular, I have argued that strategic planning activities are not necessarily restricted to space or to time, but are about defining and then moving towards goals and objectives in particular localities with their own particular and interlocking sets of circumstances and people, an understanding of which is critical to successful strategic planning activity. Thus, strategic planning, when looked at in this way, is likely to be both a context for and a dimension of most other planning activities; there is, in other words, likely to be something akin to the processes I have described going on at whatever spatial scale or type of activity is being examined. I would therefore like to conclude with a few words about these relationships.

To use again the example I have quoted on several occasions, it may be interesting to see how the Manchester Olympic Bid process, which I have characterized as a strategic planning process, found expression (or did not) in the other elements of the statutory planning policy framework:

- *Central government planning policy* – said very little about the Olympic Bid process, although central government decision-making about resource allocation certainly was very helpful in assisting primarily with the funding of facilities. However, this is not to say that central government planning policy was irrelevant to the process of bidding for the 2000 Games or would equally be irrelevant to the process of bidding on a future occasion. Indeed, one of the keys to our decision to change the facilities package significantly between the 1996 and the 2000 bids, in the hope of getting some of those facilities constructed, was a recognition of the need to put more emphasis on urban regeneration if we were to have any real hope of securing government funding, or from our own point of view if we were to integrate the Olympic bidding process more effectively into what we were trying to do anyway in rejuvenating the city. We have good reason to believe that Manchester's success in this, and the clear evidence that all sectors and the general public could unite behind a goal of this kind, were important elements in the government's decision to institute the City Pride initiative, which in its invitation to the city and also London and Birmingham to produce a prospectus of what needs to be done to regenerate the city over the next 10–15 years (well, this is how we are interpreting it, anyway), is arguably another example of an attempt to generate a strategic planning document that is not like anything else. Other central government policies for planning and about the planning process will impact on such strategies in various ways, but by their general nature this is much more likely to affect how we go about things rather than what we do.
- *Regional planning policy* – until recently, a section dealing with regional planning policy in the North West would have been a blank page. More recently, the North West Regional Association has produced a regional economic strategy, and subsequently has produced reports on regional transport strategies and on regional environmental needs, and has been the instrument through which the local planning authorities have got together to work on regional planning guidance. In all of this, the Olympic Bid was an important element in the regional shopping list of potential major matters that could improve the regional economy in the regional economic strategy; but by the time the follow-up papers began to emerge, the International Olympic Committee awarded the 2000 Games to Sydney and thus these reports downplayed the matter. Now that we have secured the English nomination for the Commonwealth Games of 2002, however, future documentation out of this stable will no doubt pick all this up again. In all of this, therefore, regional activity has been following the strategic planning process in Manchester, although its endorsement of our actions has helped.
- *Structure planning policy and local planning policy* – I am taking these together because in the conurbations they both form parts of our Unitary Development Plan. In preparing the Manchester UDP, we found ourselves

135

in the position of wanting to give expression to and to move forward the emerging Olympic Bid, but not wanting to do things that imposed a rigidity on an evolving situation that may have proved less than helpful when push came to shove. To take an obvious example, the work on the stadium area in east Manchester was still very fluid when the UDP was being drafted in its deposit form, and therefore what we wanted to do was to provide a framework for action that would set down some helpful principles while being both flexible and durable. We therefore decided to declare it one of the city's Major Urban Regeneration Areas, one of three such designations in the city where major change was expected, which would mainly be handled by informal briefs set in the context of the UDP. These tensions between clarity and flexibility were mirrored many times in the UDP preparation process, and while obviously we think we attained the balance as near right as we could, this then falls to be tested by the UDP inquiry process. The 400 or so objections from the DoE, mainly about the way we had worded policies in our attempts to tackle this sort of balancing job and at the same time to be as clear as possible about our intentions, did not really help in these terms, although they too fall to be tested through the inquiry process. At the time of writing, with the inquiry inspector's report very recently published, this balancing act looks to have survived this process in its essentials.

This quick tour through what was being done to relate the Olympic Bidding process to formal planning policies illustrates the point that the latter found it very difficult to keep up with the former, and on the whole did not try. The test often became the need to avoid writing difficulties into a rapidly evolving process, rather than the need to add value to what was already under way. This perhaps makes the point that reliance on formal planning processes has its limitations, and that maybe planning strategies are really about reaching the parts that other planning activities cannot reach.

CHAPTER 9

Interpreting planning law

Ian Gatenby & Christopher Williams

Introduction

The purpose of this chapter is to explore the relationship between planning law and planning policy, and to ask whether, in some cases, there is a relationship at all. The aspect, which will be dealt with in most detail is a review of planning law and policy relating to the role of the development plan in planning decisions, exploring the legal background to Section 54A of the Town and Country Planning Act 1990, and its relationship to national planning policy as contained in PPG1 *General policy and principles* (DOE/WO 1992a). Other aspects that will be covered are the use of Grampian conditions, contrasting the approach of the Secretaries of State and the courts, and recent developments in the field of planning advantage. The overall thesis is that in reaching development control decisions in several different respects, the identification of relevant issues for the decision-maker is largely a matter of law, but the manner in which they are applied remains largely a matter of policy. Broadly, as long as the planning decision is approached in a legally correct way – for instance, asking the right questions, taking relevant factors into account and excluding irrelevant factors – the courts will not interfere with the judgement of the decision-taker. A key factor is asking the right questions.

Policy–law relationship

It would be foolish to attempt a one-paragraph summary of the interface between law and policy in planning, not least because the courts have been attempting to do this for several decades, they are still developing their approach, and the answer itself will vary depending on which part of planning law one is considering. Also, a whole new branch of planning law is emerging in the form of material deriving from the European Union. Whereas in the UK the traditional approach to planning is that:

- planning "rules" are almost entirely in policy documents, which can be changed relatively quickly, and
- planning authorities have great discretion, so that for example they can approve today a policy couched in relatively absolute terms and then tomorrow lawfully take a planning decision to make an exception to that policy.

The European influence in planning is starting to make itself felt and is very different in two critical respects. First, where the UK Government is giving effect to EU Directives, it must do so by law. For example, we have the Conservation (Natural Habitats, etc.) Regulations 1994, which give effective to the Habitats Directive. Since the regulations are law and not policy, they cannot be changed with anything like the ease with which policy can be changed. Secondly, since they are law and not policy, planning authorities can only make an exception to them in so far as they are specifically allowed to do so. Unlike general planning, where they have an almost unlimited discretion to make exceptions from policy, where the policies are contained in regulations, their discretion is limited by the terms of the regulations themselves. With the growing influence of the European Union, it is to be expected that this trend will continue. The following comments, discussing the interface on law and policy, do not apply to this new type of EU-derived planning law. The broad role of the law is to set out general rules within which the planning authority must operate. Policy guides the planning authority on how it should operate within the limits set by the law. Thus, for example, the law indicates what is or what is not a material consideration. Planning authorities must take into account what is material and not pay attention to something which was not legally a material consideration. On the other hand, policy can properly indicate what weight is to be given to a material consideration.

This is easy to say, but in practice it is not an easy matter to decide what a planning authority in fact has to do when the law tells it to take a factor into account, but the policy tells it to give little or no weight to that factor. The comments further on in the chapter (on Grampian conditions) provide a graphic illustration of the problems.

The development plan

In February 1992 we published an article in the *Journal of Planning and Environment Law* (*JPL*) exploring the implications of the then new Section 54A of the Town and Country Planning Act 1990 (Gatenby & Williams 1992). This section had become law in September 1991. It states:

Where, in making any determination under the planning Acts, regard is to be had to the development plan, the determination shall be made in accordance with the plan unless material considerations indicate otherwise.

This has to be read together with several sections of the 1990 Act, which require that regard should be had to the development plan, and particularly Section 70, which states that in determining an application for planning permission the planning authority must "have regard to the provisions of the development plan, so far as material to the application, and to any other material considerations". The difference in emphasis between the old formulation of Section 70 and that of Section 54A reflected the government's desire in 1991 that the development control system should once again move towards a plan-led basis, and away from the philosophy of market-driven or appeal-led planning that had predominated during most of the mid- and late 1980s.

Although there was considerable alarm at the prospect of the enhanced role of the development plan in development control decisions, we took the view in 1992 that Section 54A would in fact be quite muted in practice. In particular, we concluded that the legal position was unlikely to be greatly changed, as there would almost always be material considerations apart from the development plan, and the weight to be given to them would be a matter for the judgement of the decision-maker, who would be entitled to decide that in any particular case there were material considerations that overrode the development plan.

Since that article, and over the course of the previous three years, there have been several judicial decisions on Section 54A that have gone some way towards clarifying the question of its correct legal application. As one might expect, in some areas the cases pull in opposite directions. An analysis of the most pertinent judgments follows. What, we believe, will emerge as an overall conclusion is that, by and large, our view expressed in 1992 remains broadly correct.

The first cases involving the effect of Section 54A on planning inquiries were reported in the *JPL* in January 1993. However, the bench sidestepped the issue in these cases by finding the inspector's decision to be in accordance with the development plan. It fell to David Widdicombe QC, sitting as a Deputy Judge, to clarify the effect of Section 54A in the judgment on *St Albans District Council vs Secretary of State for the Environment and Allied Breweries Limited* (1993) (*JPL* 374). In this case, Counsel for the Appellant had drawn attention to paragraphs 25 to 27 of PPG1, and in particular the sentence "an applicant who proposes a development that is clearly in conflict with the development plan would need to produce convincing reasons to demonstrate why the plan should not prevail". In other words, it was suggested that the development plan had to prevail unless there were "strong contrary planning grounds". However, Mr Widdicombe held this to be a mere gloss on the statute, and that although undoubtedly Section 54A did set up a presumption in favour of the development plan, for its rebuttal it was sufficient if there were material considerations that indicate otherwise. In other words, the Deputy Judge preferred to stick to the words of the statute. Not surprisingly, the Judge said that to treat the development plan as merely one material consideration would reduce Section 54A to the level of the pre-existing provision of Section 70, but the Court was not prepared to indicate how weighty the material considerations indicating otherwise would have to be to overcome the provision of the development plan. Thus, the weight to be attributed to the relevant factors in a decision is first and foremost a matter for the decision-maker.

Mr Widdicombe QC also held in the St Albans case that failure by the inspector to refer to Section 54A was not fatal, so long as the requirements of the section were met. However, he did observe that failure to refer to Section 54A did suggest that in that case the inspector had not considered that there were material considerations that justified the departure from the development plan, but had instead used the methods set out in Section 70 in weighing up all relevant factors to reach the conclusion. The appeal was not allowed on the grounds that had Section 54A definitely been followed, the outcome would have been the same in any case.

Another important decision on Section 54A is that of Michael Harrison QC (now Mr Justice Harrison) sitting as Deputy Judge in *South Lakeland District Council vs Secretary of State for the Environment* (1993) (*JPL* **644**). In this case the Deputy Judge held that it was not necessary for the Inspector to refer expressly to Section 54A. What was required was for it to be possible to look at the decision letter as a whole and see that the Inspector had reached the decision in a manner consistent with the provisions of Section 54A. Nothing in Section 54A requires the section itself to be referred to explicitly by any decision-maker; what is required is to do what the section says, that is, to determine an application in accordance with the provisions of the development plan unless material considerations indicate otherwise.

The relative weakness of the statutory wording in Section 54A is demonstrated by the judgment of Malcolm Spence QC sitting as Deputy Judge in *Sainsbury plc vs Secretary of State for the Environment and Bexley LBC* (1993) (*JPL* **651**). The report of this case indicates that it was accepted by all concerned that the planning application in question did not comply with the development plan. Nevertheless, the Deputy Judge clearly accepted that the application could be granted if it was not going to cause demonstrable harm. Thus, following judgment in the St Albans case, it supports the view that, where an application is not in accordance with the plan, this does not of itself amount to demonstrable harm. The decision-maker can still use lack of demonstrable harm to other interests of acknowledged importance as a material consideration to overturn the presumption in favour of the plan. What the inspector in this case placed importance on was not whether there was a technical breach of the plan, but whether the application would cause demonstrable harm to the objectives of the plan.

Section 54A has, on the other hand, been used to give extra weight to the development plan in one case. In *British Railways Board vs Slough Borough Council* (1993) (*JPL* **678**), David Widdicombe QC as Deputy Judge held that

he had no doubt at all that (designation of the site as a wildlife heritage site) had to in practice constitute a formidable barrier to any residential development of the site, especially in view of the presumption in favour of the development plan as required by Section 54A of the Town and Country Planning Act 1990.

Taking this judgment with Mr Widdicombe's earlier pronouncements in the St Albans case, it would appear that there is a degree of presumption in favour of the development plan, but that this can be overridden by material considerations, and that the courts have not been prepared to indicate how strong those material considerations have to be in order to override the plan. It will clearly fall to be a matter of judgement in each case for the decision-maker. Mr Widdicombe therefore rejected the argument that Section 54A created a strong presumption in favour of the plan.

Going one stage further, the question of whether Section 54A creates a presumption in favour of the development plan at all has twice been considered by Roy Vandermeer QC sitting as a Deputy Judge. The first case is *Gateshead Metropolitan Borough Council vs Secretary of State for the Environment, Evans of Leeds, and Safeway plc* heard in September 1992 (only one year after the enactment of Section 54A) but not reported until 1994 (*JPL* **55**). The timing of this judgment therefore preceded the decision of David Widdicombe QC in the St Albans case previously referred to. It was argued on behalf of the local planning authority that the effect of Section 54A was that if there were any breach or conflict with the development plan, then there was a presumption against the development that needed to be displaced by the Appellants. Mr Vandermeer QC stated that "I think it would be wrong for me not to express my own grave reservations about this approach". However, this was not a point that required to be determined in the case, and so the judge said nothing more about the reservations in his judgment. Subsequently, Mr Vandermeer has had a further opportunity to consider these matters in the judgment in *Bylander Waddell Partnership vs Secretary of State for the Environment and Harrow London Borough Council*, decided in November 1993 and reported in 1994 (*JPL* **440**). The Inspector's decision letter stated "in this case, the fundamental question is whether the development complies with the development plan as required by Section 54A of the Act, and I have concluded that it does not". In Mr Vandermeer's judgment, it was clear that the provisions of Section 54A only come into play when regard is to be had to the development plan. It is first necessary to determine whether the provisions of the development plan were material. If they were not, then Section 54A was irrelevant. This confirms our argument (1992) *JPL* 113, as summarized by Purdue (1994), that Section 54A only applies, in the case of planning applications and appeals, when the policies in the plan have something to say about the particular type of development. This judgment is also consistent with government advice in PPG1 (DoE/WO 1992a: para. 28) to the effect that, where the plan does not contain a policy relating to a particular development proposal, the planning application or appeal should be determined on its merits in the light of all the material circumstances.

Mr Vandermeer also took the opportunity to consider the earlier judgment of

Mr Widdicombe QC in the St Albans case. From the report of the case in the *JPL*, it appears that if Mr Vandermeer had any reservation about the way that Mr Widdicombe had expressed the decision in the St Albans case, it was in relation to Mr Widdicombe's comments that there was a presumption in favour of the development plan. Mr Vandermeer was quite clear in his view that the concept of a burden of proof is not in general terms helpful or relevant in planning cases. What matters is the judgment of the inspector or the Secretary of State upon the material placed before them. Where there was a material provision in the development plan to which regard had to be had, it was best to avoid the language of presumption and burden of proof and to keep to the language of Section 54A itself. Therefore, where there is a provision in the plan to which regard must be had, the decision-maker is instructed to determine the application in accordance with the plan unless material considerations indicate otherwise. In the judgment of Mr Vandermeer QC, it is for the decision-maker to judge whether material considerations do indicate otherwise, and the amount of weight to be given to any material consideration is a matter for the judgement of the decision-maker, whether inspector or Secretary of State.

As Purdue comments (1994: *JPL* 447), it is quite clear from this case that Mr Vandermeer considers that Section 54A should not be taken to have created a presumption against development that is contrary to the policies in the plan. Even if there is a presumption that the application should be refused, that does not mean that the application has to be refused, as it may be that material considerations indicate otherwise. As Purdue comments "the importance of the Deputy Judge's approach is that it removes any idea that the policies in the plan have to be given any special weight . . . ".

We now turn to the relationship between judicial interpretation of Section 54A, and government planning policy as contained in PPG1. PPG1 states that

> applications for development should be allowed, having regard to the development plan and all material considerations, unless the proposed development would cause demonstrable harm to interests of acknowledged importance. (DoE/WO 1992a: para. 5)

This is a statement of government planning policy, which retains the well known presumption in favour of development. Furthermore, as PPG1 itself reminds us at paragraph 20: "The Courts have held that government statements of planning policy are material considerations that must be taken into account, where relevant, in decisions on planning applications . . . ". The position is therefore as follows: there is no legal presumption in favour of granting planning permission. Nevertheless, there is government policy that planning permission should be granted unless to do so would cause demonstrable harm. Such government policy is, as a matter of law, itself a material consideration. More specifically, the absence of demonstrable harm is clearly a material consideration that has the potential to indicate that the provisions of the development plan should not prevail in any particular instance. Thus, in the St Albans case, Mr Widdicombe QC found that lack of demonstrable harm was a material consideration amply sufficient to justify a departure from a particular development plan policy, even allowing for the Section 54A presumption in favour of the plan.

Therefore, although it has been suggested in the past that there is apparent conflict between the provisions of PPG1 and the law in Section 54A, in our view this conflict, if such exists, is one of technicality rather than practical application. The *Sainsbury vs Bexley* case is another example of how both propositions can be applied in practice. The provisions of the development plan clearly have to be taken as the starting point, and are to be followed in the absence of any material considerations. However, one of these material considerations is the general presumption in favour of development, and the presence or absence of any demonstrable harm that would result from the development. So far, the indications are that courts will uphold the decisions of inspectors in allowing development that conflicts with the development plan, so long as there is a lack of demonstrable harm. This does not mean that an inspector or local planning authority will be obliged to allow a proposal that conflicts with the development plan, merely because there is no evidence of demonstrable harm. Section 54A would still allow them to refuse planning permission in those circumstances, so long as they took into account the fact that there was no demonstrable harm. Equally, however, it would be open to the decision-maker to decide that the absence of demonstrable harm did justify a decision contrary to the development plan. Thus, the conclusion is that the weight to be attached to the various factors remains, as it always has, a matter for the decision-maker, and this principle is not swayed in any way by the presence of Section 54A, nor recent judicial interpretation of it. Debating the theory and philosophy of Section 54A therefore, leads one on a convoluted path. We therefore turn to a more practical approach.

The practical application of Section 54A

From the above analysis, we suggest that the application of development plan policy in accordance with the statutory tests of Section 70 and Section 54A involves two stages: first, form a view of the proposal in the light of the development plan and, secondly, then see if other material considerations cause one to modify the first view. These stages can be broken down into the following steps:

1. Identify the statutory development plan applicable to the location of the proposed development; the fact that the development plan may be about to be superseded by a new one does not alter what is the development plan for legal purposes, although plainly this would be a material consideration that might indicate that the development plan should not be followed.
2. Determine whether the development plan contains policies or proposals relevant to the proposed development. If a form of development has not

143

been considered in the development plan, it cannot be said in this context that the development plan has any policies in relation to it; in these circumstances Section 54A does not apply. PPG1 paragraph 28 indicates that, where the development plan is not relevant because (for example, it does not contain a policy relating to a particular development proposal), the plan does not provide a clear guide, and the planning application or appeal should be determined on its merits in the light of all the material considerations. Thus, the test of Section 54A applies only where the provisions of the development plan are then material to the application.

3. If there are policies that deal with the proposed development, then determine whether the development is in accordance with the development plan, or not, or whether the policies pull in opposite directions. For these purposes, the plan must be read as a whole. It would not be unusual for the plan to have several relevant policies, some pointing in favour of the development and some against it. In those circumstances it appears to us that Section 54A is of little practical effect. This view is borne out by paragraph 28 of PPG1, which indicates that, where there are material policies in the plan that pull in opposite directions so that the plan does not provide a clear guide for a particular proposal, then the proposal should again be determined on its merits in the usual way, giving whatever weight is thought appropriate to the various development plan policies. Otherwise, if the development is in accordance with the development plan, then it should be permitted unless there are any other material considerations, in which case these have been weighed against the development plan and a judgement reached by the decision-maker. If the proposed development is not in accordance with the development plan, then it should be refused unless there are any other material considerations, in which case these have to be weighed by the decision-maker against the development plan policies.

4. What if the development plan policy conflicts with national policies? This question has two aspects. First, where national policies pre-date the development plan, so that for example a local plan has been decided in full knowledge of national policies at that date, then if the local plan is inconsistent with national policies it is arguable that the local plan should prevail. On the other hand, where national policies emerge after the development plan, they would be a material consideration that might indicate that the development plan should not be followed. Secondly, as a matter of practice the Department of the Environment has indicated in PPG1 (DOE/WO 1992a: para. 29) that the Secretary of State will examine development plans closely to ensure that they accord with national policies, and he will intervene where he thinks that they do not. Where he does not intervene, local authorities can take it that the Secretary of State will uphold the planning policy on appeal, even if it is contrary to national policy.

5. Have relevant factors occurred or come to light since the plan was prepared? If so, and they have not been taken into account before the plan is adopted, they could constitute material considerations that could justify a decision contrary to the development plan.

6. What is a material consideration in this context? Whether something is capable of falling in this description is a legal question. A material consideration in this context, in our view, is a factor relating to land-use planning that has arisen since the plan was approved or a factor arising before then that had not, or not fully, been taken into account by the plan-making authority. The question whether a site should be used for housing is a land-use factor; the local need for housing is a material consideration, but the questions who should live there and whether the housing is affordable are probably not land-use factors. An authority that took into account factors not material to planning, when determining a planning application, would be acting contrary to law even though they acted in accordance with their own policy.

7. Do the material considerations indicate a decision contrary to the development plan? Many local authorities may interpret this as meaning that the development plan will be upheld unless there is overwhelming evidence to the contrary. However, in our view, Section 54A does not have this meaning, since "indicate" is a relatively weak word in this context and it gives the decision-maker a wide discretion whether to override development plan policy because of other factors. There is no doubt that the degree to which a factor is to be regarded as material in any given case is a question for the planning authority. But an authority may be treated as ignoring a material factor, thus making its decision open to legal challenge, if it treats a material consideration as being of little or no significance, i.e. if it purports to consider it but does not realistically do so.

The legal position, in summary, is that the decision-maker must, where there are policies material to the application, give effect to those policies unless material considerations indicate otherwise; but when the policies are not material to the application, the decision-maker should reach his decision based on a balance of all other material considerations, having regard to the general presumption in favour of development contained within PPG1.

It is clear that two critical questions are: is the development plan policy "material to an application"; and what is the meaning of "indicate". In most practical situations, the legal implications of Section 54A may well be limited, since in most situations there will always be material considerations apart from the development plan, and in our opinion the weight to be given to them will be a matter for the judgement of the decision-maker who will be entitled to decide that they override the development plan. How decision-makers exercise that judgement as a matter of practice depends upon the changing flow of government policy.

So, although it has given rise to much analysis over the past few years,

145

including from ourselves, the application of Section 54A is rather more clear and straightforward than may at first have been thought to be the case. We concur with the views of the then Chief Planning Inspector, Stephen Crow, expressed at the 1993 Town and Country Planning Summer School that there are two basic steps for decision-makers to take (Crow 1993): first, to consider how a proposal measures up to the plan, and to reach a view on that. Secondly, to consider the other material considerations that will almost certainly exist, and to determine whether they override the conclusion already reached about the proposal in the context of development plan policies. The amount of weight to be put on the conclusion of the first step against the material considerations in the second step is a matter of policy. This will be considerably influenced by the government guidance of the day: in the mid-1980s there was government policy emphasis on the presumption in favour of development; now, there is emphasis on the plan-led system.

Conflicts between plans

One particular difficulty that can arise when assessing the extent to which local plans are a material consideration is when there is a conflict between them and other plans, such as structure plans, mineral plans, waste plans, or a local authority's corporate plans. However, the only case where statute has intervened is in the relationship between the guidance in structure and local plans.

Section 46 of the 1990 Act requires that the proposals in a local plan shall be in general conformity with the structure plan, and that the local plan cannot be adopted unless a certificate has been issued that the proposals conform generally to the structure plan. However, once a local plan has been adopted, Section 48 of the 1990 Act prescribes that where there is a conflict between any of the provisions of a local plan in force for an area and the provisions of the relevant structure plan, then the provisions of the local plan will prevail for all purposes. Since the legal requirement is general conformity with the structure plan, there may well be instances where the local plan is inconsistent with the structure plan.

The only exception to this rule is where policies and the structure plan are changed after a local plan has been adopted. This may have the effect that the local plan no longer conforms generally to the new policies. To deal with this possibility, Sections 47(5), 47(6), and 48(2) contain a procedure whereby a county planning authority shall, on the approval of proposals for the alteration or replacement of a structure plan, consider whether the local plans for the area affected still conform generally to the new structure plan policies. The county must then draw up a list of local plans that in their opinion do or do not conform generally. This list must be sent, within one month of the date of approvals of the new structure plan policies, to the Secretary of State and the district planning authorities responsible for the relevant local plans, and the consequence of a local plan being put on the non-conforming list is that in the case of conflict between the structure plan and the local plan, the local plan will not prevail as is normally the case, until a proposal for the alteration of the local plan, or for its repeal and replacement, has been adopted or approved by the Secretary of State, and the alteration, or replacement plan has come into force.

One further possibility is that changes to the structure plan policies may be contemplated at the same time as a local plan is being prepared or alterations proposed. It would certainly serve to defeat the object of conformity between plans if local plan policies had to conform generally with outdated structure plan policies that were about to be repealed. The solution provided by the Act is that, where proposals for alterations to the structure plan had been submitted to the Secretary of State for approval, a local planning authority may seek a direction from him under Section 47(2). The result is that the preparation and adoption of local plan policies can take place on the assumption that the proposed changes to the structure plan have been approved, and that the local plan policies can in fact be adopted before the structure plan changes are approved.

However, such a direction from the Secretary of State ceases to have effect, should he decide to reject the proposed changes to the structure plan, and the assumption that proposed changes to the structure plan are approved must adapt as modifications to the county's proposal are proposed to the county by the Secretary of State. Furthermore, if after the local plan is adopted the changes to the structure plan are approved in a form that means that the local plan no longer conforms generally, the local plan would not then prevail over the structure plan.

In all other circumstances, if there is conflicting policy guidance in any particular case it is a matter of planning judgement, not a question of law, which policy guidance the decision-maker should adopt, or how he should deal with the particular conflict. Conflicts may exist within a plan itself, between a plan and its proposed replacement, between a plan policy and policy guidance recently adopted by a local planning authority, and between local and national planning policy. How such conflicting guidance or policy statements are to be treated are matters of planning judgement for the decision-taker. Provided he has regard to such considerations as are material, there is no room as a matter of law for a rule as to how such considerations are to be treated. There is no rule of law that the Secretary of State's policy cannot prevail in the face of other material considerations. Such a rule would require statutory provision and there is none (see Lord Scarman in *Pioneer Aggregates vs Secretary of State* (1985)).

The issue of conflict between the provisions of a structure plan, local plan, minerals local plan, or waste local plan, is considered by PPG12 *Development plans and regional planning guidance* (DoE 1992b). There are four broad propositions:

- Where there is conflict between the provisions of a minerals local plan or a waste local plan and those of a structure plan, the provisions of the minerals/waste local plan will prevail unless the structure plan has been altered or replaced, the structure plan authority has issued a statement to local planning authorities in the area that the minerals/waste local plan is not in general conformity with the altered or new structure plan, and the minerals/waste local plan has not subsequently been altered or replaced.

- Where there is conflict between a local plan and a minerals local plan or a waste local plan, the more recently adopted (or approved) provisions prevail.

- In the event of conflict between the provisions of a local plan and those of a structure plan, the former prevail unless the structure plan authority has stated that the local plan is not in general conformity with the structure plan, and the local plan has not subsequently been altered or replaced.

- In the event of conflict between the provisions of a structure plan and a local plan made by the same authority (the Peak Park Joint Planning Board and the Lake District Special Planning Board), the provisions of the local plan prevail unless the structure plan has been altered or replaced.

Grampian conditions

One area that the law will scrutinize is whether a factor is material or immaterial. The recent case of *British Railways Board vs Secretary of State for the Environment* is an illustration of how planning policy can be divergent from the legal interpretation of the courts, in this case relating to Grampian conditions. Grampian conditions are negative conditions imposed on a planning permission, prohibiting the carrying out of development works unless and until a certain set of circumstances (outside the control of the developer) has come into being.

The Department of the Environment Circular 1/85 (DoE 1985b) admitted that imposing a positive condition upon a developer requiring the carrying out of works on land within the application site, but not at the time of the grant of permission under the control of the applicant, could give rise to difficulties, and perhaps be *ultra vires* on the grounds of unreasonableness.

To circumvent this problem, paragraph 34 of the Circular stated that

> although it would be *ultra vires* . . . to require works which the developer has no power to carry out, or which would need the consent or authorization of a third party, it may be possible to achieve a similar result by a condition worded in a negative form, prohibiting development until a specified action has been taken. The test of whether such a condition is reasonable is strict; it amounts to whether there are at least reasonable prospects of the action in question being performed.

Use of these conditions pre-dates Circular 1/85, and the leading case is *Grampian Regional Council vs The City of Aberdeen District Council* (1984) 47 P&CR 633. Lord Keith said, in his leading speech:

the reasonableness of any condition has to be considered in the light of the circumstances of the case. In this case the proposals for development put forward by the First Respondents were found by the reporter to be generally desirable in the public interest. The only aspect of them which was regarded as disadvantageous was (a traffic problem) . . . That problem was capable of being solved by the closing of the southern part of Wellington Road, something that had at least reasonable prospects of being achieved under statutory powers to that effect. In the circumstances, it would have been not only not unreasonable but highly appropriate to grant planning permission subject to the condition that the development was not to proceed unless and until the closure had been brought about.

Lord Keith's words had the unfortunate effect of creating the impression, at least in the Court of Appeal, that the reasonable prospect of a condition being met was essential to the reasonableness of that condition. Notably, Lord Justice Purchas in the decision on *Jones vs Secretary of State for Wales and Ogwr Borough Council* (1990) 61 P&CR 238, stated that:

in my reading of the speech of Lord Keith, he clearly had in mind that a condition of this kind would be reasonable and, in certain circumstances, more than reasonable, but only if and insofar as it was established that there was a reasonable prospect of the removal of the obstacle being achieved.

This was echoed by the judgment of Lord Justice Nourse, who said "it must be unreasonable to impose a condition which at once shuts out any reasonable prospect of the permission's being implemented". The same logic was applied by Lord Justice Glidewell in *Medina Borough Council vs Proberun Limited* (1991) 61 P&CR 77.

These decisions did not meet with universal approval by developers, at least some of whom would have been happier to receive a flawed planning permission and take the chance of negotiating the necessary rights, rather than receiving no planning permission at all. However, the Court of Appeal continued in its approach, in *British Railways Board vs Secretary of State for the Environment and London Borough of Hounslow* (1993) (*JPL* **342**). In that case, Lord Justice Dillon expressly stated that:

it was . . . a nonsense to grant a planning permission subject to a condition which the planning authority, or the Secretary of State on an appeal, knew perfectly well there was no reasonable prospect of the applicant being able to satisfy.

The Secretary of State was not bound to grant planning permission subject to a condition that would have made a nonsense of it. Lord Justice Kennedy agreed, citing Grampian as:

authority for the proposition that planning permission might be refused if there were no reasonable prospects of the applicant being able to fulfil the condition because, for example, the owner of the adjacent land simply would not sell.

The approach of the Court of Appeal has now been swept away by the decision of the House of Lords on appeal from the decision in *British Railways Board vs Secretary of State for the Environment et al.* (1994) (*JPL* **32**). Their Lordships held that the Jones case was wrongly decided and should be overruled. In Grampian it was stated that the reasonableness of a certain condition depended on the circumstances of the case. The owner of the land to which the application related might object to the grant of planning permission for reasons that might or might not be sound on planning grounds. If they were unsound, the mere fact that the owner objected and was unwilling for the development to proceed could not in itself necessarily lead to a refusal. The planning authority's role was to decide whether the proposed development was desirable in the public interest; its decision should not be affected by the consideration that the owner of the land was determined not to allow the development so that permission for it, if granted, would not have reasonable prospects of being implemented. Therefore, the mere fact that a desirable condition appeared to have no reasonable prospects of fulfilment did not mean that planning permission ought necessarily to be refused.

This approach of their Lordships would seem to make good sense because, although the courts have emphasized that consent cannot make reasonable what is unreasonable, it is not unreasonable to impose a condition that enables the development to take place, just because it may be difficult to achieve the precondition. It at least gives the developer five years in which to try to negotiate the necessary rights.

Although Lord Keith's speech makes clear that a negatively worded condition will not be automatically invalid just because there may not be a reasonable prospect of achieving the precondition, it leaves a little unclear the extent to which the authority still has a discretion to refuse on the grounds that there is no prospect of the development taking place, because the condition is very unlikely ever to be satisfied. Lord Keith at one stage in his speech states:

> If he (the applicant) considers that it is in his interests to secure planning permission notwithstanding the existence of such difficulties, it is not for the planning authority to refuse it simply on their view of how serious the difficulties are.

However, elsewhere he seems to be saying that there is still a residual discretion to take into account the improbability of the permission, if granted, being implemented. Later he states "What is appropriate depends on the circumstances and is to be determined in the exercise of the discretion of the planning authority". So the position must be that there is a discretion to refuse on the grounds that there is no reasonable likelihood of implementation, but that it is for the authority to have good reason why they consider this justifies complete refusal.

The decision of the House of Lords is a welcome step in the direction of commercial reality. However, the DOE has announced the interim decision of the

Secretary of State on the Hams Hall Freight Terminal, in which it is stated that the Secretary of State has decided to maintain as a matter of policy that for negative conditions to be imposed there should be at least reasonable prospects of the action in question being performed within the time limit imposed by the planning permission. It follows that, whatever the House of Lords may say on the matter, the Department of the Environment is sticking with the Court of Appeal's approach.

We pause for comment here on the legality of the Secretary of State's proposed approach: the law is now not in any dispute and the House of Lords decision in *British Railways* is the leading statement of principle. As a matter of policy the Secretary of State has announced that he chooses to disregard the House of Lords judgment. In our view, unless the Secretary of State proposes to amend the relevant primary legislation (the Town and Country Planning Act 1990), his announcement will give rise to considerable conflicts between local planning authorities and developers regarding the appropriate drafting of conditions.

Local planning authorities will clearly rely on the Secretary of State's announced policy, and continue to require at least reasonable prospects of a Grampian condition being fulfilled. Developers will take comfort in the House of Lords to argue that such reliance by local planning authorities on the Secretary of State would be unlawful. Indeed, if the Secretary of State himself were to decline to grant planning permission on appeal, in line with his own policy, on the basis that there was no reasonable chance of a Grampian condition being fulfilled, such a decision could quite properly be challenged in the High Court, which would doubtless follow the new leading authority. Planning authorities are in a difficult position: on the one hand they must give genuine consideration to a condition that has little apparent prospect of being fulfilled, because that is the law; on the other hand they must give genuine consideration to a policy that says that such a condition should not be imposed. Having thus faced in two contrary directions, they must then take the decision. They would be entitled to give little weight to the condition, as long as they consider it properly. Those drafting advice to planning authorities will need great skill.

Planning advantage

In the light of recent court decisions, the extent to which an item of planning advantage is a material consideration has been uncertain, with court decisions being apparently in conflict with government policy. The law was considered in the Court of Appeal judgment in *Tesco Stores Limited vs Secretary of State for the Environment and others* (judgment 25th May 1994). The case is due to be considered in the House of Lords in March 1995, and so the following points should be regarded with caution, since they might be changed in the light of the judgment. The importance in the present context is that if an item of planning gain is material to a planning decision, the planning authority must consider it, but if it is not material then it should not be considered in the context of that decision. Failure to observe these guidelines would open the planning decision to legal challenge.

DOE guidance on planning advantage set out in Circular 16/91 (DOE 1991a) had been widely interpreted as meaning that one had to ask (*inter alia*) whether an item of advantage was necessary, for instance, needed to overcome some planning objection; on this basis, an offered item of planning advantage that failed the test of necessity would not, it was suggested, be a material consideration. The Tesco case confirms earlier decisions that this is incorrect. It would be wrong to overlook planning advantage that failed the test of necessity. DOE guidance may therefore need revision. Planning advantage is relevant, whether necessary or not, if it has a connection with the relevant planning proposal, and is for a planning purpose.

The judgments in the Court of Appeal throw some light on how the decision-taker might approach matters. An applicant offered to fund a major new local road. The Secretary of State concluded that the relationship between the proposed development and the road was tenuous, not needed to enable development to proceed, and such that it would have been unreasonable to seek even a partial contribution to the cost of the road. In short, it squarely failed the test of necessity. The court decided that the Secretary of State had fairly considered the offered planning advantage, and in deciding to give it little weight he was entitled to apply his own published policy. If the Secretary of State had said that he would ignore the offer of planning advantage, because it failed the test of necessity, he would have acted unlawfully, but because he did consider it, he was entitled to give it little weight in the light of his own policy, and his decision was lawful.

The line between giving something little weight and ignoring (or effectively ignoring) it may be a fine one, but it is a distinction that the law makes and which planning authorities must observe. The judgment of Lord Justice Beldam clarifies that failure to have regard to a material consideration may occur either when the material consideration is overlooked or ignored altogether, or when it is considered but regarded as of no, or not significant, weight in making the particular decision. In the first case the maker of the decision will not have paid regard to a consideration capable of being material; in the second he will have regard to it but discounted its weight or significance wholly or partly in arriving at his conclusion. In the words of the judgment:

> the distinction is in my view, important when the court is asked to declare invalid a decision made by the Secretary of State on a question involving policy and judgment that are essentially his preserve.

Conclusions

In this chapter we have sought to draw a distinction between the application of planning policy (whether contained in national guidance or the development plan) by the decision-taker, and the approach of the courts in determining whether other material considerations exist, and the extent to which these have properly been taken into account by the decision-taker in coming to his conclusion on a particular planning application or appeal. In each of the three areas covered we have explored the suggestion that the law may differ from published government policy. We have dealt with the traditional approach and not the new approach that is having to be adopted in relation to European Union Directives relevant to planning.

In the case of Section 54A, and the general presumption in favour of development stated in PPG1, we have concluded that any conflict that exists is one of technicality rather than practical application. The correct application of material considerations that indicate otherwise is a question of law, but the subsequent weighting of various factors in coming to a decision is a matter of judgement for the decision-taker, as a question of policy.

Similarly, in the field of planning advantage, the correct identification of whether an offer of planning advantage is a material consideration or not is a question of law; but the weight to be attached to any offer correctly identified as a material consideration is a question of judgement for the decision-taker as a matter of policy, within which context it will be open to the Secretary of State to apply his own policy set out in Circular 16/91.

Finally, in the case of Grampian Conditions, we have pointed to an area of actual conflict between the leading House of Lords authority and the policy that the Secretary of State proposes to adhere to. This may well receive further examination by the courts.

By and large, the courts are reluctant to intervene in planning decisions. As long as the planning authority asks the right questions, considers relevant matters and disregards irrelevant matters, the courts will rarely intervene. Although on occasion conflicts may apparently exist between law and policy, the courts have shown themselves anxious to leave questions of policy for decision-takers, provided they approached the questions within the correct legal framework.

PART THREE

Constraints and opportunities in the policy process

CHAPTER 10

Members and officers in the planning policy process

Sue Essex

Defining roles

Ian Gatenby & Christopher Williams have highlighted in Chapter 9 the duty of the decision-maker in applying relevant weight to policy considerations in planning decisions. "The decision-maker" is a term that can easily apply to an individual within the local planning authority. But it is also applicable to the two sets of actors within planning, both of whom are responsible for taking decisions on behalf of the authority as a whole. Although the duty of the decision-maker is broadly set out by legislation, legal cases and government policy, it is not always clear how the actors – members and officers – identify their roles in the policy- and decision-making environment. Britain's system of local government is founded on the principle of representative democracy. Although the functions of a council democratically rests with locally elected councillors, the management and running of these activities is delegated to paid officers. The relationship between members and officers in the planning system is an interesting and somewhat under-assessed area of examination.

It is difficult to give a precise and clear definition of the roles of members and officers in local government and consequently their respective activities are often blurred in practice. In terms of policy-making the definition can often be particularly obscure as overall political direction becomes integrated with technical considerations, subsequently refined through dialogue between officers and members, to become policy statements.

The National Local Government code (para. 23) makes some attempt at clarification in the section entitled councillors and officers:

> Both councillors and officers are servants of the public, and they are indispensable from one another. But these responsibilities are distinct. Councillors are responsible to the electorate and serve only so long as their term

of office lasts. Officers are responsible to the council. Their job is to give advice to councillors and the council, and to carry out the council's work under the direction and control of the council, their committees and sub-committees.

In reality there is also a wide variation between local authorities as to how this definition of roles is implemented. Factors such as the political style and leadership of the council, the geography, and the social and economic characteristics of the area can each play a significant part, and the management style of the chief executive and senior officers will also influence the way the roles are defined. In addition, there may not be a consistent pattern within local authorities themselves. There may well be very different approaches between functional areas of the council, depending on the personality and viewpoints of individual chief officers and chairpersons of council committees.

There have been attempts in the past to clarify the situation and to try and make clear distinctions between officers and members and their interrelationship, and several of these attempts at guidance and clarification need to be highlighted.

In 1967 the Maud Report felt "there should be a clear division between members and officers". This clear cut view did not find favour in the Bains Report written just five years later, and one of the most influential reports advising local government practice. Bains felt that "it is necessary for members and officers to forge effective partnerships with mutual appreciation of their respective roles". This idea of partnership between the elected member and the paid officials, working together to achieve the objectives of the authority, struck a chord in practice and in many authorities officers and members developed ways of partnership working that was beneficial.

The 1980s was a period when there was considerable hostility between local and central government, often as a result of different political ideologies between the Conservative central government and Labour-controlled local authorities. It sometimes resulted in open warfare over issues of centralization and local autonomy, particularly with the introduction of strong financial controls for local councils. The Thatcher years were also characterized by rate capping and town hall revolts. One of the aspects of local government practice that the government took a strong dislike to was the decision of many Labour leaders and members to have a much more direct "hands-on" approach to the running of their councils. This often meant in practice that this was not simply restricted to the control of strategic policy-making, but also included day-to-day decision-making. In order to achieve this degree of hands-on control many local politicians literally became full-time or professional politicians in the style more frequently seen in other European countries.

One of the steps taken by the government to exert some control over local politicians was to revisit this issue of members' roles and the manner in which local government functioned internally. The Widdecombe Report on local government was written at the height of this central/local conflict in 1986 and concluded that "increasingly politicization of local government has placed strains on the statutory framework between councillors and officers". The report sought to distinguish the role of the politician and, perhaps more importantly, the political leadership from that of the officers, and particularly emphasized the role of the Head of Paid Service in terms of responsibility within councils.

The Widdecombe Report also highlighted the issue of twin-tracking, that is the situation where a senior officer in one authority is also an elected member for another local authority. This practice, disliked by Widdecombe, in effect gives lay politicians the opportunity to use their professional skills and experience, whether it is in planning, social services or another field in their role as elected members. Many of the recommendations in the Widdecombe Report were eventually incorporated into the Local Government and Finance Act, which sets the current legal framework.

One further report subsequent to this Act, which is worth referring to, is the 1993 Working Party on the Internal Management of Local Authorities in England, set up by the government (DoE 1993h). This working party looked again at the operation of local government and considered new models of arrangements and roles for elected members, including radical options for decision-making structures. The report concluded that "the representative role of the Councillor is indivisible from his or her role in policy formulation or the scrutiny of performance". Specifically in terms of policy development the report stated that there are ways in which all councillors can become involved in the development of policy in their authority. There is an equally important role for councillors in monitoring and reviewing the performance of their authorities in meeting predetermined performance standards and objectives.

The value of these statements is that they recognize the multidimensional aspects of councillors' workloads and functions, of how in practice it is impossible to separate actions from policy, and policy development from policy review, and why it is necessary when considering the role of the councillor to involve all these areas. It is also the reality in practice that officers will possess similar multidimensional aspects to their work.

The Internal Management Report has not been acted upon by central government in any official way at the time of writing, but recent considerations on local government reorganization have focused attention on internal management within local authorities and inevitably on the role that senior officers and members will perform in the newly created authorities. The need to create new councils does provide an opportunity for reassessment.

Looking specifically at the way in which member and officer roles apply to the planning service, the same complexity in practice tends to occur. In the UK, local government is the principal mechanism for dealing with the town and country planning and other allied complementary legislation. Within the framework of local democracy, the roles of elected members should be to achieve their objectives through the planning decision mechanisms of their authority.

Defining responsibilities

Perhaps in planning more than any other area of local government, there has been real concern and conflict over the distinction between member and officer roles, partly as a result of central government changing the balance of responsibility between each group in recent years. This has been most obviously seen in the emphasis that is now being placed on officer recommendations by the government, notably for planning applications, without any clear guidance as to the way in which elected councillors should respond.

A limited attempt was made in Wales in 1993 with the publication of the *Development control good practice guide* (WO 1993a), as part of the multifaceted Citizens' Charter initiative. In terms of good practice for development control, the booklet states:

> the importance of elected members cannot be overemphasized. They have the power and the responsibility to create conditions within which a well run efficient development control service can evolve and be maintained. Creating the right attitude and culture towards development control is perhaps the single most important factor in the production of a fair, speedy and efficient service.

Following this theme through, the charter guide states that it is the responsibility of officers, particularly the chief officer, to ensure that resources within that environment are optimally developed and utilized.

These statements, although to a certain extent useful, do not shed much light on the relationship between officers and members in delivering development control and certainly do not provide a clarification in terms of making difficult decisions on planning applications. Many councillors feel that the essential point is that the quality of the decision-making is crucial (i.e. outcomes of the process), rather than the process itself, which is where the charter document concentrates. It is the division of responsibility, and the balancing of opinions between members and officers in decision-making, that is still very ambiguous.

It is interesting to note that in the more recent "Planning Charter Standards", introduced jointly by the Department of the Environment, the Welsh Office and National Planning Forum (DOE/WO/NPO 1994), the references mentioned above have disappeared, giving even less guidance to elected members than the previous publication. There was some help to members previously in the Audit Commission study *Building in quality: a study of development control* (Audit Commission 1992), which included a summary sheet for members but started with a massive understatement: "Serving on the planning committee is one of the most demanding roles for councillors". The report recognized the pressure facing councillors, stating: "At the local level the councillors are at the cockpit of these pressures." However, the bulk of the advice refers to the role that members have in making sure officers deliver a quality service. Only in the last sentence does it refer to the role of members:

Members have key roles, not only in arbitrating individual applications but also in keeping the planning department in good repair to meet rising public expectations and the next surge in application pressure.

Although the study concentrated on development control, there is a strong inference that being an elected member is really a managerial task and not one of policy determination. It would seem to many councillors, however, that keeping the planning department in a good state of repair is really the responsibility of the chief planning officer rather than the elected member.

The issue of ward responsibilities and representation can also be problematic for elected members, particularly when local constituency interests may not be in accord with the perceived wider public interest. Representation can be even more difficult when there are different interests operating at a very local level. This may require members to make judgements between one sector of the community and others, or even one neighbour against another. The lack of clarity in the local government system does not help, and the difficulty for elected members to separate their ward responsibilities from the wider responsibility to the council as a whole is a recurring issue (see Benyon 1982 for an interesting account). The National Code of Local Government Conduct for elected members states that it is the duty of councillors to represent everyone in the administrative area: "You have an overriding duty to the whole community."

The interesting point is that the area referred to in the code is the whole area, such as the district, and since the election of councillors takes place at a ward level, many councillors are faced with a dilemma of representation. The National Code refers to this only by saying: "You have a special duty to your constituents, including those who did not vote for you." When making judgements on planning applications, this dilemma can be a difficult one to resolve, often balancing local disadvantage with the wider community good. In such circumstances the term "public interest" can be a very indistinct phrase.

The geographical definition for elected members and the need to represent a local community are crucial differences in the respective responsibilities of members and officers, and can explain the often divergent ways members and officers respond to the same issue. For instance, consultations on planning applications for an officer may appear a straightforward exercise in eliciting whether or not there are valid planning objections. For the local member, consultation on a planning application may also be an opportunity for raising community awareness.

In the wider context of local government, the long-held traditional view is that elected members provide the policy direction and that paid officials implement the policies. One of the complications to this simplistic view is increasing central government control through financial allocations, legislation and advice notes, which has increased significantly.

The view from local government of all political parties has been that the increasing centralization of decision-making has undermined local democracy and restricted the freedom of local councillors to respond adequately to their own local circumstances. This feeling has also been reinforced by the introduction of compulsory competitive tendering, which has strengthened the role of local government as one of enabling, with local councils taking responsibility for the preparation, letting and overseeing of contracts, rather than being the direct providers.

Issues of conflict

The issue of increasing centralization of policy decision-making by the government, which has frequently led to strong differences between central and local government, can in practice undermine the relationship between officers and members. An obvious example of this in the planning system has been the government's attitude in past years to out-of-town retail superstores. Until the introduction of the revised Planning Policy Guidance Note 6 on retailing (DoE/WO 1993), along with Planning Policy Guidance Note 13 on Transport (DoE/DoT 1994), the government took a relaxed approach to retail development regardless of its location. Many local councils took an opposing point of view but then found that locally determined policies on shopping, aimed at keeping town and city centres viable, were overruled on appeal when national policies were given greater weight than locally derived policies. Planning officers have consequently found themselves in the unenviable position of trying to balance national guidance with local policies or objectives, frequently leading to recommendations on planning applications that have not found favour with the elected members.

For a few authorities the conflict between officers and members has caught the headlines. Two district council planning authorities in particular, North Cornwall and Ceredigion, are worth highlighting as they have been two of the most celebrated cases in recent years, with their activities coming under scrutiny.

Ceredigion, a small rural district in West Wales, where there is considerable concern for the economic and social future of local communities, allied with concern for the Welsh culture and language, was considered by the House of Commons Welsh Affairs Committee in its Third Report on Rural Housing in 1993 (House of Commons Welsh Affairs Committee 1993). The committee looked at many issues on rural housing and the way that the planning system works. The report was critical, investigating and highlighting many issues of real concern over planning practice and decision-making. But significantly, the report considered the issue of disagreement between members and officers in the planning system:

> Where a planning committee approves significant numbers of planning applications against the advice of their planning officers (and on occasions

their legal officers too), the relationship between officers and members is bound to be put under some strain.

This view was encapsulated by the Welsh Affairs Committee in their belief that an "air of conflict" between members and officers existed in Ceredigion. On the issue of representation and the dual loyalty of councillors, the committee also looked at decision-making and concluded that, in Ceredigion, members sitting on the planning committee were giving too much weight to personal circumstances and insufficient regard to policy issues, the committee finding that "excessive weight was being given to the views of local ward members". In one of the hearings for the select committee, the Commissioner for Local Administration in Wales said:

> Some councils are making decisions not on the basis of adopted plans, but on an arbitrary basis, not infrequently based on the untested assertions of individual councillors, most commonly the councillor representing the ward where the development takes place.

However, one can see the dilemma of a councillor in a district such as Ceredigion where the local councillor knows most of the people in the area, where the needs of longstanding local residents may seem to be more important than adhering rigidly to policy statements or national guidance. It is in these circumstances that the conflicts of role and responsibilities can be most acute for councillors. In the hearings, one of the Ceredigion councillors expressed this conflict in terms of the difficulty of complying with the Dyfed County Council Structure Plan: "If we strictly follow the structure plan policies we will be driving people out of the rural areas to live in places that are 10, 12 or 15 miles away." In terms of Welsh Office policy guidance, the same councillor maintained that, when the council disagreed with the guidance, "surely we are entitled to do so as a democratically elected group of people". The select committee response to this statement was to reiterate the supremacy of parliament, not something that is likely to be music to the ears of local councillors, wherever they represent.

There were similar issues of conflict in North Cornwall, which, following a television documentary inquiry in December 1991, resulted in the setting-up of an official enquiry into the operation of the planning system within the district by the Department of the Environment (DoE 1993a). The report, more commonly referred to as "the Lees Report", recognized the issue of helping local people.

> Many councillors have genuinely been trying to help disadvantaged local people, but on occasions they seem to have been going about it the wrong way. For instance, instead of granting planning permission for inappropriate developments in open countryside, the council should adopt formal land-use policies."

The North Cornwall report is instructive in that there is a long list of recommendations setting out suggested revisions of procedure and aspects of good practice that have relevance way beyond the boundaries of North Cornwall and are specifically designed to resolve some of the conflicts that frequently occur within local authorities.

Devising good practice

It is essential for any planning authority to think through and clarify members' roles, and to continually assess the operational framework for their action. Only then can methods of best practice be addressed. The framework is complicated in planning by its seemingly high technical content. The effect of legislative control on the planning system, compounded by the use of public inquiries and judicial decisions, all serve to give an impression that can be very intimidating to the lay member. The reality is that most newly elected councillors enter local government with only a rudimentary knowledge of planning and yet it is frequently a controversial and high-profile area of local government, where elected members are expected to act as referees between strongly opposing sides. In this kind of scenario, some authorities have tended to leave planning more and more in the hands of officers or alternatively have delegated responsibility to interested (and sometimes trained) elected members. The opportunity of delegation is frequently quoted as good practice and a means of achieving greater efficiency. It is likely to have advantages in terms of speeding up planning procedures and decision-making; however, there may be a cost in terms of local democracy if delegation results in a restriction of access to elected members that inhibits councillors' ability to represent people properly. This is always the trade-off with increased delegation and it is certainly true in practice that members of the public expect their elected representative to be involved in making planning decisions. It is interesting in the report on North Cornwall that Audrey Lees recommended more delegation to officers, but simultaneously points out that:

> successful delegation can normally work well only where there is a firm background of policy, a record of consistent recommendations and decisions and where there is mutual confidence between members and officers and also between public and council.

Delegating planning to relatively few members has also been attempted by some local authorities, generally in the form of a small planning committee with directly delegated powers. This allows those interested and committed councillors the opportunity to specialize in planning and to acquire the essential knowledge and training that is necessary. There are many local councillors around the country who have made great efforts to become skilled in planning and who recognize the value of lay members possessing the necessary expertise. This knowledge-base can develop over a period of time, but frequently needs to be added to by direct training. This clearly requires a budget to be set aside to cover the costs, but training does not always mean sending people on expensive conferences. There are ways that costs can be reduced by arranging seminars or preparing information notes within the authority with the needs of the members in mind. Too often the opportunity to do this is by-passed in the standard approach of committee structures, and thought should be given to the use of seminars, discussion groups or specially organized training sessions. There are arguments in favour of this approach, not only where there is a delegated planning committee, but also where powers are in the hands of the full council. This may be particularly relevant to ensure that all members have an understanding of development plan policy issues as well as development control.

Developing policy

The renewed emphasis on local planning policy espoused by the government and reiterated in reports, such as Lees on North Cornwall and that of the Welsh Affairs Select Committee, requires local authorities to think more carefully how plans and policies are put in place, approved and implemented. In terms of development plans, the impetus given in the Planning and Compensation Act 1991 and associated Planning Policy Guidance Notes has put the onus on planning authorities to prepare and approve up-to-date local plans and to use these as a basis for decision-making within development control. The government's requirement for councils to prepare a district-wide local plan, when placed alongside the need for other strategic and operation statements such as social care plans, economic development strategies and housing strategy documents, has emphasized the need to formulate policy development.

Local authorities have responded in different ways to the need to think and plan strategically. The corporate approach, popular in the 1970s, was largely discarded in the 1980s as being too over-planned and deterministic. However, in recent years, local authorities have tended to move back to the need for more internal corporate working, often prompted by the requirements of outside agencies. For example, the Strategic Development Scheme, the Single Regeneration Budget, City Challenge and European bids such as URBAN, all encourage local authorities to think in an integrated corporate way, often combining resources with outside agencies. All this requires strategic direction for local authorities, necessitating elected members to set the political framework for officer action.

In addition, the conflict between the wider public interest and local concerns can partly be dealt with by giving the council a strong policy base that is processed through to implementation. In this way, a policy direction that may be determined at the central planning core of the authority can provide the framework for the councillor to act locally.

However, the pressures on councillors to respond to the demands of their local community can be very strong, often to the point of undermining strategic policies. A typical example of this is where a local housing authority may have policies on identifying and releasing land for social housing. These policies, to which the council subscribes overall, may break down in implementation owing to individual sites causing local concern. This concern more often or not erupts at the submission of the planning application. In these circumstances, councillors often feel a conflict of interest between the council's overall policy objectives while representing the concerns of local residents. Such instances may reflect that the local authority, at either local level or member level, has not adequately consulted the public at the policy development stage or perhaps has failed to implement public consultation exercises adequately. In the case of land identified for housing development this may well be included in housing strategy documents. In recent research carried out for the Welsh Office by colleagues at the Department of City and Regional Planning, University of Wales College of Cardiff, the opportunity to advertise and publicly consult on housing strategies was identified as a possible means of good practice for local housing authorities (Littler et al. 1994). This makes the point that many other important strategic statements produced by local councils, unlike development plans, do not have requirements for public consultation.

The development plan is a vital cornerstone of the strategic direction for the local authority, but in many cases member involvement tends to be limited. In the research mentioned above, a survey of Welsh district councils revealed that there had been a very limited involvement of members in the production of local plans. Many officers expressed disappointment that this was the case, contradicting the often held belief that officers like to keep members at arm's length. Officers frequently stated that they preferred a situation where members were involved in strategic policy direction as a way of discussing policy options at a very early stage. This in practice gives a confidence to officers and a belief that they are operating in an agreed policy framework.

Experience suggests that it is still very difficult to motivate the public in general to become involved in policy development, particularly on a strategic and authority-wide basis, and it is not until the specific details of planning applications come into the public arena that the public start to become actively involved. Various techniques have been used to try and foster this member involvement, including seminars, visits, public meetings, and so on. Cardiff City Council has used a seminar approach for its members. At key stages, all members, not just those on the planning committee, were invited to seminars led by officers developing the local plan. These seminars were seen as particularly important in the early stages as a means of agreeing policy options that were then refined, following discussion. In addition, this approach was followed in the course of reconsideration of the plan during the process of consultation. In this way, all those members who wished to be involved could be, and it gave the plan strong political direction. The frustrations emerged when agreed policy wording developed during this careful process of officer and member working was disputed by the Welsh Office and in their consultation comments.

Looking back over the process, it has proved to be a good model of officer member working, which produced accord and allowed the local plan to be the product of the local authority, rather than solely of the planning department. The process did not exacerbate delay in decision-making and there was a real feeling of a co-operative effort involving many people. The irony of the local plan approval system, however, is that the city council had to wait 14 months following the local plan inquiry for the Inspector's report on the plan.

In reviewing the policy process in Cardiff, a process that is still continuing, there has been considerable interaction of members and officers in the process, hopefully facilitating a better understanding of and between both sides. The members set the parameters and objectives of the plan, and both officers and members had worked through together to refine policy statements and land allocations. However, it should be pointed out that throughout the process of plan production there had been a continual modification of locally derived policies drawn up to reflect the views of the council, local people and agencies to statements that accorded more fully with central government policy guidance. The government's centralization process, introduced through the use of this policy "guidance", has to some extent undermined locally formulated policy (largely unseen by the general public and then reinforced by the inspector in his report) which has left rather frustrated those of us who have lived closely with the process of local plan preparation.

Conclusions

There are many advantages to members and officers working in partnership while respecting one another's respective responsibilities.

Joint working in local plan preparation is a good example of how members and officers working together can achieve a good working relationship and satisfactory outcomes. Seminars, away-days and study visits are all ways in which officers and members can work together, often in an informal setting, building up effective partnerships. However, there is also a need to recognize that members' time is limited, particularly when they are also holding a full-time job or have strong family commitments. There is a need to reassess the way that members operate. Perhaps the traditional committee report can sometimes give way to a discussion on planning issues. Similarly, the occasional visit around the authority's area can provide the opportunity for members and officers to view some of their past decisions, an opportunity to review their own performance. But most importantly, there should be a recognition that to make members more effective they need training. That need not mean sending members away on expensive conferences, especially where there are restrictions on time and budgets. The training could be provided by officers of the authority themselves, where there is not the opportunity of bringing in an outside person.

Above all, it should be recognized that the advice to members on their role, their responsibilities, dealing with issues of conflict, and so on, is at times woefully inadequate. The role of local councillors is also continually undermined by central government directives. Planning, probably more than any other local government service, exposes members to these pressures. Clear statements are needed of the standards expected of local councillors but also more consideration of the differing roles and responsibilities that councillors have.

CHAPTER 11

Public participation in planning

Huw Thomas

Introduction

The vagueness of the term "public participation" is by now notorious, and a discussion of public participation in planning could quite reasonably consider in some detail power relations within the planning system as a whole. Alternatively, and, again, without overstretching the meaning of the term, it could focus on the minutiae of current legislation or governmental regulations relating to publicity and consultation in development planning or development control. The discussion in this chapter will be located somewhere between these extremes. Its chief concern will be the ways in which local planning authorities should consider the issue of "public" influence over planning decisions in general, and development plan-making in particular, but it does not consider semi-judicial processes such as public inquiries (where it has been shown that outcomes appear to favour those with knowledge of the planning and development process; see Adams et al. 1990).

The background to the discussion is the trend within the statutory planning process to limit opportunities for public participation, whereas outside it community involvement is being encouraged (albeit within strictly defined limits and, on occasion, with some cynicism). What are the implications for planning of changes in local governance, changes that can affect both the structures within which policies are formulated and delivered, and the relationships between "the public" and the state? Can planners – at one time regarded as in the vanguard of public participation – learn from some of the new practices in other fields?

Participation is about influence and power, and the state of policy in planning or other policy areas must be understood in the light of power relations in our society and their broad implications for planning. This introductory section will sketch these, albeit very briefly. The next section considers the variety of objectives that "public participation" or "public involvement" might try to secure, locating these within a discussion of democratic theory. The underlying theme of both sections is that participation is not a purely technical exercise, and success is not assured by acquiring a certain expertise. Public participation – even when relatively narrowly defined by government planning regulations – is a particular kind of relationship between the state (its bureaucrats and its elected politicians) and the rest of society, and this relationship has built into it a certain distribution of power and influence. Put somewhat crudely, public participation can be about giving most people some greater say over planning (implicitly, thereby, reducing the power of whomever had a greater say previously), or it can be about giving some people, or social groups, more say, or it can be about appearing to give some or all people more say (while, in reality, existing power relations remain in place). Consequently, the very meaning of the term is likely to be a focus for political struggle and debate in particular instances, and a discussion of public participation in planning needs to be located within an understanding of broader power relations in the planning system and outside it, and of differing views as to how power and influence should be distributed in society and the role of participatory mechanisms in achieving this.

Analyses of the planning process from the 1970s onwards have concluded in broad terms that the distribution of power and influence within the planning system reflects the significance of power structures within society at large. In a society in which a major corporation typically has more political clout than, say, a tenants group on a peripheral housing estate, then it might not be surprising that the organization representing developers of private housing (the House-builders' Federation) has more influence over national planning policy than, say, the National Gypsy Council. Healey et al. (1988: 245) conclude their thorough analysis of planning in the 1980s with the remarks that:

> As a machinery for promoting policies, meeting the demands of specific interest groups, and balancing competing interests, the contemporary planning system is biased in favour of certain powerful interested parties.

Specifically, these are:
- the agriculture industry
- the mineral extraction industry (especially the coal industry)
- some industrial firms (particularly those in established premises or able to mobilize national or local support)
- knowledgeable property developers (particularly those well connected to either local authorities or central government)
- all land and property owners interested in the appreciation of their property holdings
- well organized community and environmental pressure groups (defending established images of urban and rural environments).

Such a list illustrates the interrelationship between power and influence in planning and other areas of political and economic life, but it also underlines the fact that there is not a complete correspondence between the distribution of power and influence within planning and that in other policy areas.

169

In the first place, the planning process is not of equal importance to all-powerful economic interests. For example, for the development industry, financial interests, the agricultural industry, and the mineral extraction industry, the decisions and scope of the planning system are central to their economic wellbeing; this is not the case for many other economic interests, who pay correspondingly less attention to the planning system. The lack of interest by at least some powerful interests may open up space for a more diffuse public influence, as public opinion surveys in diverse areas and across social classes have shown planning to be of more interest to "the public" than any other policy area (Parry et al. 1992: 356ff.). Secondly, as Healey et al. (1988) demonstrate, the structure of policy and decision-making within planning can be complex, allowing several different points of access at which (to varying degrees) influence may be brought to bear by different kinds of interests.

Although similar points of access may be available in other areas of state activity, their mix and significance may well differ, thus benefiting (or not) different kinds of social and economic interests, even within the broad category of the relatively powerful. It is within this context that the opportunity for public participation is especially significant.

Compared to most other areas of public policy (consider, for example, health case policy or policing, at one extreme) planning has for some time been characterized by its giving formal and regular opportunities for general public involvement or participation in policy formulation. It has been argued that in some cases the influence of such public participation has been considerably less than, say, more informal contacts between members of local socio-economic elites (Simmie & French 1989), and there is widespread agreement that, generally speaking, public participation in local planning has expressed the voice of middle-class residents (Cloke & Little 1990) and often male middle-class residents (Boaden et al. 1980). Nevertheless, the public participation process opens up a potential avenue for influence, an arena of political struggle over planning, that may sometimes allow more influence in planning for some interests than they have in other policy areas. For example, even those sectors of the middle class who are influential within planning by virtue of organizing themselves as local amenity societies, environmental groups and so on (Lowe & Goyder 1983) are likely to exercise considerably less influence over local policing strategies or local health case policy. This is because the ability of middle-class residents to mobilize effectively through public participation "exercises" depends not only on their having better access to resources that can often help them – time, familiarity and confidence with bureaucratic procedures, personal contacts in key places, money for campaigns, private transport in order to attend meetings, and so on (Parry et al. 1992) – but also on there being such "avenues for influence", in the terminology of Healey et al. (1988), there being such a policy process.

Of course, the significance of public participation within planning is not uniform over space or time; in some places, it may be regarded as a mere formality to be undertaken as quickly as possible (see e.g. Swinbourne 1991, Thomas

1992a, for examples of "consultation" as a means of legitimating decisions already taken); in others, it may be accorded considerable significance, but perhaps over a defined range of issues (Alty & Darke 1987). These differences will themselves be the consequences of that complex of socio-economic, political and historical factors which helps define and distinguish "localities" (Duncan & Goodwin 1988, Healey et al. 1988, Cox & Mair 1991). We can conclude, therefore, that the significance of public participation cannot be "read off" from a general account of power structures in British society at large, nor should it be assumed to be the same in every place, and over time. Public participation takes place in a society where power and material resources are unequally distributed, and it would be naïve of any planner to ignore this fact. But this leaves open some area of discretion for local planning authorities to decide how significant public participation should be in their locality. The first step in making such a decision is to ponder what is wanted from the public participation process. Some options are discussed in the next section. The chapter then goes on to consider the UK's current planning regulations and government advice on public participation, before concluding with suggestions about appropriate strategies, illustrated by some examples of current practice.

Participation and democratic theory

Since the 1960s the term "participation" has been a part of the vocabulary of international planning. By the late 1970s, Fagence (1977) could document research and discussion in several countries, and contributions to discussion of the theory and practice of participation have included illustrations from the USA (an early example being Arnstein 1969), Holland (e.g. Hague & McCourt 1974) and the UK (e.g. Bruton 1980, Alty & Darke 1987). Inevitably, detailed case studies have had to be sensitive to the institutional (and legal) context within which the practice of participation has been conducted, but key issues of general concern have also emerged. The most significant are an interconnected trio:

- that the term "participation" is ambiguous
- that different interpretations of what participation amounts to will often have different political philosophical bases, and
- that different interpretations of what participation amounts to will have their own implications for what are regarded as appropriate techniques for encouraging or facilitating participation.

The latter point should be taken to include the idea that the role of the professional planner in the process of participation is open to discussion and dispute, and that perspectives on that role will differ according to interpretations of what participation involves (which, in turn, often depends on philosophical differences). The remainder of this section will discuss the ambiguity of the term "participation", relate this to philosophical positions, and sketch their implications

171

for techniques (for what planners might do). In the light of conceptual distinctions drawn in the section, subsequent sections will consider the current legal governmental policy requirements in relation to participation in planning, trends in local governance, and review evidence of what seems to be happening "on the ground".

An early and detailed classification of the different meanings that might be attached to the term "participation" is Arnstein's (1969) use of the metaphor of a ladder of participation with eight rungs (see Fig. 11.1).

As a description of the very different degrees of direct public influence or power over decision-making that can shelter under the participation label, Arnstein's discussion is acute, and justly celebrated. It can be argued that a more topical "ladder" should use different terms (Wilcox 1994a), admit to different possibilities, and certainly show that it is easier to move between certain rungs that it is between others (Burns et al. 1994). But Arnstein's prototype has the same basic virtue of dissecting the ambiguity surrounding the term and getting across the notions that planners be clear in their own minds about the kind of participation that is being offered, or demanded, in specific instances, not shelter ambiguously behind standard phrases, and realize the specific implications of offering or encouraging a particular kind or degree of participation.

An example of an attempt to encourage participation that was almost derailed by a lack of clarity in this respect is provided by du Boulay (1989). Discussed is an initiative by Coventry City Council to involve Black people in policy formulation. As initially conceived, however, the initiative – the creation of a "community forum" – left the city council in control of agenda-setting. This was perceived by those invited to be involved not as unqualified participation but as participation that was – in Arnstein's terminology – too low on the ladder, in effect a kind of tokenism. The result was dissatisfaction and the possibility of the initiative collapsing. By way of contrast, Alty & Darke (1987) detail the realism of officer and councillor assessment of the degree of participation that Sheffield City Council was prepared to encourage in local plan-making. For our purposes, what was "on offer" is less significant than the fact that the city council appreciated that the idea of participation was ambiguous, and that there needed to be clarity – in their minds, and those of the public – about precisely what the term meant in relation to their plan-making: what decisions were councillors already committed to, and what decisions could the participating citizenry actually influence. Needless to say, there can be disagreements about what is deemed closed to participation should be closed, and such political debate and struggle is healthy. Whatever its outcome, the participation that ensues will be the more meaningful for the clarity that has been created.

Discussion of the different kinds (or degrees) of participation that are possible leads to consideration of why one kind, or degree, might be preferred to another. It then becomes clear that underlying such choices are political–philosophical analyses to do with the purpose, nature and value of democracy, particularly in relation to influencing patterns of land use. Arnstein's ladder is not only intended

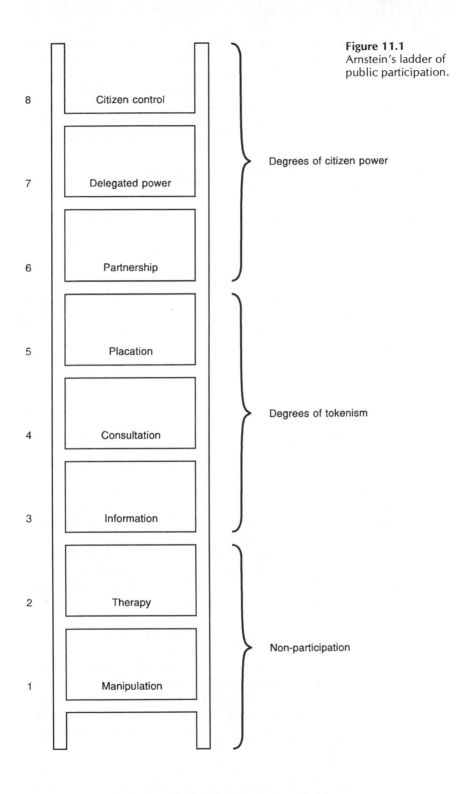

Figure 11.1
Arnstein's ladder of public participation.

as a classificatory device; underlying the metaphor that there is also a particular philosophical and political analysis: a natural implication of the ladder is that the higher rungs are the ones to which planners should aspire. This means – to cash the metaphor – that planners should aim at facilitating the maximum amount of direct citizen control over decision-making in planning. But this view is the only one of several political–philosophical opinions about the desirable relationship between a citizenry and state activity (in this case, state land-use planning), and each will have prescriptive implications for public participation in planning. If we agree with Held (1987: 1) that "nearly everyone today says they are democrats", then such a discussion is in effect, a discussion within the theory of democracy.

As Held (1987) illustrates, there are a substantial number of "models of democracy", but it is more plausible to regard some, rather than others, as influential within the politics and profession of planning. Hague & McCourt (1974) argue that two conceptions of democracy are particularly salient to discussions of planning. The first – democratic elitism – regards democracy as involving competition between political elites for the periodic support (typically, through voting) of the public at large. This Schumpeterian vision (e.g. Schumpeter 1967) rests upon a low opinion of the capacity of ordinary individuals either to engage with or to understand policy questions and decisions; as Held (1987) notes, it has a tendency towards technocracy. A characteristic of technocratic attitudes is that they portray the technocrat/professional as having a comprehensiveness of view denied to the public at large (which pursues sectional interests) (Hague & McCourt 1974; Fischer 1990: 24ff.). Public participation then becomes a way of keeping abreast of sectional concerns, but there can be no question of their determining the outcome of policy processes. There might be many reasons why technocrats or elite politicians might wish to tap into popular views in this way. They might see it as a way of identifying deeply or widely held beliefs and values; once these are known, then decisions can perhaps avoid cutting across them and thereby forestall widespread popular opposition. Alternatively, it may be seen as a way of legitimizing potentially controversial decisions by ostensibly incorporating likely dissidents into the decision-making process (albeit on strictly limited terms). These essentially manipulative intentions were ascribed, by some commentators, to the Skeffington Report's (1969) proposals for increased participation in the planning process (Damer & Hague 1971), whereas Buchanan's (1982) account of the preparation of the Suffolk Structure Plan presents a picture of key decisions being taken by a small group of officers and politicians, with public participation used as a way of securing wider support: the techniques and timing adopted appear to have been chosen in order to "constrain debate, engineer support, and exclude opposition" (p. 12). In essence, only a limited range of organizations were canvassed for their views at early stages, whereas in later stages comments were invited during the summer, when responses are notoriously low. Moreover, no attempt was made to encourage comments or involvement – those who failed to respond for whatever reason were deemed to have no objection to the plan.

Hague & McCourt's (1974) counterpoise to democratic elitism was the model of participatory democracy. This model has been discussed at some length (e.g. Pateman 1970, Held 1987) and only its defining characteristic will be emphasized here: that direct involvement of citizens in decision-making in key social institutions (including, of course, the state) is essential for, but also an expression of, the self-development of individuals. Participation is thus viewed not so much as a means to an end, but as part of the end (the creation of a society where individuals can develop to their full potential). This view of democracy sees participation as considerably more significant than an occasional episode or stage in a policy-making process; rather, participation is advocated as a characteristic of the process. Policy-making takes place, in this model, within a continuous interaction between the state (in our case, the planning authority) and the population at large. And a key objective of a participation programme within this view of democracy would be to develop the capacity of individuals and communities to involve themselves in, and exercise a greater control over, decisions affecting their lives. Such an objective will influence the kinds of techniques or methods used in the participation process, with an attempt being made to avoid those that emphasize, and/or perpetuate, a distinction between "lay people" and professional "experts" (and a dependence of the former on the latter).

The process of capacity-building is not easy and it requires sensitivity to the particular circumstances and histories of individual communities as studies such as those of Hastings & McArthur (1995), Campbell (1993) and Gibson (1993) show. The very idea of a "recipe book" for success is a dangerous one in as much as it suggests there might be a formula that can be applied irrespective of circumstances. Gibson (1993: 34–8), is prepared to offer general guidelines, based on years of experience, and some strands within these are of particular significance for planners considering public participation. The importance of trust and confidence-building is emphasized: within communities, and between communities and outside agencies such as local planning authorities; he stresses the need for clarity in decision-making processes, so people see how their input fits in; and the outside "enabler" is reminded that their task is to assist the community to take on the job of community development and management. Much of this resonates with a discussion by Burns et al. (1994). They analyze an exciting innovation in the London Borough of Islington, which since 1986 has tried to increase public influence over policy-making and implementation as part of a conscious political project to increase participatory democracy. Neighbourhood forums, composed of local residents, are active throughout the borough in discussing and advising on council policy. They describe how the political leadership in the borough has sought to pursue the underlying principle of the decentralization initiative without ignoring the potential constraints of day-to-day life. There has been an awareness, for example, that neighbourhood decision-making can still be exclusionary and unfair to those who find themselves in a minority, or simply lacking the resources to be involved. Steps have been taken, therefore, to ensure that principles of equal opportunities are not submerged in an enthusiasm for "local democracy". In legal terms, the forums remain advisory bodies, but Burns et al. (1994) suggest that their influence is increasing as years go by, and both council officers and elected members take their responsibilities to report and answer to them seriously. And the researchers were in no doubt – having witnessed forum discussions of planning applications – that "it is perfectly possible to involve local people in decision-making about issues affecting their area, even when this involves the exercise of regulatory functions" (Burns et al. 1994: 186).

Two other models of democracy are also worth noting, because there is evidence that they have won some political influence in the UK in the 1980s. The first is the neopluralist model that regards the democratic polity as one where contending interest groups vie for influence over individual decisions and policy areas, although not under conditions of equality. The classic pluralist model, pictures decision-making as an area of conflict and debate between interest groups that recompose and realign from one policy area to another (Dahl 1961). Such accounts ignore the systematic imbalances of power in society that can structure the very terms in which debates over policy are conducted to the consistent benefit of particular groups (Lukes 1974). Neopluralist models are sensitive to these concerns: as a result, they place an importance on measures that provide means of counteracting (if only on particular occasions) imbalances of power: "public participation" is such a means. The approach of Sheffield City Council to public participation, which was mentioned above, is a good example of neopluralism in action: the city council aimed to create conditions in which the voices of social groups that rarely had access to the loci of power could be heard. There was no guarantee that these voices would be decisive in decision-making, but they were given a better chance to compete for influence than would otherwise be the case. The groups identified by the council were women, parents with young children, elderly people, people with disabilities, unemployed people, the low paid/trade unions, young people, Asian communities, and Afro-Caribbean communities (Alty & Darke 1987: 9).

The final model of democracy to be discussed is the New Right model, which arises from a current of political thought that has been extremely influential in the UK's politics (and the politics of planning) in the 1980s and 1990s (Thornley 1993). The New Right model of democracy regards the central feature of the democratic state as the "rule of law", which limits state interference in social and economic life to the maintenance of law and order (and in particular, the defence of property) and the defence of society against external aggressions (Held 1987, Low 1991). On this view, the role of state-sponsored town planning is at best minimal and, arguably, is otiose (Jones 1982). To the extent that planning of land use might take place in a state organized on New Right principles, then "participation" is construed as affording individuals whose rights might be affected by planning policies opportunities to make representations to this effect; presumably, in most cases the relevant rights would be property rights. This line of thought, although by no means found in a pure form in the UK's politics even in the 1990s, has nevertheless been one strand in the development of planning

176

throughout the twentieth century. McAuslan (1981) documents the way in which the protection of private property rights has remained an important principle in planning law, even when political (and professional) fashions have promoted concern for "the public interest" or "public participation".

The New Right's mistrust of state bureaucracies may well have had a further indirect effect on public participation in planning. A general thrust of the policy of Conservative central governments towards local government has involved attempts to make them more open to comment, or criticism, from the public. An example of their ethos has been the proliferation of "Citizen's Charters", which define minimum standards for aspects of public service delivery and invite users of the service to complain and/or seek redress if these standards are not met. Many local planning authorities have adopted Citizen's Charters.

Although such initiatives usually have only a slight connection to development plan-making and public participation, it is a plausible speculation that they help create and sustain a climate of opinion in which planning authorities, as public bodies, are expected to be open to, and responsive to, public comment and criticism. However, further research is needed before this speculation can be tested more rigorously.

National policy and legislative guidelines

Some commentators have documented the way in which successive Conservative governments, broadly influenced by a New Right agenda, have attempted to reorientate the planning system by reducing its intervention in market processes (and interference with property rights, more generally) (e.g. Griffiths 1986, Thornley 1993). This process has been erratic, with political expediency dictating that planning controls remain strongly interventionist in some circumstances (notably in relation to curbing development in green belts and other areas of acknowledged significance); however, with respect to public participation, the New Right ethos has not had to be qualified to any noticeable extent. As a result, there has been a consistent diminution of the significance accorded to general public participation in policy formulation, as part of an effort to "streamline" the system and reduce delays that are supposedly costly to developers and create uncertainty (Thornley 1993). Thus, the latest legislation governing the preparation of development plans contains no requirement for public consultation prior to the preparation of the version of the plan that is to be placed on deposit. Although government and other authoritative guidance recognizes the benefits of some "consultation" and "involvement" (not necessarily participation) before that state (e.g. DoE 1992b,c), the "streamlined" legislative framework establishes an important principle that public involvement in plan-making can be adequate even if it is largely reactive, rather than helping to shape a plan at its formative stages (see Fig. 11.2).

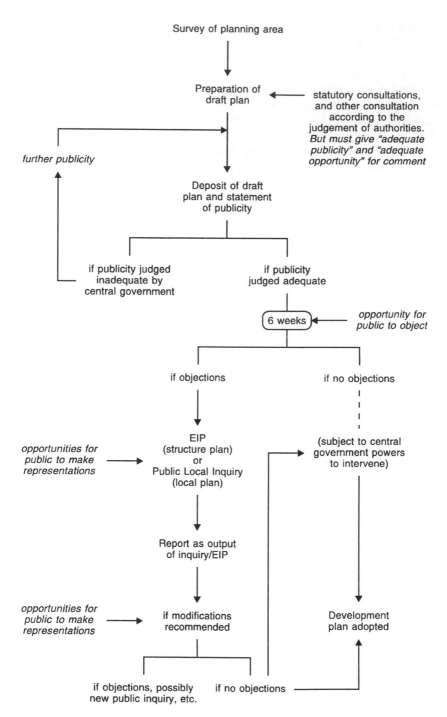

Figure 11.2 Public participation in development plan preparation.

So in relation to the pre-plan survey, for example, the government's professed desire to see local residents shaping a plan from the outset (DoE 1992b: para. 4.10) sits uneasily with its reminder to authorities that the public has a right to view the data collected, on request, but with no encouragement to involve the public more significantly in the process of survey work, which – inevitably – has built into it presuppositions about the kinds of planning issues facing the area. And although the official *Good practice guide* (DoE 1992c) contains a section on consultation that talks a great deal of sense, it consists of only 15 paragraphs out of nearly 60 in a chapter on plan preparation.

There is no sense, then, of participation being promoted as part of a commitment to participatory democracy, or even to a pluralist or neopluralist view of democracy. Consider the government's advice in PPG12 *Development plans and regional planning guidance*:

> 4.7 Authorities will wish to bear in mind the desirability of resolving points at an early stage of plan preparation and of minimizing objections once the plan is on deposit.
> 4.8 Against the background, the Secretary of State emphasizes that it is important for authorities to give their proposals adequate publicity and to give people an adequate opportunity to comment on them. In addition, authorities should *consult organizations with a particular interest in the plan proposals, including conservation and amenity groups and business, development and infrastructure interests.* [emphasis added]

Here is clear encouragement to make the dominating ethos in consultation first, the pragmatic desire to manage urban or rural change and to defuse potential dissent (with echoes of democratic elitism); and second, to focus consultation and participation on particular interests. The list illustrates those who have influence within the Conservative government – amenity interests (typically middle-class White "Middle England", Short et al. 1986), and the development industry.

The message of efficiency and management being keys to good practice certainly seems to have been influential in local government circles. For example, the *Good practice note* on local plan preparation prepared by the Association of District Councils and the District Planning Officers' Society (ADC/DPOS 1994) runs to 20 pages and by its own admission focuses on the period between putting the draft local plan on statutory deposit and receiving the Inspector's report (p. 3). Thus, it contains no advice on public participation. This focus is justified as the period that causes most delays in the plan preparation process.

The emphasis on speed has also been a prominent strand in central government policy on development control, with local authorities being urged to manage the system more effectively, and "league tables" being compiled of speed of decision-making (Thornley 1993). The development control process is, in any event, one with notoriously few opportunities for public involvement (see Fig. 11.3; Healey 1990).

179

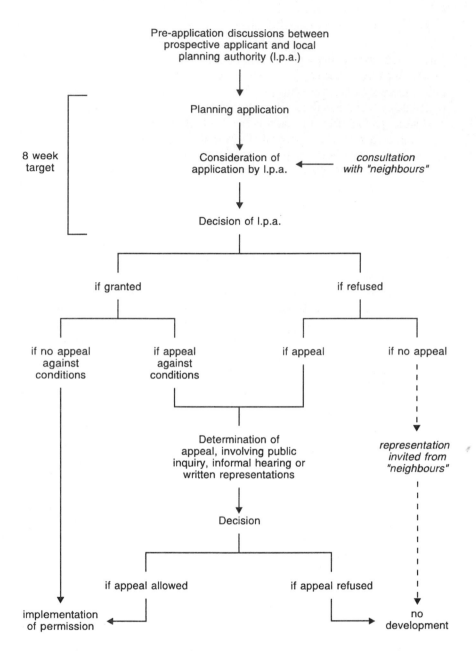

Figure 11.3   Public participation in the development control process.

It has been argued by Thompson (1987) that this focus on speed and "stream-lining" places at a disadvantage those who are unfamiliar with the planning process, and unfamiliar with (or lacking confidence in) bureaucratic processes more generally. As such people are unlikely to be among the more powerful members of society, the obsession with speeding up processes, and cutting down on opportunities to voice opinion, is likely to reinforce existing power structures. Yet although government has been pushing in this direction in relation to the land-use planning system, in neighbouring policy fields there are, at least, intimations of greater public participation.

In urban policy, for example, the City Challenge programme (in England) has emphasized that the local community should have a role in urban regeneration. In Tipton, this has meant – *inter alia* – setting up a "young people's forum", to which people are elected and which feeds views and advice into the City Challenge management process. Those involved describe a three-stage process of "trying to get the group together, then providing it with the support, confidence and wherewithal for it to feed its ideas into the mechanisms of City Challenge. And finally, withdrawing from the scenario and letting the young people get on with it themselves" (John Parkes, quoted in Minton 1994: 11). In practice, "there are discernible differences in the culture of the different City Challenge organizations, and this does seem to have an impact on the weight they give to community involvement" (NCVO 1993: 46). Nevertheless, it is clear that some City Challenge teams are working hard at opening up decision-making processes to community gaze and involvement, and in particular, working to increase the representation of Black and other ethnic minorities in key decision-making areas (NCVO 1993: 34–6). Some urban development corporations (UDCs) too are displaying a degree of sensitivity to local wishes for involvement. In response to local pressure Tyne and Wear Development Corporation (TWDC) has set up Monitoring Panels in three areas where major developments are planned. The panels are essentially reactive, as they receive information about the schemes and ideas proposed in their area, and are able to make suggestions and comments. Their influence is limited because ultimately UDCs are committed to regeneration led by private sector property development, but what influence they can have appears to be growing. Robinson et al. (1993: 41) conclude that for all their limitations, "The Panels have been successful in keeping community needs firmly on TWDC's agenda".

The City Challenge ethos of community involvement is consistent with a more general trend towards involving voluntary citizen assistance in governance. From parent governors of schools to Neighbourhood Watch and Groundwork Trusts, the "public" is being invited to involve itself – sometimes in localized policy-making (as in education), more often in implementation of policy. This is not the appropriate place to discuss the reasons for what some have termed a shift from local government to a fragmented local governance (see, for instance, Stoker 1990, Goodwin et al. 1993), but it looks set to continue.

In particular, there are reasons for supposing that community involvement in

181

governance will remain on political agendas. For example, in environmental policy, the pursuit of sustainability has been linked to increasing participation in, and commitment to, policy formulation, in initiatives such as Local Agenda 21 (see *Town and Country Planning* 1994: **63**(7)). Meanwhile, the European Union is exploring the significance of public involvement in governance as a way of increasing social cohesion (European Foundation 1994). The trend, and individual initiatives, raise important questions about who, or what, the "community" is, on which this chapter will touch later, but the general thrust is unmistakeable. Some reasonably well established aspects of planning practice – for example, the use of area-based advisory conservation groups, or access groups to advise on disabled access (Mannion 1991) – are consistent with the trends in local governance, but in relation to mainstream development planning and development control we have noted that planners have been subject to quite different pressures, and impressionistic evidence is that after 20 years of statutory public participation, planners can be quite as cynical as the public about its value.

Nevertheless, even if the overall tenor of government advice is clear, it is also the case that local authorities have considerable discretion as to how they relate to the public in the development planning process. The *Good practice guide* (DOE 1992c: 17–8) acknowledges that undertaking consultation may be done for several reasons, and suggests that different techniques may be appropriate according to the objectives of the local planning authority. However, as Alterman (1982) points out, it is not only the local planning authority that will have a perspective on what participation is for, and how it should be undertaken; so will many others with an interest in the planning process – politicians, the "public", sectional interests such as developers, and so on. Participation is a contested concept. She argues that this conflict makes it more necessary to take a systematic approach to the key dimensions along which (implicitly or explicitly) decisions are taken, which in total constitute a "participation strategy", for coherent political struggle and debate to take place. The remainder of this chapter will discuss these dimensions, illustrating their significance, where possible, with contemporary examples.

Participation strategies

The type of issues

Alterman argues that the type of issue to be discussed should influence the participation strategy adopted. Several variables are identified by which issues can be categorized. Two of the variables are particularly significant: first, the degree of technical knowledge required to understand and participate; secondly, the time range involved and tangibility of outcomes

In relation to the first, Alterman points out that participation can occur on highly technical questions, but appropriate techniques must be used. Two examples of this might be the Sheffield City Council strategy of devoting officer time to supporting groups of citizens (Alty & Darke 1987) and the Greater London Council's funding technical support for the formulation of a "People's Plan" for part of London's Docklands (Brownill 1988). These are important initiatives, but certain issues still remain: providing technical "advice" need not always empower or educate those being advised. On occasions, it can amount to simply representing their interests in essentially technical (or techno-rational) policy arenas (see Thomas 1992b on styles of planning aid). This is an important issue because technical perspectives and language carry with them a set of values, and it may be that participants' interests are actually best served by challenging the assumptions and values embedded in the current technical orthodoxy. Thus, for example, it has long been recognized that objectors to highway proposals that are the subject of some kind of cost–benefit analysis might need to object to the assumptions embedded in the technique itself, not simply understand how to do it. In environmental policy, there is considerable debate about whether indicators devised as parts of local environmental strategies need to be legitimized to a scientific audience, a "lay" audience, or both (Hams 1994, Church & McHarry 1994). So the provision of "technical support" is a matter to which careful attention needs to be devoted, and the questions asked: who is this support empowering, and how?

The second significant variable along which issues can be categorized might be captured by the view that "the making of structure plans is often seen as the aspect of planning which is of the least importance and least interest to the local community" (Short et al. 1986: 19). Strategic planning, which considers the medium and long term, does not have the same immediacy for the public, it is often claimed. Indeed, such views were put forward by both planners and elected members at the "Planning policy in the 1990s" conference at Cardiff in 1994 which was the trigger for the production of this book. Specialized techniques have, of course, been developed to "tap into" public attitudes about the future (e.g. Fagence 1977), but it does seem to be the case that active engagement with strategic planning issues is less congenial for the general public. At the time of writing, an attempt to address this issue by the Brecon Beacons National Park is being evaluated by Mark Tewdwr-Jones and myself. The National Park authority has held a series of parish meetings throughout its area to discuss the kinds of issues that residents would like to see included in its local plan. Influenced by the experience of "Planning for real", the planners have used large-scale maps of the area as a focus for, and spur to, residents to formulate their ideas in informal community-based sessions, where they are encouraged to express their views on planning and development issues in straightforward ways (typically, by placing cards on a map or model (for a discussion of "Planning for real", see McGhie 1991: 51). However, initial impressions from the Brecon Beacons suggest that residents remain more comfortable discussing the future of particular plots of land rather than strategic, park-wide objectives (indeed, the use of maps

– intended to bring the exercise to life – may have contributed to this outcome). An interesting question is whether a more appropriate set of techniques for an authority clearly interested in taking participation seriously might not have been those developed by the "strategic choice" school, the latest manifestation of which was set down in textbook fashion by Friend & Hickling (1987).

To these two points can be added a third, which has been touched upon earlier in this chapter: who is it that will be allowed to define the nature of the issues to be discussed? Who controls the agenda? It must be acknowledged that the scope of planning is defined, in broad terms, by governmental policy, statute and judicial decisions, and these constrain what a local planning authority can consider putting in a development plan. But the degree of constraint can be exaggerated – both housing land allocations, as opposed to environmental improvement schemes, are planning tasks, for example, but different groups in the population may have views about which should be the issues to which attention is devoted in public participation and in day-to-day planning activity. And there is no reason why public participation for plan-making cannot be combined with public participation on other matters, if this helps engage the interest of "the public".

Goals and objectives

Goals and objectives have received some attention in the section on democratic theory. In brief, a programme of participation will involve, and have implications for, relations between the state and society at large; implicitly or explicitly, a decision is made about the manner in which the participation will change or reinforce existing relations. Within these general goals, more detailed goals can be formulated: for example, is the participation intended to educate the public (perhaps, as part of a process of increasing its influence *vis-à-vis* technical officers)? Or is it intended to garner popular support and legitimacy for a set of policies that are already formulated by technical experts? As Wilcox (1994a: 7) puts it "ask yourself what you wish to achieve, and what you want to help others achieve". As with the other dimensions of a participation strategy, different interests involved in the planning system may have different goals and objectives; these differences will, in turn, inform their evaluations of the process of participation.

The definition of the "public"

The definition of the "public" is also vital for decision-making for a participation of strategy. Put crudely, it is necessary to decide who is being enabled to have some involvement in policy-making. The decision must be sensitive to the realities of social and economic life. Thus, if a public participation programme seeks to enable each and every individual in a given area to participate, using a traditional standard method, such as exhibitions and public meetings, then it is very likely that in practice only those sections of the population most confident and experienced in dealing with bureaucracies will respond: these will tend to be middle class and hence more likely White (Boaden et al. 1980: 87ff.). As Wilcox (1994a: 7) remarks "There isn't one 'community' but a multitude of different interests, each with their own agenda". If the trend towards community involvement in governance continues, then it will become increasingly important that planners hang on to this idea (Buckingham-Hatfield (1994) makes this point forcefully in relation to environmental issues). For if "community involvement" becomes just another piece of window-dressing to impress central government grant-givers, whereas in reality hitherto inhibited voices in the "community" remain unheard, then the existing cynicism about public participation in planning will simply be compounded. So planning authorities need to recognize the likely bases of social identity and distinctive interests in any community-paid employment (and the lack of it), gender, age, ethnicity and disability, for example.

Authorities need to remind themselves of the heterogeneity of community interests and, from time to time, to take stock of which ones seem to be finding expression in whatever forums are available. Such work requires an understanding of a community; this cannot be developed over night, and planning authorities may see value in projects such as Cardiff City Council's community planning initiative on its St Mellons housing estates, where planners have a base in the community. Or a local authority might decide – as Sheffield did – to target its programme at defined sectors of the community, so that their voice may be better heard. Sheffield focused on groups the council regarded as relatively disadvantaged; other authorities might choose to focus on other sectors. However, the point is that "the public" needs to be defined; a programme then needs to be consciously designed with the particular public in mind, a "public" with a certain vocabulary, background, history, culture, set of interests, patterns of life, and so on – all of which will influence the drawing up of a public participation programme that can engage with that "public". For example, Greed (1994: 175ff.) argues that lessons from feminist theory and practice have included methods of participation that emphasize "reaching women in their own territory, on women's side of the public/private dichotomy, in the shops, schools and gathering places, rather than in public halls at mainstream meetings" (p. 175).

The stage in the planning process

There may seem to be little to discuss in relation to the stage in the planning process, but its importance should not be overlooked: a coherent programme of public participation must be clear about the stage in the planning process at which involvement is being sought. This allows those who are participating to gauge how their current involvement relates to action "on the ground". It also raises the issue of why involvement might be expected/requested at one stage and not

185

at another, that refers us back to goals and objectives, above. Finally, considering this dimension forces a planning authority, and other interested parties, to confront the extent to which a particular participation "episode" is part of a longer-running dialogue (or relationship) with those invited to participate. As Krishnarayan & Thomas (1993) have argued in relation to involving ethnic minority communities, it is unrealistic to expect people to respond positively to isolated invitations to "participate".

What is open to influence?

Alty & Darke (1987) and more recently Wilcox (1994a,b) emphasize the importance of clarity about what is and is not open to influence through public participation. Openness on this question will influence the presentation of ideas and proposals to the public: a degree of cynicism develops among the public if people feel they have been misled about the scope of their likely influence in decision-making; a well designed public participation programme should make it clear what the scope for influence is. It is plausible to speculate that often planners are coy on this question simply because, in reality, very little influence indeed is likely to be exercised through any public participation programme. For example, Swinbourne (1991) recounts her – unwilling – involvement in a public participation exercise that was simply a legitimation exercise for planning proposals that were already formulated. But even if little influence is likely, it is short-sighted and self-defeating to obscure the fact: it will not take people long to realize the truth, particularly in an age of suspicion of professionals (Giddens 1990). Of course, the planning authority's view of what is, or should be, open to influence may well be contested, with other groups seeking to broaden the scope of the influence of the public participation programme. Such is the stuff of local politics.

The types and amount of resources

Decisions on this dimension inevitably have implications of the nature of the public participation programme. O'Grady (1994) estimates the cost of the local plan preparation in Stratford-on-Avon as close to £200000 (excluding local authority officers' time). Although this figure includes the cost of studies by consultants, it is plausible to suggest that the production of a video and successive rounds of consultation and public meetings in a large number of rural parishes constitute a substantial proportion of it. Not all authorities may feel able to budget on this scale, and alternative methods of achieving their goals may then need to be considered. Every method or technique of participation has its drawbacks and benefits, so budgetary options need to be related directly to their implications for the nature of the participation programme. As with other dimensions of a participation strategy, there may be differing views of, and struggles over, the appropriate level of resources for participation.

Conclusions

The central theme of this chapter has been the need for clear thinking by all those engaged in participation initiatives about the purposes of participation and about various key dimensions of the (implicit or explicit) "participation strategy". Of course, these groups and agencies will have to decide whether, for tactical and/ or ethical reasons, they wish to make public their clear thinking. They may choose not to, for participation is about gaining power and influence, and there can be losers as well as winners (nevertheless, it would be difficult to justify a lack of openness by elected local authorities). But whatever public muddiness and "fudge" results from the cut and thrust of political debate and struggle, participants can only benefit from private clarity of thought and perception.

Having belaboured the need for clarity, the remainder of this section will pick up a different theme, although one also highlighted earlier in the chapter. This is the contrast between pressures within the planning system to "streamline" procedures and processes, and trends in community governance more generally, that offer at least an opportunity for increasing public participation. Because planned land use is central to a comprehensive environmental or urban policy, gross differences in working practices, and degrees of openness, between these policy areas are likely to be unsustainable in the medium and long term. How the differences are resolved will be decided by political struggle. In the meantime, however, it is conceivable that activists in environmental policy and urban policy (and "activists" can include – among others – state agencies, non-governmental organizations and individuals) will ignore planning, and its narrow focus on speed and efficiency, and work through other instruments and institutions that might be more open to influence, more positive about public participation. This would be unfortunate, for two reasons. First, the overall effectiveness of environmental or urban policy is weakened if land-use planning is ignored; second, for practising planners, many of whom entered the profession with ideas of helping create a better society, the side-lining of planning when the great environmental and social issues are addressed would be a personal disappointment (Thomas & Healey 1991).

Such a consequence can be avoided if public participation in planning becomes one strand in the complex web of relationships between agencies, groups and individuals that is the emerging system of local governance. The episodic nature of traditional public participation "exercises" militates against large or enthusiastic public involvement, particularly by groups who have little (or unhappy) experience(s) of participation (Krishnarayan & Thomas 1993, Hart 1994). People are more likely to devote time and energy to an invitation to "par-

187

ticipate" if the specific invitation is part of a broader relationship between them and "government" (not necessarily a specific agency, but perhaps a collection, or network of agencies). Although it is only sensible to recognize that the UK's political culture has not encouraged or supported citizen involvement in local governance (Rallings et al. 1993), there is currently interest across the political spectrum, for different reasons, in increasing citizen involvement. For those who wish to increase public participation in planning, then the challenge is clear: ensure that planning agencies – departments, policy groups, area teams – engage with the changes in the nature of community governance and involve themselves in debates and initiatives on decentralization, improving service delivery and inter-agency networking.

CHAPTER 12

Planning policy and the market

Andy Thornley

Introduction

Planning has always had strong links to the market, or more precisely the various different land and property markets. In contrast to many other policy areas where policies are formulated purely within the public sector, planning policy has always had to address its relationship with the development process (Adams 1994). However, the exact balance in the relationship is not fixed and it can vary over both time and space, with parts of the development process being drawn into public control or influence. As Lindblom (1977) notes, in a liberal democracy there are two main interrelated centres of authority: the democratically accountable government and the asset-owning private sector. Although the public sector cannot control business decisions, it has various means to influence them. In the UK, public control has only ever been partial and the main motive force in development has been the market. However, the means available to the public sector to influence the market depends upon the powers provided through the political process (Smith 1988). Hence, the planning–market relationship is heavily influenced by the stance taken by a particular government. Thus, the analysis has to be extended to cover the political approach to the planning–market balance at both a national and a local level. In this chapter I will discuss the way in which planning's response to the market has varied in the period since 1979, when a strong market-orientated ideology was initiated. I will explore the changes in the statutory planning process but, as we shall see, much planning activity has taken place outside this process. A broader coverage is required and I will also explore approaches to urban regeneration. The way in which planning policy has changed over the period has been conditioned by broader forces. Very little illumination would be achieved by examining the planning processes in isolation and so the first part of the chapter sets out this broader context. I start with a discussion of the relationship between planning and the market.

The planning–market relationship

Planning has often been criticized, particularly by economists, for not being sufficiently aware of market processes and hence of the effects that planning policy has had on market conditions (Healey 1992). It has been said that, in the past, planning has expected the market somehow to fit into its own framework built around non-market objectives. This raises the issue of the purpose of planning: to what extent should it be orientated towards market-supportive activity? I will return to this normative question in a while. Clearly, planning actions can have direct implications for development, the control over the location of activity can affect commercial fortunes, and detailed design requirements or delays in the process can sometimes have financial implications. Brindley et al. (1989) demonstrate the way in which different relationships between planning and the market can lead to different planning styles, such as regulatory, trend or leverage planning. They refer to the different kinds of market conditions in an area and the different attitudes to the relationship, either market critical or market led. Healey (1992) in discussing development plans, identifies three approaches, each with a different relationship to the market, either following market trends, managing the market or creating a market. These typologies provide a useful way of identifying the variation in the planning–market relationship and it would be interesting to explore more fully the causes of the variation.

One causal factor already mentioned is the condition within the market itself. How do the fluctuations in the fortunes of the property markets, set within broader economic changes, influence the relationship? It has been shown (e.g. Hobbs 1992) that the fluctuations in post-war planning can be linked to broad economic conditions. So, "in periods of economic austerity or recession (such as the late 1940s and between the mid-1970s and the mid-1980s), the emphasis on the narrow, physical aspects of planning control tended to increase" (Hobbs 1992: 292).

Conversely, in periods of economic growth such as the 1960s and early 1970s, the scope of planning widens to include a broader range of social and economic issues. However, the picture is complicated by several different dimensions. There is first a timelag between economic change, the development process and the planning response. There are differences between the economic conditions in different parts of the country and the different land and property markets' different tendencies (Healey et al. 1992).

A second general influence on the planning–market relationship relates to the political context. How do political pressures change the view about what the "correct" relationship should be? This is a question of political ideology. The resolution of the question will be influenced by the pressure that different interests can exert on the government and therefore overlaps with the economic issues outlined above. The ideological view of the right relationship between the market and planning will imply a particular interpretation of the "proper" purpose of planning. During the post-war period, planning can be seen to have fulfilled a variety of different purposes, although these have been implicit rather than explicit and have often involved internal contradictions. Some of these purposes have been geared to aiding the market process, such as providing information, co-ordinating infrastructure, or ameliorating adverse "externalities" or "neighbourhood effects". Some have been related to the quality of the environment – this can be of a fairly local nature such as preserving local amenity and visual appearance or of a broader nature concerned with long-term environmental sustainability. The first of these purposes is often linked to NIMBY (not in my back yard) protectionist lobbies, whereas the latter is advocated by environmental pressure groups and in more recent years by the European Union. Finally, there is a set of social policies that may be orientated to groups that are seen to be disadvantaged by the market processes, to deal with locational imbalances or to generate participatory approaches to planning decisions. The period since 1979 has been one in which there has been a strong right-wing political ideology, often termed Thatcherism, through which the balance has shifted towards greater freedom for the market. This has given greater weight to the planning purpose of aiding the market. Socially orientated aims have been rejected on the grounds that social issues would be dealt with by the trickle-down resulting from the beneficial effects of promoting a more buoyant economy. Thus, there have been changes in the planning–market relationship, as it has been considered a good thing to shift some of the decision-making from the planning arena into the market and at the same time to restrict the accepted purpose of the planning system (see Thornley 1993 for more details). However, in recent years a new discussion has arisen. To what extent can another shift be detected in the planning–market relationship with a greater emphasis on planning spurred by the widespread concern over environmental matters? Thus, for a full picture of the way in which economic changes influence the planning–market relationship, detailed research is needed of different kinds of area, different property sectors, different stages in the boom/bust cycles, the variation in lobbying power and the resultant political ideology.

The next section will consider in a little more detail some of the economic and political changes to affect the planning–market relationship over the past decade or so (for a discussion of these relationships at a European level, see Newman & Thornley 1996). It is necessary to explore this context and to extend the discussion beyond the statutory process. There are several reasons for this. First, planning cannot operate in isolation from its economic, political and social setting. Planning reflects the resolution of these broader forces. Secondly, planning activity has increasingly occurred within other initiatives that have had considerable national political force behind them. In many ways, statutory planning has been subservient in those areas where such national initiatives have occurred. The deregulation of statutory planning, and the greater importance given to market criteria accompanied by the 1980s emphasis on projects rather than plans, contribute to the need to explore beyond the confines of the statutory system if we are interested in how cities and countryside have been developed in recent years.

191

The economic and ideological environment

Throughout the developed countries, the major economic change of the previous two or three decades has been the shift from manufacturing to service activity. This has been accompanied by the globalization of the economy, the concentration of the economic control functions in a few centres, with the increased decentralization of manufacturing and back-up office functions. This trend has led to the restructuring of economic activity between locations and has increased the contrasts between regions and cities. A feature of recent years has been the competition between different localities each trying to attract the growing sectors of the economy to their area. This increased competition between cities and regions has been given a particular boost by the opening up of markets within Europe. In trying to attract inward investment, cities and regions need to address the global nature of the economy and the resultant decrease in importance of national markets and national government influence. This competitive environment also has an effect on political structures and, ultimately, planning policies.

City governments have adopted new approaches to increase their competitive advantage, often termed "city marketing" (Ashworth & Voogt 1990). A key element in the strategy is to enhance the image of the city and ensure that it is in the public eye. A good image, an impression that the city is exciting and dynamic, means that it is more likely to appear on the lists of potential new locations prepared by corporate decision-makers. City marketing or "civic entrepreneurship" grew rapidly in the USA during the 1970s (Barnekov et al. 1989). Mayors and city administrations took the initiative in promoting business priorities and sought to demonstrate the attractions of their particular city for inward investment (Harvey 1989). These strategies of "civic boosterism" were epitomized by public–private sector partnerships and the attempt to generate wealth through new development. During the 1980s, these "boosterist" strategies also became common throughout Europe. According to Parkinson, "the search to improve competitiveness of cities has meant that strategies to achieve economic growth have dominated the policy agendas of many European cities" (1992: 179).

A major feature of the city marketing exercise is to show that the city is dynamic and in tune with contemporary needs. This results in the development and promotion of highly visible and "modern" projects – often referred to as "flagship projects" (Bianchini et al. 1992). From such developments it is hoped that a sense of confidence can be established that will then lead to further investment in additional projects. The assumption is that the benefits will also extend to the surrounding communities and solve the social, physical and environmental problems of the city in what has been termed the "trickle-down" effect. Such a strategy replaces direct expenditure on the social needs of such areas and instead the city finances can be concentrated upon aiding the development of the flagship projects through for example, infrastructure or financial inducements. Planning policies will be expected to conform.

The city marketing approach has been accompanied by new forms of urban governance in which the private sector has played a leading role. Molotch was one of the first to give a label to this evolving phenomenon based upon the experience of the USA in the 1970s. The grouping that formulated this new entrepreneurial approach was called a "growth coalition" (Molotch 1976, Logan & Molotch 1987). This is a particular grouping of people that come together to advance the image of the city, set priorities for attracting investment and co-ordinate the projects. The coalition comprises the leading business interests who set the agenda and the leading members of the political elite who organize the political decisions to ensure that the local government support is geared towards it. The unions are often drawn in on the promise of job prospects, and the media and academia provide publicity and respectability. The latter elements in the group are important in generating consensus around the strategy and convincing the local population that everyone will benefit.

However, many authors have shown how this concept cannot be automatically transferred to the UK experience of the 1980 and 1990s (e.g. Lloyd & Newlands 1988, Harding 1991, Imrie & Thomas 1993b). In Britain there is far less autonomy given to the city government level, and central government is far more involved in urban policy. The structure of the private sector also differs, with companies in the USA often having much closer ties with a particular city, whereas in the UK companies tend to operate at a national scale. A third difference is the closer ties between business and city politicians in the USA including financial support for election campaigns. Several authors have suggested that the concept of "urban regimes" has greater value in making comparisons between countries (Keating 1991, Newman 1995). This concept, as developed by Stone (Stone 1989, Stone et al. 1991), is formulated in a broader fashion than "growth coalitions" and in fact the latter can be seen as just one kind of urban regime. Economic interests can combine with urban political power structures in many different ways. Each kind of regime is defined as the particular way in which an informal group can gain access to institutional resources, with some degree of stability, and have a sustained influence over urban decisions. However, the balance of interests, the types of resources accessed and the means by which the group is constituted can vary from place to place. Cities that adopt a city marketing approach are usually characterized by an urban regime in which a group, with a strong private sector presence, is responsible for formulating the strategic agenda and ensuring that there is a coherent pattern of decision-making to support it. The "vision" and resultant priorities are then "sold" to the cities' inhabitants as the best way forwards in the competitive environment, usually employing "city pride" sentiments to obtain consensus.

It has to be questioned whether such strategies and the resultant flagship projects benefit certain groups over others. The removal of decision-making from the "normal" arena of politics into elite discussions, supported by consensus-seeking marketing, tends to mask conflicts. It has also been noted that, as the development process moves from promotion to implementation, the differential effects on different sectors of the population become more evident and the

193

consensus of the early stages is destroyed (Saunders & Stone 1987). The consensus is therefore likely to be a temporary and artificial construct, and recent evidence shows a backlash against competitive and "flagship" style approaches as it is seen that they increase social polarization and environmental deterioration (Loftman & Nevin 1992, Parkinson 1992).

I will now examine in more detail the way in which these economic and political trends have influenced planning policy.

A new plan-led approach?

National policy has provided a supportive environment for these trends towards a market orientated approach in urban governance. Since Mrs Thatcher's election in 1979, central government pursued an approach that incrementally restructured the planning system (Thornley 1993). The net effect of this was a deregulation of the system, giving greater freedom to the market and a downgrading of the importance of development plans. This was accompanied by an increase in central government control of the planning system through its increased involvement in appeals, issuing of a growing amount of Planning Policy Guidance including Strategic and Regional Guidance and initiatives such as Urban Development Corporations. Another feature of the period was the fragmentation of the system. Different kinds of planning approach evolved in different areas, each with its particular planning–market relationship (Brindley et al. 1989). During this period the government found it difficult to reconcile the increased freedom for the market with the environmental objective, and the NIMBY attitudes of many of its supporters. One way of by-passing this dilemma was to create a different kind of planning system in areas with environmental quality such as national parks, conservation areas or green belts. Such areas were excluded from the deregulatory regulations and so over time the power of planning to control the market in these areas became markedly different from the rest of the country. There was then a further division based upon the degree of local political control over planning decisions. In some areas such as Urban Development Corporations, Enterprise Zones, or Simplified Planning Zones the local political involvement was either removed or reduced. As a result, the market was stronger in these areas, as it was not possible to impose other decision-making criteria through the local political system. However, several events occurred in the late 1980s and early 1990s to disturb the confidence of this ideological thrust. There was the removal of Mrs Thatcher in 1990, the increasing concern over environmental issues and the slump in the property market.

The Planning and Compensation Act of 1991 gave renewed importance to the development plan and encouraged planners to enthuse about the start of a new era. As has been discussed by Alan Jones, Ian Gatenby and Christopher Williams elsewhere in this book, the Act stated that planning decisions should be taken in accordance with the plan unless other material considerations indicate otherwise. The plan is therefore the prime consideration, although the door is still open to uncertainty through the interpretation of the above phrase. The courts will be the final arbiter in the relationship between the plan and "other material considerations", and it has been suggested that the plans will have strength only if they avoid being vague or ambiguous (Grant 1991). The government has also extended the scope of the plans by requiring them to include a section on environmental sustainability; however, they have also reiterated the need for them to be "efficient, effective and simple in conception and operation" and confined to land-use aspects (DoE/WO 1992a). One of the issues arising from the change is that of scope – can the plans include more non-market objectives? PPG12 states that the needs of particular groups in the population can be taken into account and it lists ethnic minorities, religious groups, elderly and disabled people, single-parent families, students, and disadvantaged and deprived people in urban areas. It is noticeable that women are not included. In deciding the significance of this social dimension it is necessary to see whether these aspects extend beyond the background justification into policies themselves. Here, the words of the then planning minister, Sir George Young, should be born in mind, reiterating that "non-land-use matters should not feature in plan policies and proposals at all". Many local authorities have been experiencing difficulties in getting the agreement of the DoE to some social aspects of their plans, such as social housing policies or those relating to the disabled. Meanwhile, some local authorities are placing increasing emphasis on seeking the views of the private sector. This is one expression of the aim to make plans more "market aware". Thus, in the preparation of the South Warwickshire Local Plan in the late 1980s, the authority invited consultants, landowners and agents to register their development interests. The 400 responses were fed into the plan preparation process (O'Grady 1994). In 1994, Wokingham distributed standard forms to developers and those with an interest in land requesting information on sites considered suitable for development. These sites were ranked against the council's own criteria and formed part of the plan preparation process. Thus, in current developments it is possible to detect both a move to greater market awareness and also a rekindling of interest in social aspects. However, the resultant scope and content of the plans will be very dependent upon the autonomy of the local authority and the degree of central government interference.

The move to a greater emphasis on local-level policy implied in the Planning and Compensation Act had been developing during Mrs Thatcher's last years in government. It was in 1989 that Chris Patten, the Secretary of State at the time, introduced the notion of "local choice". This arose as a strategy to escape from the contradictory position he found himself in when considering the appeals over the refusal of some new settlement proposals. At this time, several applications had been submitted to build new villages in the countryside near major towns, particularly in London. The applications were usually opposed by local authorities and went to appeal where they then had to be decided by central government in a very exposed and publicized manner. Patten found himself caught between two lobbies, both natural supporters of the Conservative Party, the housebuilders and the residents of the shires. The residents had been showing their displeasure through a Green Party protest vote in the European parliamentary elections. It was a "no-win" situation. The idea of "local choice" allowed such difficult decisions to be shifted to the local level.

So, development plans can again become the arena in which the difficult job of balancing different interest groups can take place. However, how much autonomy will they have? Central government having devolved this responsibility still retains the ability to control and monitor the process. It formulates the strategic and regional guidance to which the development plan must conform, it can intervene in the preparation of structure plans if it thinks the scope of the issues covered is inappropriate, and it has the powers to call in the plan if it is considered controversial. Then, of course, it exerts much influence over the process through the Planning Policy Guidance Notes (PPGs). Although not legally binding documents, these statements of central government control the rest of the planning policy hierarchy because of the way they are treated in any appeal (Tewdwr-Jones 1994a,b). Thus, although development plans may have regained importance, they can use this power only if they conform to the boundaries set by central government. Alongside the higher status of the development plan sits the increased intervention of central government in the details of planning policy.

Central government's changing attitude to the relationship between planning and the market can be usefully traced through an examination of the Circulars and PPGs over the years. In the 1980s the emphasis in the Circulars was on deregulation and ensuring that the market was given greater importance. For example, one of the aims of Circular 22/80 *Development control policy and practice* was to give greater power to housebuilders and it stated that planning should "create the right conditions to enable the housebuilding industry to meet the public's need for housing" (DoE 1980: para. 11). Planners were also told to "bear in mind the vital role of small-scale enterprises in promoting future economic growth" (para. 13). This period was epitomized by Michael Heseltine's claim that many jobs were locked up in planners' filing cabinets. The stress placed on market-based decision-making continued through the 1980s and the White Paper *Lifting the burden* (HM Government 1985) was followed by Circulars stressing the importance of allowing greater freedom for businesses: "it is for market forces to determine whether there is a demand for such premises" (DoE 1986: para. 7).

By the end of the decade environmental issues were becoming more important as a result of international and European initiatives. The government's response in the form of the White Paper *This common inheritance* (HM Government 1990) filtered through to the PPGs of the following years. So in PPGs 1 and 12, produced in 1992, there is much greater emphasis on environmental protection, although it is stressed that sustainability depends upon continuing development and economic growth (DoE 1992b: para. 6.8). It is said that planning should be careful not to distort market competition without good reason.

196

It is not the function of the planning system to interfere with or inhibit competition between users and investors in land, or to regulate the overall provision and character of space for particular uses for other than land-use reasons (DoE/WO 1992a: para. 6).

The purpose of planning is to balance market needs, by making adequate provision for development, while also protecting the natural and built environment (DoE/WO 1992a: para. 4; DoE/DNH 1994: para. 1.2). Since 1992 the issue of sustainability has pushed the balance even further towards the environmental side. Thus, the revision of the PPG on retailing (PPG6) stresses the importance of revitalizing town centres and minimizing the need to travel. However, it also reiterates that "it is not the function of the planning system to preserve existing commercial interests or to inhibit competition between retailers or between methods of retailing" (DoE/WO 1993: para. 3.2). The sustainability objective is taken even further in the later PPG on transport (DoE/DoT 1994) in which the aim of reducing the need to travel, especially by car, is made a central priority. Thus, a pattern emerges. Whereas throughout the period both development promotion and environmental protection are accepted as aims, in the 1980s the emphasis was on opening up the planning process to a degree of market acceptance, whereas the agenda for the 1990s has been on trying to graft onto the system a greater concern for sustainability. However, the guidance assumes that it is possible to combine both economic efficiency and environmental goals, and it sidesteps the question of inherent conflict. There is also considerable ambiguity in the policies, leaving much still to be resolved through practice.

Another conditioning factor on the development plan results from the competition position between cities described earlier. The desire of a particular city to promote itself in the game to attract investment can condition the role and content of the plan. It may become part of the city marketing publicity, that is, demonstrating that the city has a plan that encourages investment and provides locational opportunities that match the needs of companies and developers. Too strict a regulatory planning regime could divert interested parties to another city. For example, the 1993 Unitary Development Plan for Birmingham seeks to set out a vision statement for the city. It aims to secure for the city a national/international status equivalent to that of other major European provincial capitals (Birmingham City Council 1993). However, the past practice of building flagship projects, such as the International Convention Centre, has attracted criticism for diverting priorities from social programmes (Loftman & Nevin 1992) and contributed to a political backlash and change of city leadership. The plan has to try and combine the economic requirements of a city wishing to "sell itself" to prospective investors while also dealing with the pressures exerted by local citizens demanding satisfaction of their social and environmental needs. Such a balancing act may be impossible to reconcile and led Chris Patten to impose "local choice" in the first place.

It has not been so easy for central government to escape the contradictions.

Apart from the scares caused by the urban riots of the 1980s and the pressure from some clerics, it has managed to avoid having to address the social dimension and the contradictions this might pose for a market-dominated approach. The conflicts between environmental objectives and a liberal development regime are becoming more difficult to contain. This is illustrated in the contents of recent PPGs.

The local autonomy that has been accorded to local authorities through the "local choice" approach and the greater importance of development plans has to be regarded as circumscribed. Freedom to formulate policies in the plan is highly constrained by both the boundaries set by national government, reflecting their ideology, and the competitive economic environment that often determines the local political priorities. However, more scope for local initiative could arise as the former consistency of central government directives breaks down.

So far I have concentrated on planning policy contained in the statutory planning process. As we have seen, this process is restricted to land-use matters and is very legalistic, making integration with broader social and economic policy-making difficult. Since the 1960s, other policy instruments have been adopted to deal with the complex issues of urban regeneration, involving many different government departments. In the 1980s, with the market-led approach, these instruments often incorporated different and more relaxed planning regimes. Thus, much of the "development action" took place outside the statutory system. Let us now look at whether the trends in this sphere of planning policy are similar to those described above.

New directions in urban regeneration?

During Mrs Thatcher's time, policy towards urban regeneration followed a fairly consistent pattern. Central government would announce an initiative that they would administer and control through financial and regulatory powers. They would use this power to open up decision-making to market influence and reduce local democracy. The Urban Development Corporations epitomized this approach. A major aim behind the initiatives was to provide the infrastructure, financial inducements and decision-making processes that would attract private sector investment. Through creating the conditions attractive for the property industry, it was expected that development would ensue and that this would create a spin-off effect. This property-led approach to urban renewal has attracted much critical attention (e.g. Healey et al. 1992, Turok 1992, Imrie & Thomas 1993b) in particular for the way in which it ignores many of the dimensions necessary for city revitalization and its dependence on the cycle-prone property market.

The government has not put much emphasis on the monitoring and evaluation of its many initiatives. However, the two government sponsored reviews undertaken both had critical comments to make. In 1989 the Audit Commission said that the "the programmes are seen as a patchwork quilt of complexity and idio-syncrasy" and called for a more coherent approach (Audit Commission 1989: 1). The government commissioned research to evaluate the success of the vari-ous urban policy initiatives implemented during the 1980s and this reported that the economic and environmental emphasis of the policies ignored problems of social disadvantage and that the local voluntary sector and local government should be more involved (DOE 1994a). The research could find no evidence that property-led developments had produced any trickle-down benefits for poorer areas. During the Thatcher period, urban regeneration policy was ideologically dominated by a belief in the superiority of the market and a discrediting of the public sector (Lawless 1988, Parkinson 1989, Thornley 1993, Atkinson & Moon 1994). As mentioned above, the approach was one of simplifying the process for developers, such as liberalizing the planning regime or removing local politics, and providing various incentives whether financial or infrastructural. This pro-vided a national framework in terms of ideology, legislation and finance that matched the aim of many cities to compete in the game of attracting investment and developing flagship projects. Was there any shift in this position in the 1990s?

A new government initiative was launched in 1991, called City Challenge, which involved several new elements (Bonshek 1992). One of these was the competitive bidding approach, since extended to other initiatives, in which local authorities were invited to enter a competition to try and win a limited number of awards. The approach has been criticized for involving much time, money and effort in producing impressive bid documents but, as there have to be many los-ers, this can often be unproductive. Government sets out guidelines for the bids and of course selects the winners, although they give no explanation for their choice. In setting out the guidelines the government made it clear that a high pri-ority was placed upon attracting the commitment of private business to ensure good financial leverage and self-sustaining growth for the area. This requirement clearly influenced the choice of projects in the bids – the emphasis has been on those that would be economically viable rather than those that might meet the social needs of the area. The focus of the initiative on small areas also meant that problems that might pervade a wider geographical area could not be addressed. However, the initiative also put considerable emphasis on involving other agen-cies, for example, the local voluntary sector, universities, Training and Enter-prise Companies and the local community. This greater involvement plus the local authorities' enhanced role in formulating the bid can be seen as a move away from the centrally directed approach of the appointing UDCs divorced from local influences. However, in setting out the brief for the competitive game, cen-tral government is still able to impose its priorities.

Many of the aspects of this new initiative – especially the incorporation of dif-ferent sectors, the role of local authorities and the greater co-ordination between departments – show a shift away from the approach of the 1980s and have been

199

welcomed by commentators (de Groot 1992, Parkinson 1993). However many of the faults of the previous approach remain, such as the concentration on small areas and the limited finance. There has also been considerable doubt cast upon the degree to which the voluntary sector and local communities have been involved (Mabbott 1993, NCVO 1993). Evidence suggests that, whatever the new rhetoric, the initiative is still geared to property-led physical regeneration (Bonshek 1992).

Although the City Challenge initiative had not involved any new expenditure, being "top-sliced" from the urban regeneration budget, it fell foul of government public expenditure cuts in 1992. New rounds of the initiative were suspended. Meanwhile, another initiative was announced in 1992, called the Urban Regeneration Agency, renamed English Partnerships in 1993. This body has statutory powers to reclaim derelict land and property and is allowed to operate anywhere in England. Initially it was feared as a possible "roving UDC". Peter Hall, adviser to the government at the time, described it as a major new initiative that could apply the City Challenge approach on a larger scale (Hall 1992), but its importance does not seem to have materialized. Probably of greater relevance is the government's attempt to create better co-ordination between all the different programmes as suggested by the Audit Commission in 1989. There are two elements to this: a Single Regeneration Budget (SRB) and integrated regional offices of government departments. Both came into effect in 1994. The regional offices will prepare an annual regeneration statement setting out key priorities, administer the SRB and continue to be responsible for regional departmental programmes. The new budget, involving no extra resources, encompasses in one pot the myriad programmes of the five government departments involved – Environment, Trade and Industry, Employment, Education and Home Office. The new budget will continue the competitive philosophy of the City Challenge initiative; the government will set out the guidelines and invite bids. Recipients will be expected to make a significant contribution from their own budgets and maximize contributions from other sources such as the private sector and Europe. A Cabinet Committee on Regeneration will agree the resources and set the guidelines for its allocation. Another initiative was also announced at the same time, called City Pride. Manchester, Birmingham and London were invited to compete for resources through preparing a "city prospectus" which will set out promotional activities and a vision for the city over the next ten years. It will require a partnership with the private sector. Here we see again the competitive element and also a clear link between the government's allocation of resources and the city marketing approach.

So, do these newer initiatives indicate a change of direction? Certainly there is more devolution of responsibility to local authorities who are responsible for formulating and co-ordinating the City Challenge and SRB bids. There is also a greater acceptance of the need to involve local communities and the voluntary sector, although the actual practice has yet to emerge. However, such local autonomy is again much constrained. Central government has a strong hold over the process through setting the guidelines and judging the bids, and it could be said that its priorities are still orientated towards creating the necessary climate for private sector investment rather than addressing the social needs of the areas. If local authorities wish to win in the competitive game, they have to show they are conforming to these priorities, and the requirement for local partnerships with the private sector will help ensure this. The City Pride idea is perhaps the clearest indication that the government is encouraging cities to prepare strategies that will make their areas attractive in the international competitive arena.

Conclusions

So has there been any change in the relationship between planning and the market over the period? In the early years of the Thatcher period, the emphasis was on thinking the unthinkable and challenging the well ingrained values of the post-war welfare state. This ideological campaign involved a forceful presentation of the merits of the market, individualism and self-help. The aim was said to be the rolling back of the state, and countering bureaucratic power, epitomized by Heseltine's comment about the jobs locked up in planner's filing cabinets. However, as the 1980s unfolded it could be seen that what was taking place was not so much a dismantling of the state but its reorganization. Government has not retreated from policy concerns. The approach is to set the framework and then to regulate it – a free economy but a strong state (Gamble 1988). This can be seen across a wide range of policy areas (Wilding 1992), including the formulation of the National Curriculum and national testing at different ages, the new status for the government's Social Services Inspectorate, the activities of the Audit Commission and the Citizen's Charter.

Similarly, it has been noted that the government's attitude to local government underwent a significant change in the late 1980s from one concerned with cutting expenditure to one of restructuring (Bulpitt 1989). In this restructuring a similar regulatory approach is being imposed upon local authorities who are required to adopt an enabling role rather than a providing one (Ridley 1988). Thus, a new pattern for the state is created with far less direct provision of services and far more monitoring and control of the activities of a variety of other agencies, whether private or voluntary. Such an approach can be compared to business management ideas. In their much quoted book, *In search of excellence*, Peters & Waterman (1982) looked at what they considered to be the most successful businesses, such as MacDonalds, to try and identify common characteristics in their management approaches. They discovered that a pattern emerged of a central team setting priorities and general strategy combined with decentralized flexible area management close to the consumer. Decentralized area management had considerable autonomy as long as they conformed to the framework set by the centre. These principles are being applied to the public sector, sometimes linked to the concept of "post-Fordism" (Stoker 1989), which implies a new approach to economic production involving flexible production and segmented marketing. However, providing public services involves criteria different from supplying hamburgers and it can be argued that local authorities have a role beyond simply providing services because they also should be setting priorities through the local democratic process.

These general trends concerning the restructuring of the state can be seen to have affected planning. A change can be identified from the late 1980s, whereby central government has been willing to allow greater freedom to local authorities to adopt planning policies. This has been seen in the "local choice" idea and the renewed power of development plans. It can also be detected in the shift from excluding local authorities and community groups from urban regeneration in the UDCs to the partnership approach of the City Challenge and SRB. However, this greater local autonomy and flexibility is set within even greater central government constraints. The centre is spending more time in formulating its priorities and strategies to which the decentralized bodies have to conform. These regulatory instruments include strategic guidance, regional guidance, the Citizen's Charter, guidelines for City Challenge & SRB bids, and the potential role of the regional offices of central government. This strategic framework is used to ensure that the market-orientated philosophy is maintained. The government can also regulate this planning–market relationship through legislation, Planning Policy Guidance Notes, financial control and through placing private sector personnel in positions to influence decision-making priorities. As an example, let us see how this is affecting planning policy in London.

The 33 London boroughs are busy preparing their Unitary Development Plans, which will now have enhanced status in development control decisions. However, they are having to do this within a London-wide context and are represented on the London Planning Advisory Group (LPAG) who prepare a strategic document. However, this body is only advisory and their views are only one input into the government strategic guidance for London. LPAG is also influenced by the private sector, as is evidenced by the report it commissioned, *London world city* (Coopers & Lybrand 1991). This was largely based upon the views of leading financial and business managers and it influenced LPAG's strategy. Over recent years there has also been considerable pressure from the private sector for a strategic overview (e.g. Robinson 1990, CBI 1991), although not necessarily with a democratic input, and the government has set up London Forum and London First with private sector membership. These organizations can influence the strategic guidance and have, for example, been given the lead role in relation to the London City Pride initiative. The private sector is of course also taking a major role in the seven City Challenge initiatives in the capital, and many partnerships have arisen in different parts of London where the private sector is involved with local authorities in preparing regeneration strategies, often to bid for government or European money. The overall London picture is therefore one of fragmentation of planning policy with recent attempts to overcome this through subregional groupings. However, alongside this fragmentation central government keeps a firm hand on the strategic tiller, although giving the private sector considerable opportunity to influence its direction. Again this fits the pattern, already noted, of the centre controlling strategy and priorities while giving considerable decentralization of day-to-day decision-making to a variety of other bodies, as long as these conform to the central guidelines.

Thus, in the post-Thatcher years, the strong market orientation has been retained. This has been part of the central strategic agenda and has provided the framework within which the more autonomous lower-level bodies have had to operate. We saw earlier that planning has pursued several different objectives that often conflict. In the late 1980s the market supportive objective was being challenged by both the amenity protection objective, NIMBYism, and the demands for a greater consideration of broader environmental issues. Such tensions are always likely to exist, but the balance seems to be shifting towards giving greater weight to the environment. This is evident in the policies formulated by the Secretary of State for the Environment. Considerable importance was given to environmental sustainability in his approach to transport and out-of-town developments. It is too early to say whether this emphasis will continue and affect other areas of policy that are not consistent with this approach. It may be that it is a response to European pressure and the environment lobby, to be reversed when the property market picks up again. There is also some evidence that the third dimension of planning purpose, to satisfy social needs, is creeping back onto the agenda. The DOE has conducted a marketing exercise in London to find out what Londoners want in their city (DoE 1993c) and the City Pride initiative makes reference to social cohesion. However, most people look to the Labour Party for a proper consideration of the social dimension.

In September 1994, Tony Blair and Gordon Brown set out Labour's New Economic Approach. They reject both *laissez-faire* and government substitution for the market. Instead, they are looking for ways of making the market more efficient and fair, with partnership being the new slogan that will be applied to inner city and regional policy. However, there is nothing new about partnership; there have been many examples of different kinds during the previous decade (Bailey et al. 1995). The City Challenge initiative, for example, lays great stress on partnership and involvement of different sectors. There is also the question of what partnership means when applied to planning. One can say that there has always been a form of partnership between the planning system and the market, for example through negotiations over planning applications or planning gain. During the 1960s, partnership was heavily promoted as the way forward in the redevelopment of town centres (MHLG 1962). What is important is not the concept of partnership, which some have even declared as meaningless (Lawless 1991), but the balance of power within the partnership. The balance in such partnerships as the City Challenge is still weighted towards the private sector, but will the Labour Party version give more power to local authorities and the community? Will this produce a shift in the planning–market relationship and reinforce non-

203

market criteria in decision-making?

Under Keith Vaz, a Labour Party inquiry called "City 2020" has been travelling round the country soliciting views on dealing with urban problems. One of the key messages emerging from this is the need to remove central government interference and to give local authorities and local communities greater influence. The inquiry visited the USA and has been impressed by the initiatives of the Clinton administration. The central theme in Clinton's policies for the cities is "creating communities of opportunity", and two new initiatives have been started: "Empowerment Zones" and "Enterprise Communities" (Hambleton 1994). The aims behind these initiatives are to ensure that inner city communities benefit from investment and to increase citizen participation. The theme of "community" seems to have been expanding in recent years at several levels, in philosophical literature (e.g. Bell 1994), in urban regeneration through Community Trusts (Bailey et al. 1995) and in developers' schemes through the concept of "urban villages". Obviously there are many interpretations of the community theme, but it does indicate that further shifts in the planning–market balance may ensue. The extent of the shift depends partly upon whether it encompasses the idea of "community empowerment", which many are now advocating within particular communities, within political parties and within the European Union (Nevin & Shiner 1993, DCC 1994, Labour Party 1994, Liberal Party 1994).

CHAPTER 13

Planning to save the planet? Planning's green paradigm

Kevin Bishop

Introduction

Sustainability and the related term "sustainable development" are very fashionable. They are to be found in the Rio Declaration adopted at the Earth Summit. There is a new Sustainable Development Commission at the United Nations. It is in the title of the European Commission's Fifth Environmental Action Programme "Towards sustainability" (CEC 1992a). In the Environment White Paper annual report (HM Government 1992), sustainability is described as the cornerstone of national policy on the environment. Indeed, the government has published a sustainable development strategy for the UK (HM Government 1994c). A key conclusion of all of these documents is that land-use planning has a central role to play in achieving sustainable development. For some, these changes represent a new paradigm for planning practice, whereas others argue that sustainability is merely a new label for a range of concerns that have always been central to both planning law and policy.

The sustainability agenda

Although the concept of sustainability can be traced back to the Greek vision of "Ge" or "Gaia" as the Goddess of Earth, the mother figure of natural replenishment (O'Riordan 1993) it was only recently that sustainability has become the language of public policy. The publication of the "World Conservation Strategy" in 1980 signified the first really significant global statement about sustainable development and provided a catalyst for debate in the UK (and other countries) about ways in which environmental resources might be sustained. The World Conservation Strategy built on earlier work in the 1970s about anthropogenic

205

strains on the biosphere and "limits to growth" (e.g. *Blueprint for survival*, the 1972 Stockholm Conference). However, its impact on the UK government was minimal. Although there was a UK response, this was sponsored by government agencies (Countryside Commission, Countryside Commission for Scotland and Nature Conservancy Council) and certain non-governmental environmental groups (World Wildlife Fund UK [now World Wide Fund for Nature]) rather than undertaken by the government itself. "The Conservation and Development Programme for the UK" (WWF et al. 1983) did identify an important role for land-use planning in terms of managing environmental change and creating "the livable city", but this was never officially endorsed by the government and it had very little noticeable impact on planning practice.

At the global level, the World Conservation Strategy was followed by the establishment of the World Commission on Environment and Development (subsequently known as the Brundtland Commission after the name of its chairperson, Mrs Gro Harlem Brundtland) by the United Nations. The publication of the Brundtland Report, *Our common future*, in 1987 put the issue of sustainable development more firmly on the international political agenda (O'Riordan 1993) and stimulated considerable debate about the integration of environment and development. The Brundtland Report provides the most commonly used and accepted definition of sustainable development: "development that meets the needs of the present without compromising the ability of future generations to meet their own needs" (Brundtland Commission 1987: 43).

At the UK level, the Brundtland Report was important because it stimulated the government to commit itself officially to the notion of "sustainable development" (DOE 1988a, 1989f). This first official endorsement of sustainable development was elaborated further in the White Paper on the Environment, *This common inheritance* (HM Government 1990), which outlined the concept of "a full repairing lease" and identified key environmental priorities for the planning system, including the idea of locating development to minimize car journeys and the use of planning agreements to compensate for amenities lost through development. Although these environmental priorities marked an important step forwards, when compared with the changes to the planning system instigated in the 1980s, aimed at free market facilitation (Thornley 1993), they barely touch on the sustainability agenda by emphasizing a balance between development and conservation and largely ignoring the important concept of environmental capacities and limits.

The concept of sustainability is central to the sequel to the World Conservation Strategy: *Caring for the earth* (IUCN et al. 1991), which updates and extends the World Conservation Strategy. It was written to act as a catalyst for international change and to provide a framework for sustainability, and it outlines nine key principles for sustainable living. It contains a series of points upon which action by national governments is required if the principles of sustainability are to be implemented. The need for a comprehensive and environmentally based planning system figures strongly in some of the principles for sustainable living, and especially chapter 8 ("Providing a national framework for integrating development and conservation") which identifies the need for action, for example: "develop strategies for sustainability, and implement them directly through regional and local planning" (p. 66); "subject proposed development projects, programmes and policies to environmental impact assessment and to economic appraisal" (ibid.); and "ensure that their nations are provided with comprehensive systems of environmental law, covering as a minimum land-use planning and development control . . . " (p. 68).

The Fifth Environmental Action Programme of the European Community, entitled "Towards sustainability" (CEC 1992a), gives recognition at the European level to the lack of sustainability in the current model of development. As used in the Programme, the word "sustainable" is intended to reflect a policy and strategy for continued economic and social development without detriment to the environment and the natural resources on the quality of which continued activity and further development depend. "Towards sustainability" identifies a key role for land-use planning in terms of providing a framework for the socio-economic development and ecological health of a country, region or locality. A more comprehensive coverage of sustainability and land-use planning issues was contained in the earlier European Commission *Green Paper on the urban environment* (CEC 1990), which emphasized the role of land-use planning in achieving sustainable urban development through a return to the notion of compact cities and limited urban dispersion (see: Breheny 1992, Breheny & Rookwood 1994). The Green Paper emphasizes the need to integrate existing sectoral policies – from conservation, "heritage" and historic centres to air and water quality, noise and waste levels. It argues that solving urban problems also helps to alleviate global environmental problems.

The 1992 Earth Summit – the United Nations Conference on Environment and Development (UNCED) – provided further stimulus for international debate about sustainability. The key agreements reached at Rio – the conventions on global climate change and biodiversity, the statement of principles on forestry and Agenda 21 (the action plan for sustainability) – all imposed commitments on the UK government as a signatory. The UK government has published four documents in response to each of the Rio agreements: Sustainable Development, Climate Change, Biodiversity and Forestry (HM Government 1994a,b,c,d) and many local authorities in the UK are in the process of compiling their own plans for sustainable development – Local Agenda 21 – all of which have implications for the practice of land-use planning.

Sustainable development: the UK strategy (HM Government 1994c) builds upon *This common inheritance* (HM Government 1990) and the subsequent annual reports (HM Government 1991, 1992, 1994e) and is aimed at illustrating how the UK will implement the key elements of sustainable development. Land-use planning is identified as an important instrument in implementing sustainable development and, in particular, chapter 24 attempts to provide a sustainable framework for development in town and country. Important roles for land-use planning are

207

also identified in the Biodiversity Action Plan (e.g. minimizing the loss of biodiversity through development, enhancing biodiversity in open spaces) and the Climate Change Programme (e.g. protecting carbon sinks and promoting energy efficiency).

It is clear that the concept of sustainability has been widely embraced. It has been incorporated into policies at the international level, in European Union policy, in UK government strategies and, as outlined below, is increasingly at the centre of recent reforms to the planning system.

Many commentators have attributed this ready acceptance of the term sustainability to its imprecision, which allows differences to be hidden (Redclift 1991, Grove-White et al. 1993, O'Riordan 1993). However, there is general agreement among the key international documents and UK government strategies on the notion of environmental limits: the environment's capacity to support, or absorb the effects of, human activity is finite and that consideration should drive policy in all spheres (HM Government 1990, 1994a, IUCN et al. 1991).

A natural consequence of the existence of environmental capacity constraints is that human activities (and the aspirations that drive them) need to be undertaken so that they remain within these limits. Although the identification of such capacities (particularly where subjective assessment is required) may prove controversial, sustainability explicitly challenges the assumption that the environment will cope with anything thrown at it or removed from it. Land-use planning has a role in identifying and maintaining such environmental capacities (Jacobs 1993, Land Use Consultants 1993).

Sustainability implies that maintaining and enhancing the integrity and quality of the environment should be a primary objective of policy: impact upon environmental resource levels and natural assets should be the yardstick for economic activities (Pearce 1988, Jacobs 1991, Lowe & Murdoch 1993). Such considerations do not just relate to policy formulation, they should also figure strongly in development control decisions.

Sustainability also requires a shift in the reliance placed on different kinds of natural resources. These can be divided into three categories (Pearce 1988):

- *non-renewable resources* such as fossil fuels and minerals, which cannot be regenerated within human life spans
- *renewable resources* including plants, animals, air and fresh water, which can remain indefinitely provided that we do not utilize them at a rate that exceeds natural renewal or in a way that damages their self-cleansing capacity, and
- *continuing resources* such as wind and solar energy.

The need is to move away from the use of scarce non-renewable resources towards the use of renewable and continuing resources in ways that do not damage their self-sustaining characteristics. Again, land-use planning has a role in ensuring such a switch through appropriate policies based on the principle of demand management (see Phillips 1992). The use of resources normally entails the generation of wastes, which then have to be assimilated into the natural environment.

Since there are limits to the ability of the environment to absorb wastes, these must act as constraints on resource use (Lowe & Murdoch 1993). Such limitations should obviously drive both development plan policies and development control decisions.

The concern with limits reflects the intergenerational perspective that sustainability entails: we are obliged to pass on an environment that will sustain the needs of future generations. Incorporation of environmental capacities into policy-making should also take account of the distributional or equity effects of resource use and development. For many actions, therefore, sustainability includes concern for social welfare considerations and requires a commitment to a fairer distribution of wealth and resources. Development should not be at the expense of future generations (intergenerational equity) nor other groups (intra-generational equity).

These various elements of sustainability are visible, to varying degrees, in recent reforms to the planning system.

The greening of the planning system

The 1990s have witnessed some important advances in environmental policy as enshrined in planning legislation, policy and practice. Although the government rejected efforts by some environmental groups (e.g. Campaign for the Protection of Rural England) to include a legal duty to further the achievement of sustainable development in the Planning and Compensation Bill, the principle has now been accepted in national planning policy documents PPGs 1 and 12 (DOE/WO 1992a, DoE 1992b, WO 1992a). These contain identical guidance:

> The planning system, and the preparation of development plans in particular, can contribute to the objectives of ensuring that development and growth are sustainable. The sum total of decisions in the planning field, as elsewhere, should not deny future generations the best of today's environment. (DOE/WO 1992a: para. 3)

This definition, and the remit of planning, was taken a step further by the publication of PPG4 *Industrial and commercial development and small firms* (DOE/WO 1992b), which introduced the issue of intergenerational equity by stating that: The principles of sustainable development require the responsible use of man-made and natural resources by all concerned in a way that future generations are not worse off (para. 2).

The Town and Country Planning Act 1990 signified the beginning of "mandatory greening" by requiring all development plans to include policies in respect of the improvement of the physical environment, the management of traffic, and the conservation of the natural beauty and amenity of land. The Act and Regulations together also require authorities to have regard to "environmental

209

considerations" in the preparation of development plans. Although the phrase "have regard to" allows plenty of scope for differing interpretations, environmental issues are no longer an optional extra. This move to place the environment at the centre of development plan preparation was further reinforced by the publication of PPGs 1 and 12, which express the government's view of planning as a key instrument in achieving sustainable development. PPG12 on development plans contains a new section on "Plans and the environment", which emphasizes the need for a shift of attention:

> Local planning authorities should take account of the environment in its widest sense in plan preparation. They are familiar with the traditional issues of green belt, concern for landscape quality and nature conservation, the built heritage and conservation areas. They are familiar too with pollution control for healthier cities. The challenge is to ensure that newer environmental concerns, such as global warming and the consumption of non-renewable resources, are also reflected in the analysis of policies that form part of plan preparation. (DoE 1992b: para. 6.3)

PPG12 also offers support for the "environmental appraisal" of development plan options during preparation.

Other changes have contributed to this greening of the planning system. For example, the Planning and Compensation Act 1991 abolished the presumption in favour of development and replaced it with a new presumption in favour of development that accords with the provisions of the development plan (Section 54A); the acceptance in PPG12 of the "precautionary principle" in tackling potentially irreversible damage; the clear acknowledgement of carbon dioxide emissions as a material planning consideration through individual cases (e.g. the Inspectors report on the public inquiry into the application to develop a wind farm on Mynydd-y-Cemmaes) and, latterly, PPGs – notably PPG6 *Town centres and retail developments* (DoE/WO 1993) and PPG13 *Transport* (DoE/DoT 1994); recognition in PPG12 of the role of planning system in conserving finite and non-renewable resources (such as, minerals, energy and water); and new provisions in the Planning and Compensation Act 1991 concerning public consultation and the extension of planning controls to demolition.

This official endorsement of the sustainability agenda, in the form of legislation and PPGs, has been further reinforced and sometimes initiated by the commissioning of research into the environmental role of land-use planning. For example, the DoE has funded research into the role of land-use planning in reducing transport emissions, which contributed to revisions to the PPG on transport. A study into planning and pollution control led to a new PPG on this subject, PPG23. Other research, such as that on methods of environmental appraisal for development plans (DoE 1993b), has contributed to good practice guides.

In addition to this "top-down greening", many local authorities have responded to increasing public demands and concerns for environmental issues, often articulated through voluntary sector pressure groups, by producing envi-

210

ronmental action plans, environmental strategies, environmental statements and green charters that demonstrate a corporate and/or land-use planning commitment to sustainable development. For example, in July 1991 more than two thirds of Britain's 514 planning authorities were involved in some kind of "green planning initiative" (Raemakers 1991).

Planning's green paradigm?

For some the greening of the planning system witnessed in the early 1990s represents a new paradigm for planning practice, whereas others argue that sustainability is merely a new label for a range of concerns that have always been central to both planning law and policy. For example, Millichap (1993) argues that "the concept of sustainable development does not mean a dramatic shift in approach by the planning system" (Millichap 1993: 1111), yet Healey & Shaw (1993), among others, have identified a new planning discourse in the 1990s centred on the notions of sustainable development and carrying capacity.

Millichap (1993) argues that both the temporal dimension (concern about future generations) and the notion of environmental stewardship are concerns long reflected in the roots of modern British planning policy and law. The temporal dimension is reflected in the public health roots of land-use planning, where there was evident desire to avoid short-term decisions relating to urban development that would later lead to problems of slums, bad sanitation and the blighting of future generations. It is also, argues Millichap, evident in the protection afforded by planners to primary resources such as agricultural land and mineral reserves. The concept of environmental stewardship (as developed in *This common inheritance*) is also to be found, explicitly or implicitly, in the language and practice of planning. Millichap demonstrates this with reference to green belt protection, listed buildings and conservation area policy. For example, the owners of listed buildings must make "every possible effort" to "continue the present use or to find a suitable alternative use for" the listed building they wish to demolish. If they fail to fulfil their duties as good stewards then consent will not be given (quoted in Millichap 1993: 1117).

Although Millichap is correct to note that planning law and policy have long been concerned about the wellbeing of future generations and the need to protect primary resources, such concerns have often been partial and his argument underplays the potential significance of recent reforms, which have moved environmental issues towards the centre of planning policy formulation and implementation. Planning has conventionally been used as a mechanism for distributing new development and balancing competing interests – a practice that has usually ensured the dominance of short-term economic considerations over long-term environmental security. Recent reforms to the planning system have enhanced the ability of the planning system to consider the needs of future

211

generations, as dictated by the new era of PPGs, through:

- the identification of environmental capacities and limits to developments
- beginnings of a move towards managing demands and limiting supply to respect such capacities
- the acceptance of the precautionary principle where the environmental impacts of certain actions are unclear, and
- the introduction of a new scientific dimension to traditional economic, social and land-use considerations.

Although the practice of protecting mineral reserves for use by future generations demonstrates one aspect of sustainability (as argued by Millichap 1993), the demand-led nature of traditional mineral planning provision ignores the central issue of environmental limits. Prior to the revisions of Minerals Planning Guidance Note 6, which introduce the concept of managing future demand for minerals in order to safeguard environmental assets, minerals planning operated on a "predict and provide basis" (Reynolds & Burton 1994), whereby the DoE, in consultation with the minerals industry, produced forecasts of future mineral consumption requirements that were then allocated between local authorities to ensure the planning system would deliver sufficient opportunity for mineral excavators to satisfy demand.

The development of demand management as a general rather than specific planning principle is also witnessed in the new PPGs on housing (DoE 1992e) and transport (DoE/DoT 1994). The revised version of PPG3, *Housing*, not only withdrew the special presumption in favour of releasing land for housing contained in Circular 22/84 (DoE 1984), it also potentially introduces an environment-led approach to housing supply based on "environmental capacity" – an approach adopted in the Suffolk Structure Plan. An even more explicit endorsement of demand management is witnessed in the new PPG on transport, which recognizes "the need to manage demand" (para. 15) by promoting acceptable alternatives to the private car, enabling people to reach everyday destinations with less need to travel, and reducing local traffic on trunk roads and other through-routes.

Another potential sea-change has been the acceptance in *This common inheritance* and PPG12 of the precautionary principle:

> Attention must also be given to the interests of future generations. Thus, those impacts on the environment which may be irreversible or very difficult to undo should be treated with particular care in the preparation of plans: future generations may value the lost resource more than the development which it replaced. (DoE 1992b: para. 6.8)

Although the precautionary approach is again not new to land-use planning – the concept has long been applied in terms of safeguarding high-quality agricultural land – PPG12 signals its wider application and a potential switch from conventional trading off of the environment for economic growth or development. For example, the precautionary principle was accepted by the Secretary of State for the Environment in modifications to the Cheshire Structure Plan in 1992 to delete proposals for the large-scale release and development of green belt land around Chester, because of the possible harm to the historic character of the town and its setting. The precautionary principle goes directly against recent government policy that planning permission should be refused only where harm to interests of acknowledged importance can be demonstrated (Purdue 1991).

Linked to the precautionary principle has been the increased use of technical and scientific arguments in advancing the case for and against new developments. The introduction of environmental impact assessment legislation by the EC and its subsequent incorporation into domestic regulations extended the interface between planners and scientific arguments concerning environmental impacts. A new PPG on *Planning and pollution control* (DoE 1994d) and revisions to other PPGs (notably PPG13) have highlighted a role for land-use planning in controlling pollution levels and promoting energy efficiency, and have established that emission levels of some pollutants (carbon dioxide, for example) can constitute a material planning consideration. There is now discussion about the need to link strict environmental regulation systems (i.e. integrated pollution control machinery) more closely with planning controls (see Blowers 1993). The recent announcement of a new framework for local air-quality management, demonstrates this growing link between planning and pollution control. Under the terms of this scheme, which will require new legislation, national air-quality standards and targets are being established for nine individual pollutants and, if these standards are breached, then local authorities will be required to take action. The documents clearly state that local authorities will be required to have regard to the scheme's assessment of local air quality in exercising its planning, transport and pollution control responsibilities.

The 1990s have witnessed the entrenchment of environmental concerns in planning policy (Healey & Shaw 1993). Although phrases such as "have regard to" and "overriding public interest" leave considerable scope for interpretation, there is the potential that this new environmental agenda will lead to a fundamental revision of planning concepts and policy processes rather than just a reinforcement of traditional strategies as suggested by Millichap (1993).

Implementing sustainability: ship shape and Bristol fashion

Development plan preparation for Bristol illustrates the extent to which some local planning authorities are adopting and extending the new environmental agenda and provides an example of the differences in approach in the wake of *This common inheritance* and the Planning and Compensation Act 1991.

Work on the new district-wide local plan formally began in 1990 with the adoption of a project brief that identified nine main objectives for the plan. These objectives ranged from reinforcing Bristol's role as a regional shopping centre to establishing a code of community planning standards. Although there was an aim of establishing environmental and green objectives that sought to conserve energy and resources, the concept of sustainable development was not one of the original objectives. Transportation was identified as the most important issue for the new plan, despite the fact that the city council is not the highway authority. The original intention was that the new city-wide district plan would be an amalgam of existing policies, but this approach was abandoned as it would have restricted the ability to incorporate new issues and priorities.

The preparation of a "Green Charter for Bristol" (Bristol City Council 1990c) acted as an important catalyst in raising awareness of environmental issues among members and officers across a range of service directorates. The charter was produced by a working group consisting of representatives of all service directorates within the city council and the six themes upon which the charter is based (energy conservation and resources, environmental quality and control, movement and access, purchasing power, the built environment and the natural environment) provided a corporate environmental policy framework for the local plan, committing the council to certain environmental objectives that were, in part, incorporated into the plan and ensuring close liaison was maintained with other key directorates within the city council. The Green Charter encouraged a holistic approach to the environment and a partnership approach to the development of the local plan, with members kept up-to-date with a series of regular informal briefings and officers from other directorates involved in policy development.

In the introduction to the draft plan (Bristol City Council 1992) are five themes that underpin each of the policies contained in the plan: economy and regeneration, equality, quality of life, movement and identities. Although sustainable development is not an explicit theme or objective, there are strong elements of the sustainability agenda in four of the five themes. The theme of equality can be related to the ethical principle of sustainability: that development should not be at the expense of other groups or future generations. The theme of identities can also be related to the principle of enabling communities to look after their own environments. Support for local centres, which underpins the identities there, is seen as a way of reducing the need to travel, thereby minimizing energy use and potentially reducing pollution. The movement theme relates to a particular problem of road congestion and dependence upon the private motor car, with the aim of reducing the need to travel and providing alternative means to do so. However, the theme of economy and regeneration does not refer to environmental capacities or priorities, although it does relate economic development to environmental principles.

There are three chapters within the draft and deposit plan devoted specifically to environmental issues. Chapter 2, entitled "Management of the environment", focuses on planning's role in maintaining and improving the quality of the local environment through controlling the location, type, scale and design of development. There are policies to promote energy efficiency and use of renewable energy sources, minimize environmental pollution, and encourage recycling (e.g. promoting the re-use of builders' waste in the construction of new buildings and the recycling of derelict/vacant land). Chapter 3 on "The natural environment" concentrates on protecting and enhancing the city's natural heritage. Chapter 4 is concerned with "The built environment" and ensures that the quality of new development (in terms of design criteria) enhances the visual environment and meets the environmental criteria detailed in chapters 2 and 3.

Sustainability principles also underpin other chapters on movement, economy, shopping, housing and community services. The aim of the chapter on "Movement" is "to promote a more sustainable and environmentally friendly transport system" (Bristol City Council 1993a: 129) through the provision of a greater choice for movement throughout the city by giving greater priority to public transport, cycling and walking. The chapter on "Economy" explains that industrial and commercial development proposals will normally be permitted only where there is no unacceptable detrimental impact on the environment, defined in terms of local amenity, accessibility to more energy-efficient modes of transport, the level and type of traffic generated, noise and other forms of pollution, and impact on the natural environment. The chapter on "Shopping" follows government advice, as outlined in PPG6, in restricting out-of-town shopping and protecting and developing local centres in order to reduce the need to travel and ensure the viability and vitality of existing shopping centres. The "Housing" chapter also adopts the concept of compact cities as models of sustainable urban development, with the promotion of mixed-use developments and higher average housing densities through proposals for residential development on backland, under-used and derelict sites.

The impact of the new green agenda for planning is most noticeable in the principles outlined in the plan for guiding development control decisions, to ensure that development proposals are sustainable. The five principles identified in Table 13.1 mark an innovative approach to implementing development plan policies and ensuring that development proposals are sustainable. The "cradle to grave" approach attempts to apply to development proposals the concept of lifecycle analysis, or an extended process of environmental assessment. The aim is to ensure that environmental issues are considered in the initial design stage of projects and all subsequent stages of development through to the management of the development itself. "Thinking globally – acting locally" is an attempt to incorporate thinking on the international ecological footprint or shadow to the local level – the effects of decisions and actions taken at the local level transcend local authority, regional and national boundaries, and this should be reflected in planning decisions. For example, the choice of materials used in constructing and fitting out a building can have implications for tropical rainforests (e.g. the use of tropical hardwoods), the ozone layer (e.g. the use of virgin aggregates rather than recycled materials). "Working together" refers to the need for public participation in decision-making and recognition of the fact that no agency can solve environmental problems in isolation. "Prevention is better than cure" relates to the precautionary principle. The environmental implications of certain

Table 13.1 Environmental principles within Bristol's local plan.

A cradle to grave approach
Addressing environmental issues from the initial design phase, through to the operations of the completed development, including those that will occur when operations change or stop. This includes considering the environment when choosing the location of the development, formulating the general and detailed design package and in the management of the development itself.

Thinking globally: acting locally
The effects of many decisions and actions made at the local level transcend local authority, regional and national boundaries. This will be reflected in planning decisions. For example, the choice of materials used in constructing and fitting out a building can have implications for tropical rainforests (in the case of hardwood materials) and the ozone (in the case of insulation or air conditioning units).

Working together
No agency can solve environmental problems in isolation. It is vital that a partnership approach to environmental management is adopted involving close co-operation between agencies from the statutory, commercial and voluntary sectors. It is also important to ensure the active support and involvement of local people if environmental initiatives are to be successful. When determining planning applications, the City Council will ensure full and wide-ranging consultation and liaison takes place with all the relevant groups and agencies, particularly on issues of a technical nature.

Prevention is better than cure
The implications of certain actions for the environment are not always immediately clear, or easy to determine. A precautionary approach is, therefore, desirable. All the environmental costs and benefits of proposals will be evaluated before decisions are made. In this way potential problems can be identified early and appropriate measures taken in the location and design of developments to reduce any adverse impact.

The polluter must pay
The City Council supports the view taken by central government that those who cause environmental damage must bear the full costs of control. This is "the polluter pays principle". In planning terms this means development proposals will be required to include provisions for compensatory and mitigation measures aimed at removing, or reducing to acceptable limits, any environmental damage, and replacing lost or damaged resources. This can be achieved through the use of planning conditions and planning obligations with developers. For example, ensuring that the appropriate sound insulation is built into a noise-generating development.

Conserving environmental resources and local amenity
Existing environmental resources such as open spaces, wildlife habitats, rivers and watercourses, will be protected wherever possible or appropriate. Equally, the need to protect the local amenity of residents from noise and other disturbance or nuisance will be an important factor in the determination of planning applications. The acceptability of development proposals will be enhanced, if it can be shown that environmental benefits would result. For example, if a building is designed to high standards of energy efficiency.

---

actions or developments are not always clear, or easy to determine. In such circumstances the council is committing itself to proceed in a precautionary manner. The "polluter must pay" is a concept that has been central to UK pollution control policy since 1974 and the passage of the Control of Pollution Act. In planning terms this approach means that development proposals will be required to include provisions for compensatory and mitigation measures. Planning conditions and obligations are identified as the mechanism for ensuring that developers pay the cost of meeting environmental, social and economic standards. The notion of "conserving environmental resources and local amenity" begins to address the concept of critical natural capital (those areas whose loss or damage would be very serious) and continues the theme of using the planning system as a mechanism for environmental compensation/gain.

To supplement the policies contained in the statutory local plan Bristol City Council is preparing a series of Policy Advice Notes (PANs). PANs are aimed to provide positive guidance on the type of development the council wishes to see in Bristol, incorporating detailed design guidance for developers and architects on how to achieve some of the standards for development outlined in the local plan. The PANs are cross referenced in the development plan. For example, policy B10 of the deposit version of the local plan states that

> The City Council will encourage that all housing developments provide appropriate standards of facilities and amenities. Applicants should have regard to the criteria contained in Policy Advice Note – Residential Guidelines. (Bristol City Council 1993b: 112)

As well as providing more traditional guidance on design standards, the PAN also details certain environmental considerations: energy-efficient site planning, consideration of building forms to maximize energy conservation, and the use of materials in construction (preference for materials with least environmental effects e.g. timber from a sustained, managed resource rather than high energy input, manufactured products such as aluminium and plastics).

Both the draft and deposit versions of the city-wide Bristol Local Plan begin to incorporate elements of the new green agenda for planning, notably: scientific arguments on pollution and energy efficiency, the concept of demand management, the precautionary principle and enabling local communities. These elements are most clearly expressed in the guidelines for development control, which attempt to turn the rhetoric of policy into reality. Although still weak in terms of: an explicit reference to sustainable development, establishing environmental capacities and limits, determining key targets, and assessing the environmental impact of the policies themselves, the new district-wide local plan marks an important advance when compared to the draft City Centre Local Plan (Bristol City Council 1990b). Coverage of environmental issues in the City Centre Local Plan is essentially confined to more traditional concerns of habitat protection, landscape improvements and urban design guidance aimed at conservation. For example, the conservation objective of the City Centre Local Plan is "creative regeneration of the physical environment" (Bristol City Council 1990a: 15). In contrast the district-wide local plan has an aim of improving and sustaining both the built and natural environment through a range of land-use policies and plan objectives about air quality, water quality, pollution, energy use, waste management, recycling and transport and movement (May 1993).

The draft and deposit versions of the district-wide local plan, when compared to the City Centre Local Plan, indicate a significant change in the way in which environmental issues have been incorporated in development plan preparation.

Conclusions

The 1990s have witnessed a significant greening of planning law, policy and practice stimulated by top-down factors (e.g. European Union and wider international obligations) and bottom-up factors (e.g. increased environmental awareness across society and the innovative actions of some local authorities). These changes have stimulated a series of questions: What is meant by the term sustainability?; Does it represent a new paradigm for planning?; If it does, how can the planning system deliver sustainability and is the existing planning system indeed capable of delivering sustainability?

The conventional role of land-use planning has been to balance competing objectives, with "the environment" viewed as one factor to be balanced against the demand for new roads, retail premises, housing land or other developments. Sustainability means something new: it introduces the notion of environmental limits. The capacity of the environment to absorb development is finite, and that consideration should dictate policy. A consequence of identifying environmental capacity constraints is that human actions (and the aspirations that drive them) need to be managed so that they remain within these limits. The planning system has a role to play in ensuring the maintenance of such capacities, but this will not be achieved by the traditional approach of trading the environment off against other considerations. There are elements of sustainability in the way that the planning system has operated, but the actual delivery of sustainable development requires further fundamental changes in policy and practice.

There is a developing consensus on how to plan for sustainable development (see CPOS 1993, Jacobs 1993, Land Use Consultants 1993) and recent changes in central government planning guidance have started to provide a framework for environmentally sensitive planning. For example, there is a recognition in recent PPGs of environmental capacities, the need to respect such constraints and to accept the need to proceed in a precautionary manner. These changes have in some cases responded to and in others initiated local authority action. The Bristol case study demonstrates how one local planning authority has responded to the new green agenda and the extent to which this represents a new departure. However, the battle is not won, there is still a gap between rhetoric and reality at central and local government level, and even the rhetoric may not be safe. The draft guidance for the new Environmental Agency reopens the debate about what sustainable development means with its reference to the need to balance needs of the environment with development. The Secretary of State for Wales's recent *The environmental agenda for Wales* (Redwood 1995) does not even refer to sustainability. At the local level, most local authorities are at the beginning of a path towards a strong version of sustainability (see Jacobs 1993).

Although there may be consensus in advice on how sustainability considerations can be more systematically incorporated into plan- and decision-making, there is a more fundamental question about the ability of the current planning system to deliver a strong version of sustainability. Such concerns are borne out of the neutrality and pro-development bias of planning (Grove-White et al. 1993). Grove-White et al. argue that the traditional training of planners to be neutral when considering development issues may need to be revised in the light of sustainability requirements to reflect a consistent prejudice in favour of certain kinds of development and infrastructure. Following from this point, there are questions about whether the presumption in favour of development (albeit in accordance with the development plan) is compatible with sustainability. Linked to this is the land-use orientation of planning, which can potentially restrict its ability to incorporate environmental issues fully, witness the strong distinction between planning and pollution control systems incorporating PPG23. We have witnessed some remarkable advances in environmental policy as enshrined in planning law and practice after 1990. The potential impact could be significant and it certainly implies more than "a new label for traditional concerns". However, the jury is still out. The real effect of these changes will be determined by factors such as professional entrenchment (an inertia/resistance to change), central government advocacy, local politics and the commitment of planning committees, and societal pressures.

CHAPTER 14

Planning and the European question

H. W. E. Davies

Town and country planning in most of Europe started on a common basis early in the twentieth century, but diverged after 1947. In Britain, planning became more discretionary, with a tendency towards centralized control. Elsewhere, it remained more rigid but increasingly within a decentralized framework of national, regional and local planning. The new factor is the increasing interest in planning by the European Commission which, since 1992, has been given a mandate for town and country planning, although under the influence of subsidiarity no action has yet been taken. The main influence of the Commission on planning has been felt through the increasing effects of environmental regulation and the programmes of the Structural Funds in addressing regional disparities and, indirectly, through the various pilot studies and support for networks for the exchange of experience. These are leading towards a new perception of space following completion of the Single Market and a new concept of spatial planning, epitomized at the macro level by publication of *Europe 2000* and at the local scale in the increase in transnational planning across national borders. This chapter discusses these developments and asks the questions, "What effect will they have on the policies and practice of planning in the UK? Will there be a harmonization of planning systems, or a convergence, and if so what form will they take?"

Introduction

Town and country planning in the UK has nearly a century of legislative, professional and practical experience behind it. But now, at the end of the century, it is faced with new challenges in the context of the European Union. It is no longer sufficient for planners in the UK to be inward looking, satisfied that they have a uniquely effective planning system that the rest of the world looks on with envy.

The challenge of Europe comes from two directions. One comes from looking at, and being looked at in return by, the planning systems in the other member-states of the European Union. The other comes from the activities of the European Union itself, those of the European Council of Ministers, the European Commission, the European Parliament and the European Court of Justice.

This chapter reviews these two challenges and their significance for town and country planning in the UK, to use the term of the primary legislation, although it is one that is used nowhere else in Europe. This points to one of the problems, a problem of language and of meaning that bedevils any attempt at a comparative review of planning in other countries (Booth 1993).

Planning in Europe

Town and country planning started in most of Europe in the early twentieth century, for instance in 1901 in The Netherlands, 1909 in England and Wales, and 1919 in France (Davies et al. 1989). The systems shared four basic characteristics. They were all concerned with the use and development of land. Their chief instrument was a legally binding planning scheme that laid down the permitted uses of land within the area of the scheme. The systems were decentralized, with the schemes being prepared by local authorities without any higher level of plans to which they had to conform. And finally there was no attempt initially at a comprehensive coverage of planning schemes. They were to be prepared only for the extension of towns.

Planning in all of the countries evolved along broadly similar lines until 1947 when, uniquely in the UK, it shifted decisively, to follow a different course. The Town and Country Planning Act 1947 had five basic principles: a universal and discrete definition of development, a duty to prepare a development plan, a requirement to obtain permission for development, a right of appeal against a refusal of planning consent, and a power of enforcement against any breach of planning control. Each of these principles differed significantly from the earlier system in the UK, and from those that continued to be the rule in most of the rest of Europe. The result was a planning system whose characteristics differed in many respects from those in other countries.

In the first place, the new 1947 planning system was comprehensive and universal. All five principles applied throughout the country from the appointed day, without exception. Every local authority had to prepare a development plan covering its entire area; all development, with a few exceptions listed in the legislation, had to receive planning permission. Secondly, the system was highly discretionary. The concept of a legally binding plan was abolished and in its place local authorities and ministers were given a high degree of administrative discretion in determining whether or not to grant planning permission. Thirdly, this new planning system was one in which ultimate power rested with the minister, not the courts, provided the law itself was complied with. Admittedly, a chief planner to the Department of the Environment could say in 1976 that "the planning system was given by Parliament to local authorities" (Burns 1977: 684), but the minister in Whitehall retained ultimate power through his approval of development plans, and the power to decide appeals against refusal of planning consent by the local authority.

A different story holds in the rest of Europe. Planning has remained tied to the use and development of land, continuing to rely on the instrument of a legally binding plan, and staying firmly rooted at the level of the lowest tier of local government, with any appeal being to the courts on points of law rather than to ministers on points of policy or expediency. Nevertheless, there have been changes. As planners have improved their methodology and increased their understanding of changes in the use of land, so their ambition to plan and control its development has extended. Thus, they have sought to make planning ever more comprehensive, not only in its geographical coverage but also in its scope. In particular, there have been attempts to achieve greater co-ordination, whether horizontally, between different sectors at one level, or vertically, between different levels of planning, by introducing what the Danes have described as "framework management", This brings together two principles: "plans must not contradict the planning decisions made at higher levels"; but, within that constraint, there is a high degree of autonomy granted to local authorities to make their own decisions (Østergård 1994).

Thus, in every major country of the European Union except the UK, there is in place a formal system of national, regional and local planning, with elected bodies accountable to their area with responsibility for the planning of their areas. The precise degree of decentralization does vary, and is shifting with a trend towards greater decentralization, seen for instance in the 1983 reform of the French planning system in which much greater authority was given to the communes to prepare their own local plans and issue their own permits (Punter 1989).

The variety of planning systems in Europe is therefore considerable, but it is possible to point the way to a typology of planning systems. One simplistic method is geographical. There is an east/west divide between the capitalist countries of western Europe – where planning systems are decentralized, flexible and market-led to a greater or lesser degree – and those of central and eastern Europe – formerly highly centralized, sectoral and bureaucratic in their planning under the command economies. This division, purely in terms of planning systems, is breaking down as the eastern European countries attempt to adapt to a market economy. But the new problems and opportunities emerging in central Europe are giving an east–west impetus to force lines in European development as new relationships evolve between west and east, to some extent cutting across the older north/south forces.

There is nevertheless an alternative, a north/south divide in which the contrast is between the northern countries, with complex, sophisticated and accountable planning systems for which there is a high degree of public acceptance and support, and the southern countries, where planning is more fragmented and lacks the same degree of public support.

The system in each country is a response to its history, geography, stages of economic development and urbanization, and political ideology. It can be argued that a unifying feature is that many of the countries other than the UK came under the Napoleonic Code, with all that implies by way of a written constitution defining the relationships between the various arms of the state, between citizens and the state, and between citizens. It means that the rights of citizens, including in many cases property rights, are laid down in the constitution. It means a reliance on statute law in which authority is found in the constitution and legislation, rather than, as in the UK, judge-made-law. It means in the Dutch phrase the concept of *rechstaat*, the legal state, and the desire for legal certainty in the relationships between citizens and the state (van Gunsteren 1976). It is this that underlies the dependence on legally binding local plans as the ultimate source of authority about planning and control, backed by the courts.

A more formal approach towards developing a typology of planning systems in Europe, however, would identify four dimensions along which the different systems could be located. One dimension would be that between a regulatory and a discretionary system in which, for instance, The Netherlands would be towards one end with its reliance on the *bestemmings plan*, the legally binding local plan, and the UK at the other, with its system of development control tied but loosely to the development plan. A second dimension would be between the centralized and the decentralized systems. In practice, this is probably more difficult to determine as it depends on the degree of political and administrative authority that the national, regional and local governments have to make their own decisions and the extent to which that legal authority might be constrained or supported in law and the constitution. Probably, taking the same two examples, the UK would be increasingly towards the centralized end, whereas the opposite would be true of The Netherlands.

The third line of cleavage lies between planning systems that are primarily proactive, with considerable powers and resources to ensure implementation of their plans, and those that are more reactive, relying on the initiative of others, notably the private sector, for their plans to be followed and implemented. Planning in the UK in the immediate post-war years was largely proactive through slum clearance, council housing, town centre redevelopment and industrial estates initiated by central government departments and agencies, and by local authorities. Today, the dominant form is reactive planning, in which development largely is initiated by the private sector, responding to market forces. The contrast with many of the European countries is striking, even if the planning is nevertheless responding to market forces. In the case of The Netherlands, the local plan is an essential instrument in land preparation and assembly by the municipality, the funding of social housing, the laying out and development of industrial estates, and the settling of financial responsibility for the costs of providing services (Needham et al. 1993). In France, too, there are powerful instruments such as the *contrat de plan*, the formal partnership between the state and the regions, or the various techniques for promoting urban development such as the *zone d'amenénagement concerté* (Acosta & Renard 1993).

The fourth dimension is that of stability, or the extent to which the planning system is well established, changing gradually as conditions change, but without a major upheaval. This is one where, despite the changes in detail, the basic principles of the UK's system, and those of many of the others, have remained relatively constant for many years. The basic principles of the system as such have remained largely unchanged, although the ways in which the system is used and its characteristic features have shifted in response to social, economic and political change. Elsewhere, the greatest changes obviously are occurring in the countries of central and eastern Europe as they shift from a command to a market economy. But other countries have seen major changes, including, for instance, Spain, with the demise of the Franco regime and its shift towards a federal structure, or Belgium, as planning, with the great majority of other domestic responsibilities, is decentralized from the national government to the three regions.

But, if variety is the hallmark of planning systems in Europe, the major cleavage is between the British system, centralized and discretionary, and the rest of continental Europe, decentralized, legally binding and now with the addition of framework management. The key question is, what does this imply for the future development of planning in the UK? However, before that question can be tackled, a new factor must be brought into the scene, namely the European Union.

The European Union and a mandate for planning

The European Union, like the majority of its member-states, is bound by a very strict system of laws and a written constitution. Authority for any action, policy or programme by the Union must derive from its basic constitution, the Treaty of Rome 1957, as amended by the Single European Act 1986 and the Treaty of European Union 1992. Thus, in seeking whether the European Union will have any effect on planning in the UK, the answer must be found ultimately in the Treaty. And a review of the Treaty suggests that it is possible to identify three phases in the development of a concern for town and country planning, marked by the original Treaty and the two subsequent amending Acts (Davies & Gosling 1994). Between 1957 and say 1973 there was virtually no interest in planning matters. From about 1973 to 1986, there was an increasing concern about many matters relating indirectly to town and country planning, notably in regional issues and the environment. These concerns were given an explicit mandate for the first time by the Single European Act 1986, after which there was a period of intensifying interest leading up to the Treaty of European Union in 1992. Town and country planning was explicitly given a mandate for the first time in Section 130S of the 1992 Act, as part of the increasing concern about the environment. The section stated that:

the Council, acted unanimously on a proposal from the Commission and, after consulting the European Parliament and the Economic and Social Committee, shall adopt . . . measures concerning town and country planning, land use with the exception of waste management and measures of a general nature, and management of water resources.

The main interest of the six original member-states in coming together in 1957 into a European Economic Community was to foster economic growth and competition. But very soon the range of concerns began to widen into matters that might have a more direct effect on land-use planning. Regional disparities, measured by unemployment and wealth, was one concern. A European Regional Development Fund was established in 1975 and a start made on funding measures designed to correct these disparities. Funds were allocated to member-states on a quota basis for projects for industrial and infrastructure development in the various kinds of assisted areas identified by member-states. But the impact of this first regional initiative by the European Community on spatial planning was comparatively small, confined to the individual projects, without any wider implications for planning policies at the European level. Nevertheless, the concern intensified with the advent to the Community of Ireland, the UK and Denmark in 1973, and even more so with Greece in 1981 and Spain and Portugal in 1986.

The other significant area of concern in those early years was for the environment. The first mention came at a meeting of the heads of state in Paris in 1972, when it was acknowledged that an effective campaign to combat pollution, improve the quality of life and protect the environment was equally important if the basic objectives of the Community were to be achieved. A series of environmental action programmes was initiated in 1973, with a second and third programme in 1977 and 1983. From the beginning, these programmes had an interest in planning matters such as the environment of town centres or coastal areas, but their real strength was in legislation to reduce levels of pollution, maintain a satisfactory ecological balance, and set quality requirements for the environment. Regulations and directives covered matters such as air and water quality, nature conservation and major accident hazards. Other measures were of a more systematic character, notably the directive on environmental assessment of projects, which translated into the UK's legislation, has had the most direct effect thus far on the practice of land-use planning and control.

This period of growing concern for planning was given a sharper focus by the Single European Act in 1986. The prime purpose of the Act was to lay the groundwork for completion of the Single Market in 1992. But, in addition, regional policies and the environment were given an explicit mandate in the Treaty, with a consequent increased attention being given to both.

The development of environmental policy marked a continuation of the trends before 1986, but now with more authority. The Fourth Environmental Action Programme continued the work of the first three, intensifying the concern with preventing pollution and protecting the natural environment. The scope of pre-

225

ventive action was also widened by extending the ideas of environmental assessment into environmental auditing, ensuring freedom of access to environmental information, and foreshadowing the establishment of an environmental protection agency. There was also some debate about extending the role of environmental assessment back up the chain of decision-making to the assessment of policies, plans and programmes, although this did not materialize.

But the real change of direction came with the Fifth Environmental Action Programme, published in 1992 under the title, "Towards sustainability" (Commission of the European Communities 1992a). It promised a more comprehensive and proactive policy towards the environment by shifting attention away from the treatment of symptoms and problems, such as atmospheric and water pollution, towards the root causes of environmental threats by focusing on actors and agents in the key sectors of the economy: industry, energy, transport, agriculture and tourism. The earlier programmes relied chiefly on legislation to enforce standards and prevent abuses. The fifth programme proposed a wider mix of measures, including financial instruments and "horizontal" measures through integrated regional development, transport management and coastal planning.

The principles underlying the fifth programme had been foreshadowed in the *Green Paper on the urban environment*, published in 1990 (Commission of the European Communities 1990). This sought to identify the main environmental problems common to most urban areas in the Community. They included environmental pollution, the physical degradation and decay of the built environment, including the historic towns, the social malaise of the inner cities and suburbs of the larger cities, and the loss of wildlife habitats and nature. The causes of the problems that were identified included the effects of transport developments, both in making possible a wider dispersal of workplaces and population to the suburbs, and the increasing pollution thereby generated through greater use of private cars, and a segregation of land uses through the "compartmentalization and location of activities on the basis of function". The solutions included a review of town planning policies to encourage mixed land uses, denser development in cities, and a shift from private to public transport. Whether the analysis had given sufficient regard to the spatial implications of economic restructuring, the behavioural patterns of choice of home and workplace, or the nature of property development in a mixed economy, is more open to question. Arguably, the vision of the city was anachronistic, typified by the illustration on the cover of the Paper, a reproduction of a painting of a fourteenth-century city by Giotto.

The second major development was the 1987 reform of the Structural Funds (Commission of the European Communities 1989). The Regional Development Fund, Social Fund and Agricultural Guidance and Guarantee Fund were brought together into a co-ordinated policy. The Funds were allocated through co-ordinated, three- or five-year, programmes focused on particular areas designated by the Commission according to objective criteria, with a clear set of objectives, incorporating the idea of partnership between the member-states and the Commission in their preparation.

Objective 1 areas had the lion's share of the Structural Funds as they were aimed at the so-called lagging regions where incomes were less than 70 per cent of the Community's average. They included much of southern Italy and Spain, all of Greece, Portugal and Ireland and, exceptionally, for the UK, Northern Ireland. Objective 2 areas were those having to adjust to industrial decline as their levels of unemployment were above the Community's average and their economies were heavily dependent on industry. They were of great importance for the UK, receiving over 38 per cent of the total allocation of the Commission's funds for this objective. The areas covered 35 per cent of the country's population, in northeast and northwest England, west Cumbria, Yorkshire and Humberside, west Midlands, Clwyd and South Wales, and Tayside and Strathclyde in Scotland. Finally, Objective 5b was to promote the development of rural areas experiencing changes in agricultural production. These were less important for the UK, receiving only 13 per cent of the total allocation. The areas covered only 2.6 per cent of the population, in the Highlands and Islands of Scotland, mid-Wales and Cornwall and Devon.

Procedures for preparation of the programmes were lengthy and cumbersome, the final approval coming from the Commission for the so-called Community Support Framework for each area. This was a statement of the detailed aims and the allocation of funds by the Commission under different headings such as business support, infrastructure, environmental improvements and training. These funds, matched by funds from the member-state, provided the framework within which individual projects would be identified. Thus, the 1987 reform of the Structural Funds incorporated a measure of spatial planning, at least in so far as regions were identified for a form of co-ordinated programme planning. The bid for funds, which is the draft development plan, had to be submitted by the national government of the member-state, although in the first round much of the work was done by the local authorities. It took the form of a financial commitment by the Commission and the member-state for the achievement of specified objectives rather than a spatial, land-use or regional plan. However, although there was a spatial dimension to the work, the direct involvement by planning authorities as such, and the relationship between the preparation of the Community Support Framework and the statutory structure and local plans, was not necessarily very close. Ultimate responsibility for the submission of the proposals lay with a central government department, such as the Department of Trade and Industry, or the Welsh or Scottish Office. And the actual level of funding by the Commission also was not very great. The allocation for the South Wales Community Support Framework under Objective 2 for 1989–93, for example, was 107 million ECU (approximately £85 million), and for the Cornwall and Devon Framework under Objective 5b, 75 million ECU (£60 million).

In many ways, indeed, it could be argued that it was the small, residual proportions of the Structural Funds that potentially were of more direct relevance for planning practice. These were the funds allocated directly by the Commission under Article 11 of the Coordinating Regulation, the so-called Community Initiatives, and Article 10 of the ERDF Regulation, the Innovative Measures.

The Community Initiatives were designed to focus on areas or sectors necessary for completion of the Single Market or for promoting cohesion among the member-states (Commission of the European Communities 1993a). They were identified by the Commission rather than in response to bids from member-states. Eight new initiatives with a spatial dimension were identified, in addition to continuing several earlier initiatives associated with the decline of particular industries, notably coal, steel, textiles and shipbuilding. Many were designed to assist the development of Objective 1 areas, but two in particular were important for the UK. The Leader Initiative gave support for local networks of actors and interests involved in rural development in Objective 1 and 5b areas. The INTER-REG Initiative was for the development of border areas isolated within their own countries, through studies and by cross-border co-operation. At first sight, the only qualifying area of the UK could be Northern Ireland, with its border with the Republic of Ireland, and indeed a programme was developed there. But a bid for an INTERREG programme by Kent County Council, in partnership with the Nord–Pas de Calais region in France, was successful on the grounds that the Channel Tunnel in effect established a qualifying border and the French region was an Objective 2 area. And this has provided the basis for a more ambitious Euro-region, bringing in the three Belgian regions of Flanders, Wallonia and Brussels Capital, to develop greater understanding and eventually a co-ordinated set of policies for their development (Thompson 1992).

Some of the Innovative Measures were even more influential in their potential impact on planning practice. There was, in the first place, support for several urban pilot studies in different countries where the Commission's aim was to identify new techniques in urban governance for transfer to other countries (Commission of the European Communities 1992b). Given the remit of the Directorate-General for regional policy, the majority were for economic development, but there were some projects with a more specific planning interest, for instance in environmental action linked to economic goals or for the re-vitalization of historic centres, such as the rejuvenation of a rundown industrial area in Stoke, or the environmental and economic development of Belfast harbour.

Secondly, the Article 10 measures included support for the development of networks of cities and regions throughout Europe. Networking has been a complex idea that, at its simplest, has been not much more than town-twinning; but at its highest development, as intended under Article 10, it is a formal contract between several cities or regions for the exchange of ideas and experience (Camhis & Fox 1992). Thus, some 37 networks were supported, with a wide variety of interests including urban management and governance, computer technology in local and regional government, problems of urban decline and economic development, transport issues, water and energy, and for cities and regions with similar economics or common problems (Commission of the European Communities 1992c).

A sample survey of a hundred local authorities in Great Britain showed that in 1993 roughly 19 per cent were members of at least one network funded by the Commission and to that extent were learning more about other countries (Davies & Gosling 1994). Nevertheless, much of this networking was not concerned with matters of land-use planning, however broadly defined. A second crucial point was that many of these networks evolved from, or within, intermediary or representative organizations such as the Council of European Municipalities and Regions. But the third point is demonstrated by the EUROCITIES network, a group of some 42 larger cities throughout Europe that are not capital cities (Marlow 1992). This network went beyond the limited criteria of Article 10 to become an organization that seeks to influence the Commission in the development of policies and programmes affecting their interests. Thus, the Article 10 initiatives were simply for individual projects within the umbrella of the EUROCITIES network.

But in many respects the most significant development for planning in this period before the Treaty of European Union was publication by the Directorate-General for Regional Policy of the report on *Europe 2000: outlook for the development of the Community's territory* (Commission of the European Communities 1991). This marked an attempt to introduce an integrated, horizontal dimension into the review of the many factors affecting the spatial development of the European Community, and to do this in a way that anticipated the outcome of the creation of the Single Market and the intended withering away of the barriers to movement of goods, services, people and investment throughout the Community. It was a first attempt at a truly synoptic look at the geography of Europe from a comprehensive viewpoint. It was not prescriptive, in the sense of setting targets, or defining policies. Its aim was more humble, yet potentially influential as it sought to identify those Europe-wide factors and trends, about which planners in the future should be aware.

In effect, *Europe 2000* was trying to alter perceptions of space at the regional and urban levels. At the macro level, *Europe 2000* was seeking to understand the economic geography of Europe in a way that transcended national boundaries, summed up in the image of a Europe as comprising four areas. There was the traditional, industrial heartland, from London, through the Low Countries and the Rhine and across the Alps to northern Italy: the engine for economic growth and restructuring in Europe but at the same time afflicted by congestion both of land and transport, and a source of pollution for central and eastern Europe. Secondly, there was an arc on the northern shores of the Mediterranean, from Italy, through the south of France, to northeast Spain and Catalonia, a newly emerging growth zone but at the same time one risking overdevelopment, especially of the coastal regions, and pollution of the Mediterranean itself. Thirdly, there were the peripheral regions of the Community – Greece, southern Italy, much of Spain, Portugal and Ireland – where the problems were of relative poverty and isolation. And finally there were the external regions of the Mahgreb in North Africa, central and eastern Europe and the Nordic countries, the first three of which were sources of immigration and with environmental problems.

229

The key point in this description of Europe was the idea of a core–periphery relationship within the Community. The statistical evidence at the level of member-states or of major regions within the states seemed to support this concept, and was the basis for much of the priority given in the Structural Funds to the Objective 1 regions and the principle of cohesion. But it was to some extent an untested hypothesis, and further work was proposed, with a division of Europe into 11 areas for further study, drawn up fairly arbitrarily in an attempt to get away from the dictates of national boundaries. Thus, the UK lay within three areas: the Central Capitals regions, including London, Paris, Brussels and Frankfurt; the North Sea regions, from Denmark to the east of Scotland; and the Atlantic Arc, covering the west of Scotland and Northern Ireland, Wales and the southwest, and thence south to Portugal. The validity of this perception will become apparent only when the studies are finally published, later in 1995. But even a preliminary analysis of their characteristics shows that in most of the areas there is a greater degree of variation than commonality or uniformity (Gripaios 1993).

A second perception is that of a Europe of Cities. Eighty per cent of the population lives in urban areas. Again, the picture is one of uncertainty and change. Ideas of a formal, rigid hierarchy of cities and urban areas within national urban systems are being replaced by a search for a European system, and the search is complicated by the evidence of change, both in the definition of what is meant by urban areas and the stages reached in their evolution as they pass through urbanization and suburbanization to de-urbanization and in some case re-urbanization. These are all crude statements about the changing location of population and employment within the functional urban regions (Cheshire & Hay 1989). Thus, there are the older industrial cities of the traditional heartland, with their declining manufacturing and port activities, seeking regeneration through their ability to attract and retain financial and business services, cultural activities, and political power. There are also the newer growth cities of the south with their smaller, more attractive environments, cheaper land, attracting newer high-technology industries. And there are the cities of the peripheral areas with a poorly developed infrastructure and limited accessibility from the heartland, little inward capital investment, and a branch plant economy.

The distinctive feature in this pattern of cities is the absence of a simple, single hierarchy of cities (Kunzman & Wegener 1991). Instead there is a more variable pattern of success and failure in international and interregional competition with other cities, based on their economic, social, cultural and political function, and the quality of life and environment that they offer. For some cities it is their success as gateways to Europe. For others, there is the idea of the so-called "entrepreneurial city", dependent on a dynamic civic leadership, an institutional capacity for innovation, a close public–private partnership and a high degree of independence and autonomy (Parkinson 1992).

Thus, by 1992 and the Treaty of European Union, there was in place the makings of a new context for planning in Britain and other countries in Europe, that under Section 130S of the Treaty, was firmly within the mandate of what now was to be called the European Union. The questions are whether this will have any effect on either the policies or the practice of planning in the UK, and whether there will be a greater degree of integration between the UK and the rest of Europe in matters relating to planning.

European planning in the 1990s

The most direct effect of the carry-over of policies since the Treaty of European Unions is in the further development of the Structural Funds. The aims and methods for the Funds put in place by the 1987 reform have not been altered to a significant degree (Commission of the European Communities 1993b). The emphasis is still on cohesion, although there is a recognition that the core-periphery model is an oversimplification and the pattern of regional disparities within the Union is much more complex (Commission of the European Communities 1994e). Nevertheless, the spatial objectives are largely unaltered, although a new, sixth objective has been added in anticipation of the enlargement of the Union to include the Nordic countries and their Arctic territories. The procedures have been simplified, with a greater emphasis on partnership between all of the contracting parties, the Commission, the member-states through the national government, and "all of the authorities and bodies who are competent for the areas and sectors in which operations are to be carried out". Actions under the Structural Funds must in future take account of the need to protect and conserve the natural environment, so the development plans and programmes for the Community Support Frameworks must be accompanied by an environmental assessment, as well as being placed in the context of a regional economic plan.

The real change is that the proportion of the Union's budget to be devoted to the Structural Funds is to increase from 30.8 per cent in 1993 to 35.7 per cent in 1999, the majority still being allocated to Objective 1 areas, directly and through the new Cohesion Fund (Commission of the European Communities 1992d). This increase in funding means that for the UK the areas covered are extended to include small parts of London and the south of England for Objective 2 (Commission of the European Communities 1994a), parts of northeast England and Scotland, East Anglia and Lincolnshire for Objective 5b (Commission of the European Communities 1994b) and, of greatest significance, Merseyside and the Highlands & Islands of Scotland for Objective 1. As a result, more than 41.7 per cent of the country is covered by the Structural Funds (Commission of the European Communities 1994e).

Perhaps of greater significance for planning, the Community Initiatives under Article 11 have been reviewed, as a result of which there has been a greater consolidation and focusing of them (Commission of the European Communities 1994c). Two are particularly relevant for planning and the UK. The INTERREG initiative has been greatly extended throughout Europe so that it now covers all

231

internal and external border areas irrespective of whether they are in any of the Objective areas. And the possibility has been established for including maritime border areas under certain conditions. This gives legitimacy to continuing the inclusion of Kent and its extension to include East Sussex, and Gwynedd and Dyfed, on the way to Ireland. Secondly, a new URBAN initiative has been announced, although this is likely to be more important in principle than in practice for the UK (Commission of the European Communities 1994d). Its aims are very similar to those of City Challenge and other UK programmes, and the amount of funds is very small, to be spread around up to 50 cities throughout the Union. Its real significance is the recognition in spatial planning terms of an explicit urban dimension.

There are two institutional developments that could have an effect for planning. A new Committee of the Regions has been established under the Treaty, with terms of reference to advise the council on all matters affecting the regions of Europe. The membership of the Committee was subject to considerable debate in the European Parliament and elsewhere, focusing in particular on establishing that its members be the elected representatives of regional or local governments rather than the appointees of national governments (Commission of the European Communities 1993c). In the event, that became the guiding principle and, accordingly, the 24 UK members and their alternates are all councillors. But that does not hide the fact that the UK is the only one of the larger member-states without a strong, elected tier of regional government and that, for these other countries, the Committee offers the potential for becoming an important means of influencing the development of the Union's regional policies. Much will depend on whether the life of the Committee is extended beyond the next intergovernmental conference of the Union in 1996 and, if so, what will then be its role (Morphet 1994).

Secondly, within the Commission itself, a Committee for Spatial Development was established in 1990 by the informal Council of Ministers with responsibility for spatial or regional policies, with representatives of the planning ministries of member-states. The Committee was closely involved in the work on *Europe 2000* and more recently on its projected successor, *Europe 2000+*, for which a draft was presented to the informal Council in Leipzig in September 1994. The latter report, which will be published in 1995, emphasizes in particular the influence of the trans-European networks in transport, energy and telecommunications on future patterns of development, and the need for member-states to co-operate on transnational spatial and coastal planning.

In addition, *Europe 2000+* will cover the results of the 11 area studies. One possible implication to be drawn for the UK from these area studies could be a potential threat of increasing peripherality, with enlargement of the Union. The dominant force lines or axes of development around the North Sea coast are an east–west axis from Rotterdam towards Berlin and the east, with a secondary one northwards from Hanover, through Copenhagen to the Nordic countries. There is another secondary north–south axis, through the Channel Tunnel to London and north, to the Midlands and Scotland, and east to the Haven ports. But the strength of this axis is dependent on communications with the UK and on the strength of the ultimate destinations in Scotland, Wales and Ireland.

There could be a threat of peripherality for the UK too in the Central and Capitals regions where the most intense interactions are between Brussels, linked with Antwerp and Ghent in the so-called ABG-stad of Flanders, the Randstad cities, Frankfurt and Paris. Newly emerging metropolitan areas crossing national borders are creating new pressures and opportunities, namely the so-called MHAL metropolis based on Liège, Aachen and Maastricht, the Saar on the France/Germany border, and around Lille, on both sides of the France/Belgium border. In all of these areas, work is in hand on developing cross-border co-operation in planning policies. The third study, the Atlantic Arc, emphasizes the peripherality of these regions and their problem of communications eastwards into the heartland of Europe.

To a considerable extent, these developments, especially those in transnational spatial planning and development, are influenced by the different planning systems on either side of national borders. Effective planning across those borders will therefore depend on at least an understanding of the operation of the different planning systems, if not their eventual harmonization. Accordingly, the Committee has commissioned a Compendium of European Planning Systems, to provide a comparison of the planning systems and policies in the different countries, to be completed in 1995.

The point to emerge from this review of recent development is the emergence of spatial planning as a concept in the thinking of the European Union. It is there at the macro-European level with the promise of a European spatial development perspective, for which *Europe 2000+* marks a stage in its development. How far this will develop and whether it will be *dirigiste* is still open to debate. The principle of subsidiarity in the Treaty on European Union apparently sets limits to the degree of intervention, but against this are the already strong spatial influences of the Structural Funds, and the pressure for the development of European networks for infrastructure, energy and communications.

But subsidiarity is a matter for debate, as Article A of the Treaty states that it "marks a state in the process of creating an even closer union among the peoples of Europe, in which decisions are taken as closely as possible to the citizen". And the new spatial dimension is there too in the attention and support given by the Commission to promoting cross-border co-operation and planning at the most local level. Thus, on the one hand there is the move towards planning at the European level; and, on the other hand, there is the extension of subsidiarity towards a Europe of cities and regions, if necessary crossing national borders, rather than confined to nation-states.

Conclusions

The final question is: How will these developments in Europe affect planning in Britain, given the unique character of its planning system and its geographical separation from continental Europe? Will it lead to a closer integration of planning policies in the UK, with those in the rest of Europe, including the European Commission? Will it lead to an outright harmonization, or at least a convergence, of planning systems if the benefits of integration are to be obtained? Or will planning in the UK remain inward-looking, isolated from developments in the rest of Europe?

One set of answers to these questions is to be found in the evolving concern with spatial planning in the European Union. At one level there is the influence of the regulations and directives about the environment and their translation into the UK's legislation. This influence is significant, although, in a sense, it is a development that would have occurred even without the Union. The idea of sustainable development and the concern for the environment is a movement that is worldwide, as was demonstrated in Agenda 21, the final agreements by governments at the United Nations Conference on Environment and Development in Rio de Janeiro in 1992. These ideas are already spreading throughout planning, seen for instance in the White Paper, *Sustainable development: the UK strategy* (HM Government 1994c), and in the growing use of environmental appraisal in development plans. Its spatial effects in the UK can be seen in the concern about traffic and land use, or the protection of designated areas and habitats, as well as in the more general, system-wide concerns with quality of life as expressed in anti-pollution measures.

The influence of the European Union can be seen more directly in the allocation of the Structural Funds and their movement towards a more integrated form of planning based on aims and objectives, regional economic analysis, and environmental assessment. But the relationship between such planning and the more traditional land-use planning is more tenuous. Arguably, the connection in formal terms may be comparatively slight. Much of the content of a Community Support Framework is devoted to matters such as the provision of sites and premises for industry, business support services, research and development programmes, and training and education, rather than the co-ordinated, land-use policies of a typical development plan. At best, if the timing is appropriate, a structure plan could provide part of the policy framework for the bid for funds from the Commission. But the timescales of the Community Support Frameworks, whether it be the speed with which their development plans and frameworks have to be prepared, or their three- or five-year programme periods for implementation, mean that they are out of phase with the more leisurely timeframes of structure and local planning. Furthermore, the geographical areas within which the bids have to be prepared are wider than the boundaries of many local authorities and they require a regional level of action for which there is no counterpart in the UK beyond that of integrated regional offices set up by government.

There is a third area where the influence and support of the Commission can be felt, and it is one with considerable potential for integration with land-use planning. This is in the broad field of competition and co-operation between cities or regions throughout Europe, fostered by pilot studies and the development of networking to facilitate the exchange and transfer of experience, or the promotion of common interests.

Finally, there is the as yet uncharted development of a European spatial planning perspective and the ways in which it will influence policies of the European Commission and, in turn, the spatial planning in member-states of the Union. In other member-states the advent of the Single Market has led to new perceptions of spatial planning, even in advance of the European spatial perspective. Thus, in the Netherlands, the Fourth Report on Physical Planning, entitled *On the road to 2015*, had a clear, specific European perspective influencing its policies and priorities as early as 1988 (Netherlands Ministry of Housing 1988), and more recently the German government has issued a report setting the European spatial context for planning policies. In other countries with common borders, serious attempts are being made to increase co-operation and to undertake joint planning work, for instance on the borders between France, Luxembourg and Belgium (Commission of the European Communities 1993d).

Consideration of these possibilities leads on to the extent to which planning policies in the UK can demonstrate greater European awareness. Such movements have been slow to develop in the UK, with the exception of Northern Ireland. One area of the country that is attempting to adopt a specifically European dimension in its planning is Kent, where the impact of the Channel Tunnel on both sides of the English Channel has encouraged the formation of a Euroregion in which there is a real attempt to work in partnership with regions in continental Europe. But despite the common interests and the political will to co-operate, publication of the first fruits of co-operation reveals the difficulties at every level, from the problems of language and incompatible data systems to the competences of the various levels of government in the different regions (Kent County Council 1994). But at the national or regional level there is only the most general reference to a European dimension in the regional planning guidance for the South East (DoE 1994g), and almost no mention for instance in the guidance for the East Midlands (DoE 1994f).

Summing up, one way forwards towards a closer integration of the UK's planning with that in other member-states and the Commission is exemplified by the forces for convergence in the planning systems, whether the movement is by the British system or other systems. Various factors support this interpretation. In a sense, convergence can be seen in the widespread trend towards deregulation and in the moves towards a plan-led system in Britain and, elsewhere, in the shifts towards greater flexibility, for instance in ideas about *globaal* planning in the Netherlands. There are the implications of the international economy and the effects of the Single Market, especially in the desire for more open competition. If it can be shown that planning policies and procedures are working against those aims, then there may well be growing pressure for harmonization of planning systems. The effects can be seen in concern about possible variations in the spatial costs of planning through delays imposed by planning procedures, and in the conflict between certainty and flexibility in planning systems (GMA et al. 1993). Finally, there is the growth of environmentalism, especially concern about its transnational effects.

Against the convergent tendency, there are the countervailing forces resisting moves towards a greater harmonization of planning systems. National perceptions of planning and its aims in different countries are still strong and persistent, reinforced by cultural attitudes towards development and the environment. Regionalism and local democratic accountability encourage separatism, as could ideas about subsidiarity. A further deterrent could be in the different paths followed by planners in their education and training, and in their professional relationships. Planners in some countries are urban designers, closely akin to architects or engineers. In others, they may be geographers or economists, involved in regional development. And in the UK the planner is expected to have a wide-ranging competence, extending over the field from regional to local planning. But only in the UK is there a professional institute with a membership of 17,000 planners working in central and local government and the private sector. This too sets planning in the UK apart from planning elsewhere.

Despite these differences, the probability is that there will be a closer integration of planning in the UK with that in other countries. The logic of spatial planning at a transnational scale is too strong for the UK's planners to remain isolated and inward-looking. But what that planning will comprise is another matter. At one level, local planning, with its emphasis on day-to-day development control, will remain largely unchanged in its present form. Neither the systems nor the policies are likely to be much affected by moves towards integration or even convergence of planning systems. It has acquired too strong an acceptance from a public wishing to protect what it has for it to be lightly dismembered. Its combination of flexibility and regulation is too valuable and satisfies too many interests, whether they are for development or conservation.

The real challenge from Europe for planning in the UK is at the wider, regional level, whether it is in environmentalism or in economic development and urban regeneration; that is, in spatial planning in the emerging European sense of the term. It is at this level that the pressures from market forces and internationalization of economies, and the opportunities of working within the European Union, should become manifest. But the real issue in the UK before there can be a serious move towards spatial planning and its integration with planning in the rest of the European Union is the absence of a true form of what the Danish planners have described as framework management: a level of regional planning with the appropriate competences and democratic accountability.

Acknowledgements

This chapter is based in part on a study by H. W. E. Davies and J. A. Gosling on the impact of the European Community on land-use planning in the UK, commissioned by the Royal Town Planning Institute.

References

Acosta, R. & V. Renard 1993. *Urban land and property markets in France*. London: UCL Press.

Adams, C. D. 1994. *Urban planning and the development process*. London: UCL Press.

Adams, C. D., H. May, G. Pawson 1990. The distribution of influence at local plan inquiries. *Planning Outlook* **33**(2), 133–5.

Alden, J. D. 1991. *Strategic Planning Guidance: the Welsh perspective*. Papers in Planning Research 122 (October 1991: 30), Department of City and Regional Planning, UWCC Cardiff.

— 1992. Strategic Planning Guidance in Wales. *Town Planning Review* **63**(4), 1992, 429–32.

Alden, J. D. & R. Morgan 1974. *Regional planning: a comprehensive view*. Leighton Buzzard: Leonard Hill Books. [See Ch. 2 on the "Development of regional planning" and Ch. 5 on "Regional planning institutions".]

Alexander, A. 1982. *Local government in Britain since reorganisation*. London: Allen & Unwin.

Alterman, R. 1982. Planning for public participation: the design of implementable strategies. *Environment and Planning B* **9**(3), 295–313.

Alty, R. & R. Darke 1987. A city centre for people: involving the community in planning for the Sheffield's Central Area. *Planning Practice and Research* **3**, 7–12.

Arnstein, S. R. 1969. A ladder of citizen participation. *Journal of the American Institute of Planners* **35**(4), 216–24.

Ashworth, G. J. & H. Voogt 1990. *Selling the city*. London: Pinter (Belhaven).

Assembly of Welsh Counties 1990. *Strategic Planning Guidance in Wales: process and procedure*. Cardiff: Assembly of Welsh Counties.

— 1991. *The structure of local government in Wales – the Assembly's response to the consultation paper issued by the Secretary of State*. Cardiff: Assembly of Welsh Counties.

— 1993. *Strategic Planning Guidance in Wales: overview report*. Submission to the Secretary of Wales for Wales, May 1993. Cardiff: Assembly of Welsh Counties.

ADC 1990. *Closer to the people*. London: Association of District Councils.

ADC/DPOS 1994. *Local plan preparation: Good Practice Note*. London: Association of District Councils/District Planning Officers Society.

Atkinson, R. & G. Moon 1994. *Urban policy in Britain*. London: Macmillan.

Audit Commission 1989. *Urban regeneration and economic development*. London: HMSO.

— 1992. *Building in quality: study of development control*. London: HMSO.

Bailey, N., A. Barker, K. MacDonald 1995. *Partnership agencies in British urban policy*. London: UCL Press.

Barnekov, T., R. Boyle, D. Rich 1989. *Privatism and urban policy in Britain and the United States*. Oxford: Oxford University Press.

Bell, D. 1994. *Communitarianism & its critics*. Oxford: Oxford University Press.

Benyon J. 1982. The dual loyalty of councillors case study of Beverley Hills. *Local Government Studies* **8**(4), 53–63.

BCC 1988. *Replacement Structure Plan for Berkshire*. Reading: Berkshire County Council.

Bianchini, F., J. Dawson, R. Evans 1992. Flagship projects in urban regeneration. In *Rebuilding the city*, P. Healey, S. Davoudi, M. O'Toole, S. Tavsanoglu, D. Usher (eds), 245–55. London: Spon.

Birmingham City Council 1993. *Birmingham Unitary Development Plan*. Department of Planning and Architecture, Birmingham City Council.

Blowers, A. (ed.) 1993. *Planning for a sustainable environment*. London: Earthscan.

Boaden, N., M. Goldsmith, W. Hampton, P. Stringer 1980. Planning and participation in practice. *Progress in Planning* **13**, 1–102.

Bonshek, J. 1992. The 1991 City Challenge bids. *Town Planning Review* **63**(4), 435–45.

Booth, P. 1993. The cultural dimension in comparative research: making sense of development control in France. *European Planning Studies* **1**(2), 217–30.

Boyne, G. & J. Law 1993. Bidding for the local government franchise: an evaluation of the contest in Wales. *Local Government Studies* **19**(4) 537–57.

Boyne, G., P. Griffiths, A. Lawton, J. Law 1991. *Local government in Wales, its role and functions*. York: Joseph Rowntree Foundation.

Brazier, G., & R. J. P. Harris 1975. Inter-authority planning: appreciation and the resolution of conflict in the new local government system. *Town Planning Review* **46**(3) 255–65.

Breheny, M. 1992. *Sustainable development and urban form*. London: Pion.

Breheny & Rockwood 1994. Planning the sustainable city region. In Blowers (1993: 150–90).

Brindley, T., Y. Rydin, G. Stoker 1989. *Remaking planning*. London: Unwin Hyman.

Bristol City Council 1990a. *City Centre Local Plan*. Bristol City Council, Bristol.

— 1990b. *Draft City Centre Local Plan: Written Statement*. Bristol City Council, Bristol.

— 1990c. *Green Charter*. Bristol City Council, Bristol.

— 1992. *Draft Bristol Local Plan: Written Statement*. Bristol City Council, Bristol.

— 1993a. *Deposit Bristol Local Plan: Written Statement*. Bristol City Council, Bristol.

— 1993b. *Residential Guidelines: Bristol Local Plan Policy Advice Note 1*. Bristol City Council, Bristol.

Brownill, S. 1988. The People's Plan for the Royal Docks: some contradictions in popular planning. *Planning Practice and Research* **4**, 15–21.

Brundtland Commission 1987. *Our common future* [United Nations Commission on Environment and Development]. Oxford: Oxford University Press.

Bruton, M. J. 1980. Public participation, local planning and conflicts of interest. *Policy and Politics* **8**(4), 423–42.

Bruton, M. J. & D. J. Nicholson 1983. *Strategic planning and development plans*. Papers in Planning Research 70, Department of Town Planning, UWIST, Cardiff.

Bruton, M. J. & D. J. Nicholson 1987. *Local planning in practice*. London: Hutchinson.

Buchanan, S. 1982. Power and planning in rural areas: preparation of the Suffolk County structure plan. In *Power, planning and people in rural East Anglia*, M. J. Moseley (ed.), 1–20. Centre of East Anglian Studies, University of East Anglia.

Buckingham-Hatfield, S. 1994. Gendering 21. *Town and Country Planning* **63**(7/8), 211.

Bulpitt, J. 1989. Walking back to happiness? Conservative Party governments and elected local authorities in the 1980s. *The new centralism*, C. Crouch & D. Marquand (eds). Oxford: Basil Blackwell.

Burns, D., R. Hambleton, P. Hoggett 1994. *The politics of decentralisation*. London: Macmillan.

Burns, W. 1977. Minutes of Evidence, Eighth Report from the Expenditure Committee, Session 1976–77. *Planning Procedures* II, (Evidence, HC 395-II). London: HMSO.

Buxton, R. 1974. Planning in the new local government world. *Journal of Planning and Environment Law* **26**, 60–72.

240

Camhis, M. & S. Fox 1992. The EC as a catalyst for European Urban Networks. *Ekistics* **352/353**, 4–6.

Campbell, B. 1993. *Goliath*. London: Methuen.

CEC 1989. *Guide to the reform of the Structural Funds*. Luxembourg: Office for Official Publications of the European Communities.

— 1990. *Green paper on the urban environment*. Luxembourg: Office for Official Publications of the European Communities.

CEC, Directorate-General for Regional Policy 1991. *Europe 2000: outlook for the development of the Community's territory*. Luxembourg: Office for Official Publications of the European Communities.

CEC, Directorate-General for Environment, Nuclear Safety and Civil Protection 1992a. *Towards sustainability: a European Community programme of policy and action in relation to the environment and sustainable development*. (the fifth Action Programme), COM (92) 23. Luxembourg: Office for Official Publications of the European Communities.

CEC, Directorate-General for Regional Policies 1992b. *Urban pilot projects*. Brussels: Commission of the European Communities.

— 1992c. *European cooperation networks*. Brussels: Commission of the European Communities.

— 1992d. *Conclusions of the Presidency, European Council in Edinburgh, 11 and 12 December 1992* [press notice DOC/92/8]. Brussels: Commission of the European Communities.

— 1993a. *Community initiatives*. Brussels: Commission of the European Communities.

— 1993b. *Community Structural Funds 1994–99, revised regulations and comments*. Luxembourg: Office for Official Publications of the European Communities.

— 1993c. *Resolution of the European Parliament on the Committee of the Regions. Official Journal*, 6 December.

— 1993d. *Urban regeneration and industrial change: an exchange of urban redevelopment experiences from industrial regions in decline in the European Community*. Luxembourg: Office for Official Publications of the European Communities.

— 1994a. *Commission decision establishing an initial list of declining industrial areas covered by Objective 2 as defined by Council Regulation 2052/88*. Official Journal L81, 24 March.

— 1994b. *Commission decision establishing for the period 1994 to 1999 the list of rural areas under by Objective 5b as defined by Council Regulation 2052/88*. Official Journal L96, 14 April.

— 1994c. *The future of Community initiatives under the Structural Funds*. COM (94) 96. Luxembourg: Office for Official Publications of the European Communities.

— 1994d. *Community initiative concerning urban areas (URBAN)*. COM (94) 61. Luxembourg: Office for Official Publications of the European Communities.

— 1994d. *Competitiveness and cohesion: trends in the regions, Fifth Periodic Report on the social and economic situation and development of the regions in the Community*. Luxembourg: Office for Official Publications of the European Communities.

Cheshire, P. C. & D. G. Hay 1989. *Urban problems in western Europe: an economic analysis*. London: Unwin Hyman.

Christleow, A. 1994. Building on existing networks. *Town and Country Planning* **63**(7/8) 197–213.

Church, C. & J. McHarry 1994. Indications of sustainability. *Town and Country Planning* **63**(7/8) 208–9.

Cloke, P. & J. Little 1990. *The rural state?* Oxford: Oxford University Press.

Clwyd County Council 1982. *Programme Plan*. Mold: Clwyd County Council.

— 1983. *Newtech Innovation Centre*. Mold: Clwyd County Council.

— 1984. *High technology*. Mold: Clwyd County Council.
— 1985. *Wrexham Technical Park*. Mold: Clwyd County Council.
— 1987a. *Tourism strategy*. Mold: Clwyd County Council.
— 1987b. *Structure plan first alteration*. Mold: Clwyd County Council.
Collar, N. 1994. *Planning*. Edinburgh: W. Green.
Commission for Social Justice, 1994. *Social justice: strategies for national renewal*. London: Vintage.
Confederation of British Industry 1991. *A London development agency*. London: CBI.
Confederation of British Industry / RICS 1992. *Shaping the nation*. London: CBI.
Coon, A. 1989. An assessment of Scottish development planning. *Planning Outlook* 32(2), 77–85.
Coopers & Lybrand Deloitte 1991. *London world city*. London: Coopers & Lybrand Deloitte.
Council for the Protection of Rural England 1991. *Shedding hers – local government reform and the environment*. London: CPRE.
Council of Welsh Districts 1991. *The structure of local government in Wales – response to the Welsh Office consultation document*. Cardiff: CWD.
Countryside Commission 1992. *Local government reorganisation: review of Avon, Gloucestershire and Somerset*. Submission to the Local Commission.
County Planning Officers Society 1990. *Regional guidance and regional planning conferences*. London: CPOS.
Cox, K. & A. Mair 1991. From localised social structures to localities as agents. *Environment and Planning A* 23(2), 197–213.
Cross, D. T. & M. R. Bristow (eds) 1983. *English structure planning: a commentary on procedure and practice in the seventies*. London: Pion.
Crow S. 1993. The development plans, the planning inspectorate, and decision making. *Town & Country Planning Summer School Proceedings*. London: Royal Town Planning Institute.
Cullingworth, J. B. & V. Nadin 1994. *Town and country planning in Britain*, 11th edn. London: Routledge.

Dahl, R. *Who governs?* New Haven, Connecticut: Yale University Press.
Damer, S. & C. Hague 1971. Public participation in planning: a review. *Town Planning Review* 43(3) 219–32.
Davies, H. W. E. & J. A. Gosling 1994. *The impact of the European Community on land use planning in the United Kingdom*. London: Royal Town Planning Institute.
Davies, H. W. E., D. Edwards, A. J. Hooper, J. V. Punter 1989. *Planning control in western Europe*. London: HMSO.
Davies, L. 1991. An assessment of regional planning guidance. *The Planner* (8 February), 7–8.
De Groot, L. 1992. City Challenge: competing in the urban regeneration game. *Local Economy* 7(3), 196–209.
DOE 1980. *Development control – policy and practice* [Circular 22/80]. London: HMSO.
— 1984. *Memorandum on structure and local plans* [Circular 22/84]. London: HMSO.
— 1985a. *Development and employment* [Circular 14/85]. London: HMSO.
— 1985b. *Planning conditions* [Circular 1/85]. London: HMSO.
— 1988a. *Our common future. A perspective by the United Kingdom on the report of the World Commission on Environment and Development*. London: DOE.
— 1988b. *Strategic Planning Guidance for Merseyside* [PPG11]. London: HMSO.
— 1988c. *Strategic Planning Guidance for the South East* [PPG9]. London: HMSO.
— 1988d. *Strategic Planning Guidance for the West Midlands* [PPG10]. London: HMSO.
— 1989a. *Strategic Planning Guidance for London* [RPG3]. London: HMSO.

— 1989b. *Strategic Planning Guidance for Greater Manchester* [RPG4]. London: HMSO.
— 1989c. *Strategic Planning Guidance for South Yorkshire* [RPG5]. London: HMSO.
— 1989d. *Strategic Planning Guidance for Tyne and Wear* [RPG1]. London: HMSO.
— 1989e. *Strategic Planning Guidance for West Yorkshire* [RPG2]. London: HMSO.
— 1989f. *Sustaining our common future. A progress report by the United Kingdom on implementing sustainable development.* London: DOE.
— 1990. *Regional Planning Guidance, structure plans and the contents of development plans* [PPG15]. London: HMSO.
— 1991a. *Planning and Compensation Act 1991 – planning obligations* [Circular 16/91]. London: HMSO.
— 1991b. *The structure of local government in England: a consultation paper.* London: HMSO.
— 1992a. *Alternative development patterns: new settlements.* London: HMSO.
— 1992b *Development plans and regional planning guidance* [PPG12]. London: HMSO.
— 1992c. *Development plans: a good practice guide.* London: HMSO.
— 1992d. *Evaluating the effectiveness of land-use planning.* London: HMSO.
— 1992e. *Housing* [PPG3]. London: HMSO.
— 1992f. *Policy guidance to the Local Government Commission for England.* London: HMSO.
— 1993a. *Enquiry into the planning system in North Cornwall District.* London: HMSO.
— 1993b. *Environmental appraisal of development plans.* London: HMSO.
— 1993c. *London: making the best better.* London: DOE.
— 1993d. *Policy guidance to the Local Government Commission for England,* revised. London: HMSO.
— 1993e. *Reducing transport emissions through planning.* London: HMSO.
— 1993f. *Regional Planning Guidance for the Northern Region* [RPG7]. London: HMSO.
— 1993g. *The effectiveness of green belts.* London: HMSO.
— 1993h. *Working party on the internal management of local authorities in England.* London: DOE.
— 1994a. *Assessing the impact of urban policy.* London: HMSO.
— 1994b. *Nature conservation* [PPG9]. London: HMSO.
— 1994c. *Planning and noise* [PPG24]. London: HMSO.
— 1994d. *Planning and pollution control* [PPG23]. London: HMSO.
— 1994e. *Planning application fee setting* [consultation paper, June]. London: DOE.
— 1994f. *Regional Planning Guidance for the East Midlands* [RPG8]. London: HMSO.
— 1994g. *Regional Planning Guidance for the South East* [RPG9]. London: HMSO.
— 1994h. *Vital and viable town centres.* London: HMSO.
— 1995. *Green belts* [PPG2]. London: HMSO.
DoE/Department of National Heritage 1994. *Planning and the historic environment* [PPG15]. London: HMSO.
DoE/Department of Transport 1994. *Transport* [PPG13]. London: HMSO.
DoE/Welsh Office, *The future of development plans: a consultation paper,* September 1986. London: DOE.
— 1988. *General policy and principles* [PPG1]. London: HMSO.
— 1992a. *General policy and principles* [PPG1]. London: HMSO.
— 1992b. *Industrial and commercial development and small firms* [PPG4]. London: HMSO.
— 1992c. *The countryside and the rural economy* [PPG7]. London: HMSO.
— 1993. *Town centres and retail development* [PPG6]. London: HMSO.
DoE/Welsh Office/NPO 1994. *Planning charter.* London: DOE.
District Planning Officers Society 1994. *The recommendations of the Local Government Commission: memorandum of observations on the implications for land use planning.*
Docklands Consultative Committee 1994. *Community empowerment in urban regenera-*

tion. London: DCC.

duBoulay, D. 1989. Involving Black People in Policy Formulation. *Planning Practice and Research* 4(1), 13–15.

Duncan, S. & M. Goodwin 1989. *The local state and uneven development*. Cambridge: Polity.

Erhman, R. 1988. *Planning planning: clearer strategies and environmental controls*. Policy Study 100, Centre for Policy Studies, London.

European Foundation for the Improvement of Living and Working Conditions 1994. *Bridging the gulf*. Dublin: EFILWC.

Fagence, M. 1977. *Citizen participation in planning*. Oxford: Pergamon.

Federal Ministry for Regional Planning, Building and Urban Development 1994. *Spatial planning policies in a European context: approaches to a spatial planning policy at European level (1994)*. Bonn: Federal Ministry for Regional Planning, Building and Urban Development.

Fischer, M. 1977. *Technocracy and the politics of expertise*. London: Sage.

Friend, J. & A. Hickling 1987. *Planning under pressure*. Oxford: Pergamon.

Gamble, A. 1988. *The free economy & the strong state*. London: Macmillan.

Gatenby I. & C. Williams 1992. Section 54A: the legal and practical implications. *Journal of Planning and Environment Law*, 110–25.

Gibson, T. 1993. *Danger: opportunity*. A report to the Joseph Rowntree Foundation on Meadowell Community Development.

Giddens 1990. *The consequences of modernity*. Cambridge: Polity.

Goodwin, M., S. Duncan, S. Halford 1993. Regulation theory, the local state and the transition of urban politics. *Environment and Planning D* 11(1) 67–88.

Graham, T. 1990. Planning Policy Guidance Note 1 and the Presumption in favour of Development. *Journal of Planning and Environment Law*, 175–9.

Grant, M. 1991. Recent developments. *Encyclopedia of planning law and practice monthly bulletin* (July).

Greed, C. 1994. *Women and planning*. London: Routledge.

Griffiths, M. P., A. Lawton 1990. *Community councils in Wales*. Welsh Unit for Local Government: Polytechnic of Wales/Wales Association of Community & Town Councils.

Griffiths, R. 1986. Planning in retreat? Town planning and the market in the eighties. *Planning Practice and Research* 1, 3–7.

Gripaios, P. 1993. An analysis of European super-regions. *Regional Studies* 27(8), 745–50.

Grove-White, R., A. Phillips, M. Toogood 1993. *Sustainability and the English countryside*. Unpublished report to the Countryside Commission, Centre for the Study of Environmental Change,Lancaster University.

Hague, Cliff 1994. If it's not broke, don't fix it. *Town and Country Planning*, 63(1), 13–14.

Hague, C. & S. McCourt 1974. Comprehensive Planning, Public Participation and the Public Interest. *Urban Studies* 11(2), 143–55.

Hall, P. 1992. Agenda for a new government. *The Planner* 78(21), 30–34.

Hambleton, R. 1994. Lessons from America. *Planning Week* 2(24), 16–17.

Hambleton, R. & L. Mills 1993. Local Government Reform in Wales. *Local Government Policy Making* 19(4), 45–55.

Hams, T. 1994. International Agenda, local initiative. *Town and Country Planning* 63(7/8), 209–10.

Harding, A. 1991. The rise of urban growth coalitions, UK-style? *Environment & Planning C* **9**, 295–318.

Harris, N. 1994. *Planning and local government reorganisation in Wales*. Papers in Planning Research 148. Department of City & Regional Planning, University of Wales College of Cardiff.

Harris, N. & M. Tewdwr-Jones 1995. The implications for planning of local government reorganisation in Wales: purpose, process and practice. *Environment and Planning C* **13(1)**, 47–66.

Hart, L. 1994. Community involvement: addressing motivation. *Town and Country Planning* **63**(7/8), 209–10.

Harvey, D. 1989. *From managerialism to entrepreneurialism. Geografissker Annaler* **71B**. 3–17.

Hastings, A. & A. McArthur 1995. A comparative assessment of government approaches to partnership with the local community. In *Urban policy evaluation*, R. Hambleton & H. Thomas (eds), 175–93. London: Paul Chapman.

Hayton, Keith 1992. Scottish Enterprise: a challenge to land use planning? *Town Planning Review* **63**(3), 265–78.

— 1994. Planning and Scottish Local Government Reform. *Planning Practice and Research* **9**(1), 55–62.

Healey, P. 1990. Democracy in the planning system. *The Planner* **76**(19), 14–15.

— 1992. Development plans and markets. *Planning Practice and Research* **7**(2), 13–20.

Healey, P., J. Doak, P. McNamara, M. Elson 1985. *The implementation of planning policies and the role of development plans* [report to the DoE]. Department of Town Planning, Oxford Polytechnic.

Healey, P., P. McNamara, M. Elson, J. Doak 1988. *Land use planning and the mediation of urban change*. Cambridge: Cambridge University Press.

Healey, P., S. Davoudi, M. O'Toole, S. Tavsanoglu, D. Usher (eds) 1992. *Rebuilding the city*. London: Spon.

Healey, P. & T. Shaw 1993. *The treatment of environment by planners: evolving concepts and practices in development plans*. Working Paper 31, Centre for Research in European Urban Environments, Department of Town and Country Planning, University of Newcastle upon Tyne.

Held, D. 1987. *Models of democracy*. Cambridge: Polity.

HM Government 1967. *Wales: the way ahead*. London: HMSO.

— 1985. *Lifting the burden*. London: HMSO.

— 1986. *Building business . . . not barriers*. London: HMSO

— 1989. *The future of development plans*. Cmnd **569**. London: HMSO.

— 1990. *This common inheritance*: Britain's Environmental Strategy, Cmnd **1200**. London: HMSO.

— 1991. *This common inheritance: first year report*. London: HMSO.

— 1992. *This common inheritance: second year report*. London: HMSO.

— 1994a. *Biodiversity: the UK action plan*. London: HMSO.

— 1994b. *Climate change: the UK programme*. London: HMSO.

— 1994c. *Sustainable development: the UK strategy*.London: HMSO.

— 1994d. *Sustainable forestry: the UK programme*. London: HMSO.

— 1994e. *This common inheritance: third year annual report*. HMSO, London.

Hobbs, P. 1992. The economic determinants of post-war British town planning. *Progress in Planning* **38**(3), 185–300.

House of Commons Environment Committee 1994. *Shopping centres and their future* [fourth report]. London: HMSO.

House of Commons Welsh Affairs Committee 1993. *Rural housing* [third report]. London: HMSO.

Imrie, R. & H. Thomas (eds) 1993a. *British urban policy and the urban development corporations*. London: Paul Chapman.
— 1993b. The limits of property-led regeneration. *Environment & Planning C* **11**, 87–102.
Inforegio News 1994. *Europe 2000+*. Newsletter 9, European Commission, Directorate-General for Regional Policies, Brussels.
IUCN, UNEP & WWF 1991. *Caring for the Earth: a strategy for sustainable living*. The World Conservation Union, United Nations Environment Programme and World Wide Fund for Nature, Gland.

Jacobs, M. 1991. *The green economy: environment, sustainable development and the politics of the future*. London: Pluto.
— 1993. *Sense and sustainability*. London: Council for the Protection of Rural England.
Jones, A. 1991a. A new importance for development plans. *Planning* **932** (August), 14–15.
— 1991b. Equal and opposite forces in attitude to plans. *Planning* **940** (October), 14–15.
— 1991c. Local choice revived by new view of plans. *Planning* **933** (August), 16–17.
Jones, R. 1982. *Town and country chaos*. London: Adam Smith Institute.

Kavanagh, D. 1994. A Major agenda? In *The Major effect*, D. Kavanagh & A. Seldon (eds), 3–17. London: Macmillan.
Keating, M. 1991. *Comparative urban politics*. Cheltenham: Edward Elgar.
Keating, M. & R. Boyle. 1986. *Re-making urban Scotland*. Edinburgh: Edinburgh University Press.
Kent County Council 1994. *A vision for Euroregion: towards a policy framework, the first steps*. Maidstone: KCC.
Krishnarayan, V. & H. Thomas 1993. *Ethnic minorities and the planning system*. London: RTPI.
Kunzman, K. R. & M. Wegener 1991. The pattern of urbanization in western Europe. *Ekistics* **350/351**, 282–91.

Labour Party 1994. *Empowering urban communities*. Labour Party Environment Group.
Land Use Consultants 1993. *Conservation issues in strategic plans*. Countryside Commission, English Heritage and English Nature, Cheltenham.
Lawless, P. 1988. British inner urban policy post 1979: a critique. *Policy & Politics* **16**, 261–75.
— 1991. *Public–private sector partnerships in the UK*. Working Paper 16, Centre for Regional, Economic and Social Research, Sheffield City Polytechnic.
Leach, S. 1992a. The reorganisation of local government: changing directions. In *The Heseltine review of local government: a new vision or opportunities missed?* S. Leach, J. Stewart, J. Spencer, K. Walsh, J. Gibson (eds), 44–59. Birmingham: INLOGOV.
— 1992b. The disintegration of an initiative. *The Heseltine review of local government: a new vision or opportunities missed?* S. Leach, J. Stewart, J. Spencer, K. Walsh, J. Gibson (eds), 1–10. Birmingham: INLOGOV.
— 1994a. Arguments about joint arrangements. In *The local government review: key issues and choices*, S. Leach (ed), 88–98. Birmingham: INLOGOV.
— 1994b. The local government review: from policy drift to policy fiasco. *Regional Studies* **28**(5), 537–49.
Leach, S. & N. Moore 1979. County/Districts relations in Shire and Metropolitan Counties in the field of Town and Country Planning: A comparison. *Policy and Politics* **7**(2), 165–79.
Liberal Democrat Party 1994. *Reclaiming the city*. London: Liberal Democratic Party

Publication.

Lindblom, C. E. 1977. *Politics and markets*. New York: Basic Books.

Littler, S., M. Tewdwr-Jones, M. Fisk, S. Essex 1994. Compatibility of Planning and Housing Functions in Welsh Local Authorities. Unpublished report to Welsh Office, UWCC, Cardiff.

Lloyd, G. & D. Newlands 1988. The growth coalition and economic development. *Local Economy* 3, 31–40.

Lloyd, G. & J. Rowan-Robinson 1992. Review of Strategic Planning Guidance in Scotland. *Journal of Environmental Planning and Management* 35(1), 93–9.

Lloyd, M. G. 1990. Planning for enterprise in Scotland. *Local Government Studies* 16(6), 7–14.

Local Government Commission for England 1993a. *Final recommendations on the future local government of Avon, Gloucestershire and Somerset*. London: HMSO.

— 1993b. *Reviewing local government in the English Shires: a progress report*. London: HMSO.

Local Government Management Board 1993. *Fitness for purpose – shaping new patterns of organisation and management*. London: LGMB.

Loftman, P. & B. Nevin 1992. *Urban regeneration and social equity: a case study of Birmingham 1986–1992*. Research Paper 8, University of Central England in Birmingham.

Logan, J. & H. Molotch 1987. *Urban fortunes*. Berkeley: University of California Press.

Low, N. 1991. *Planning, politics and the State*. London: Unwin Hyman.

Lowe, P. & J. Goyder 1983. *Environmental groups in politics*. London: Allen & Unwin.

Lowe, P. & J. Murdoch 1993. *Rural sustainable development*. Rural Development Commission, Salisbury.

Lukes, S. 1974. *Power: a radical view*. London: Macmillan.

Lyddon, D. 1980. Scottish planning practice: influences and comparisons. *The Planner* 66(3), 66–67.

— 1985. Planning and recovery: an alternative route. *The Planner* 71(2), 26–30. [Town and Country Planning Summer School Report 1985].

Mabbott 1993. The role of community involvement. *Policy Studies* 14(2), 27–35.

McCormick, J. 1991. *British politics and the environment*. London: Earthscan.

Ministry of Housing and Local Government 1962. *Town centres: approach to renewal*. London: HMSO.

Mannion, M. 1991. Access groups – alive and kicking. *Access Action* 21, 2–3.

Marlow, D. 1992. *Eurocities: from urban networks to a European urban policy*. Ekistics 352/353, 28.

May, A. 1993. *Preface to the Deposit Version of the Bristol City Local Plan*. Bristol City Council, Bristol.

McAuslan, J. P. 1981. *The ideologies of planning law*. Oxford: Pergamon Press.

McCrone, D., L. Paterson, A. Brown 1993. Reforming local government in Scotland. *Local Government Studies* 19, 9–15.

Millichap, D. 1993. Sustainability: a long-established concern of planning. *Journal of Planning and Environment Law*, 1111–19.

Minay, C. L. W. 1992. Developing regional planning guidance in England and Wales: a review symposium. *Town Planning Review* 63(4), 415–19 and 432–4. [Also see other contributions to this special issue on regional planning guidance, 415–34.]

Ministry of Housing, Physical Planning and Environment 1988. *On the road to 2015: comprehensive summary of the Fourth Report on Physical Planning in the Netherlands* 1988 and *Fourth Report Extra* 1991, The Hague: Ministry of Housing, Physical Planning and Environment.

Minton, A. 1994. Tipton meets the challenge. *Planning Week*

(12th May), 11.

Molotch, H. 1976. The city as a growth machine. *American Journal of Sociology* **82**(2), 309–21.

Morphet, J. 1994. *European regions to make voice heard in committee. Planning* **1060**(18 March), 8–9.

National Council for Voluntary Organisations 1993. *Community involvement in city challenge: apolicy report and good practice guide.* London: NCVO.

Needham, B., P. Koenders, B. Kruijt 1993. *Urban land and property markets in the Netherlands.* London: UCL Press.

Nevin B. & P. Shiner 1993. Britain's urban problems: communities hold the key. *Local Work* **50**.

Newbury District Council 1981. *Newbury and Thatcham District Plan.* Newbury: NDC.

— 1982. *West Berkshire Rural Area District Plan.* Newbury: NDC.

— 1989. *Newbury District Draft Local Plan.* Newbury: NDC.

— 1990. *Newbury District Local Plan Deposit Draft.* Newbury: NDC.

— 1993a. *Newbury District Adopted Local Plan.* Newbury: NDC.

— 1993b. *Newbury District Local Plan Proposed Modifications Report.* Newbury: NDC.

— 1994. *Newbury District Council Newbury District Local Plan Review: Consultation Document.* Newbury: NDC.

Newman, P. 1995. The politics of urban redevelopment in London & Paris. *Planning Practice and Research* **10**(1), 15–24.

Newman, P. & A. Thornley 1996. *Urban planning in Europe: international competition, national systems and planning projects.* London: Routledge.

Norton, A. 1986. The future functions and structure of local government. In *Reports on the future role and organisation of local government*, H. Davis (ed.), 2.1–2.26. Birmingham: INLOGOV.

Nuffield Foundation 1986. *Town and country planning: the report of a Committee of Inquiry appointed by the Nuffield Foundation.* London: The Nuffield Foundation.

O'Grady, S. 1994. Managing the local plan process. In *Local planning underway*, H. Thomas (ed), 7–21. Working Paper 148 School of Planning, Oxford Brookes University.

O'Riordan, T. 1993. The politics of sustainability. In *Sustainable environmental economics and management: principles and practice*, K. Turner (ed.), 37–70. London: Pinter (Belhaven).

Østergård, N. 1994. *Spatial planning in Denmark.* Copenhagen: Ministry of the Environment, Spatial Planning Department.

Parkinson, M. 1989. The Thatcher government's urban policy, 1979–1989. *Town Planning Review* **60**(4), 421–40.

— 1992. *Urbanization and the functions of cities in the European Community: a report to the Commission of the European Communities (DG XVI).* Centre for Urban Studies, University of Liverpool.

— 1993. City Challenge: a new strategy for Britain's cities? *Policy Studies* **14**(2), 5–13.

Parry, G., G. Moyser, N. Day 1992. *Political participation and democracy in Britain.* Cambridge: Cambridge University Press.

Pateman, C. 1970. *Participation and democracy theory.* Cambridge: Cambridge University Press.

Pearce, D. 1989. *Blueprint for a green economy.* London: Earthscan.

Peters, T. & R. Waterman 1982. *In search of excellence.* London: Harper & Row.

Phillips, A. (ed.) 1992. *Meeting or managing demands on the countryside* [report of a one-day seminar on demand management held in Cardiff on 27 November 1992]. Paper in Environmental and Countryside Research 2, Department of City and Regional Planning, University of Wales College of Cardiff, Cardiff.

Planning Advisory Group 1965. *The future of development plans* [the report of the Planning Advisory Group]. London: HMSO.

Punter, J. V. 1989. Planning control in France. *Town Planning Review* 59(2), 159–82.

Purdue, M. 1989. Material considerations in planning: an ever expanding concept? *Journal of Planning and Environment Law*, 156–61.

— 1994. The effects of Section 54A. *Journal of Planning and Environment Law*, 399–404.

Raemakers, J. L. Cowie, E. Wilson 1991. *An index of local authority green plans.* Department of Planning and Housing, Heriot–Watt University.

Raemaekers, J., A. Prior, S. Boyack 1994. *A review of the emerging new Scottish National Planning Series: a report to the Royal Town Planning Institute (Scotland).* Unpublished document, School of Planning and Housing Edinburgh College of Art, Heriot–Watt University.

Rallings, C., M. Temple, M. Thrasher 1993. *Community identity and participation in local democracy.* London: Commission for Local Democracy.

Reade, E. 1987. *British town and country planning.* Milton Keynes: Open University Press.

Redcliffe-Maud, Lord & B. Wood 1974. *English local government reformed.* London: Oxford University Press.

Redclift, M. 1991. The multiple dimensions of sustainable development. *Geography* 76(1), 36–42.

Redwood, J. 1995. *An environmental agenda for Wales* [Statement by the Secretary of State for Wales]. Cardiff: Welsh Office.

Reynolds, F. & T. Burton, 1994. Resource management and sustainability through the planning system. In *Development and planning 1994*, D. Cross & C. Whitehead (eds), 123–5. Department of Land Economy, University of Cambridge.

Ridley, N. 1988. *The local right: enabling not providing.* London: Centre for Policy Studies.

Ritchie, G. J. 1979. *Local government reorganisation.* Diploma dissertation, Department of Town Planning, UWIST.

Robinson, F., M. Lawrence, K. Shaw 1993. *More than bricks and mortar?* Department of Geography, University of Durham.

Robinson, S. 1990. City under stress. *The Planner* 76(10), 10.

Rowan-Robinson, J. & M. G. Lloyd 1991. National planning guidelines: a strategic opportunity wasting away? *Planning Practice and Research* 6(3), 16–19.

Rowan-Robinson, J., M. G. Lloyd, R. G. Elliot 1987. National planning guidelines and strategic planning. *Town Planning Review* 58(4), 369–81.

RTPI 1991a. *The regional planning process.* Discussion document prepared for the Council of the Institute by the Regional Planning Working Party of the South West Branch, May 1991.

— 1991b. *The structure of local government in Wales – memorandum of observations to the Welsh Office on its consultation paper.* London: Royal Town Planning Institute .

— 1993. *Local government review – the delivery of strategic planning within a new local government structure.* London: Royal Town Planning Institute.

— in Scotland 1994. *Briefing note on the local government etc. (Scotland) Bill for the House of Lords Committee.* Unpublished paper, The Royal Town Planning Institute in Scotland, Edinburgh.

— South West Branch 1992. *Examination of local government structure: Avon, Glouces-*

tershire and Somerset. Initial submission.

— South West Branch 1993. *The future local government of Avon, Gloucestershire and Somerset*. Response to the Local Government Commission.

— South West Branch 1994. *Views of the branch to the Local Government Commission on the Review of Cornwall, Devon, Dorset & Wiltshire*.

Saunders, H. & C. Stone 1987. Developmental politics reconsidered. *Urban Affairs Quarterly* **22**(4), 521–39.

Schumpeter, J. 1967. Two concepts of democracy. In *Political philosophy*, A. Quinton (ed.), 153–88. Oxford: Oxford University Press.

Scottish Development Department 1974. *Coastal planning guidelines, north sea oil and gas*. Scottish Development Department, Edinburgh.

— 1981. *National planning guidelines, priorities for development planning*. Scottish Development Department, Edinburgh.

— 1984. *Local planning* Planning Advice Note 30, Scottish Development Department, Edinburgh.

— 1985. *National Planning Guidelines, high technology: individual high amenity sites*. Scottish Development Department, Edinburgh.

— 1987. *National Planning Guidelines: agricultural land*. ScottishDevelopment Department, Edinburgh.

— 1988. *Development opportunities and local plans*. Scottish Development Department, Edinburgh.

— 1989. *Local plan presentation*. Planning Advice Note 34, Scottish Development Department, Edinburgh.

Scottish Office 1991. *Review of planning guidance – a consultation paper*. Environment Department, Edinburgh.

— 1992. *Local plans, the planning bulletin*. Planning Services Issue 6, (November), 10–11, Environment Department, Edinburgh.

— 1993a. *Business and industry: national Planning Policy Guideline*. NPPG 2 (October), Environment Department, Edinburgh.

— 1993b. *Land for housing: national Planning Policy Guidance*. NPPG 3 (July), Environment Department, Edinburgh.

— 1993c. *Progress in partnership: a consultation paper on the future of urban regeneration policy in Scotland*. The Scottish Office, Edinburgh.

— 1993d. *Shaping the future: the new councils* [Cmnd 2267]. The Scottish Office, Edinburgh.

— 1993e. *Structure plans: housing land requirements*. Planning Advice Note 38, The Scottish Office, Edinburgh.

— 1993f. *The need for up-to-date local plans*. The Planning Bulletin, Planning Services Issue 7 (10 May), Environment Department, Edinburgh.

— 1994a. *Archaeology and planning: national Planning Policy Guideline*. NPPG 5 (January), Environment Department, Edinburgh.

— 1994b. *Land for mineral working: national Planning Policy Guideline*, NPPG 4 (April), Environment Department, Edinburgh.

— 1994c. *Review of the town and country planning system in Scotland*. Environment Department (July), Edinburgh.

— 1994d. *The planning system: national Planning Policy Guideline*. NPPG 1 (January), Environment Department, Edinburgh.

Short, J. R., S. Fleming, S. Witt 1986. Housebuilding, planning and community action. London: Routledge & Kegan Paul.

Simmie, J. & S. French 1989. Corporation, participation and planning. *Progress in Planning* **31**(1), 5–57.

Skeffington, A. 1969. *People and planning. Report of the Committee on Public Partici-*

pation in Planning. London: HMSO.

Smith, M. P. 1988. *City, state and market*. Oxford: Basil Blackwell.

Stoker, G. 1989. Creating a local government for a post-Fordist society: the Thatcherite project? In, *The future of local government*, J. Stewart & G. Stoker (eds), 141–70. London: Macmillan.

— 1990. Regulation theory, local government and the transition from fordism. In *Challenges to local government*, D. King & J. Pierre (eds), 242–64. London: Sage.

Stone, C. 1989. *Regime politics*. Lawrence: University of Kansas Press.

Stone, C., M. Orr, D. Imbroscio 1991. The reshaping of urban leadership in US cities: a regime analysis. In *Urban life in transition*, M. Gottdiener & C. Pickvance (eds). Newbury Park: Sage.

Strike, J. 1994. *Market aware development plans – principles and practice*. MPhil dissertation, Department of Land Management & Development, University of Reading.

Suttie, P. 1993. Going public. *Planning Week* 2(8), 13.

Swinbourne, R. 1991. Entering practice. In *Dilemmas of planning practice*, H. Thomas & P. Healey (eds), 63–72. Aldershot: Avebury.

Tewdwr-Jones, M. 1994a. The development plan in policy implementation. *Environmental and Planning C: Government and Policy* 12(2), 145–63.

— 1994b. The Government's Planning Policy Guidance. *Journal of Planning and Environment Law* 46, 106–16.

Thew, D. & P. Watson 1988. The future of strategic planning – unitary development plans: the West Midlands experience. *The Planner* 74(11), 19–23..

Thomas, H. 1992a. Redevelopment in Cardiff Bay: state intervention and the securing of consent. *Contemporary Wales* 5, 81–98.

— 1992b. Volunteers involvement in planning aid. *Town Planning Review* 63(1), 47–62.

Thomas, H. & P. Healey (eds) 1991. *Dilemmas of planning practice*. Aldershot: Avebury.

Thompson, R. 1987. Is faster better? The case of development control. *The Planner* 73(9), 11–15.

— 1992. Responding to the challenges of European policy and funding. *The Planner* 78(21), 24–6.

Thornley, A. 1993. *Urban planning under Thatcherism: the challenge of the market*, 2nd edn. London: Routledge.

Turok, I. 1992. Property-led urban regeneration: panacea or placebo. *Environment & Planning A* 24, 361–79.

van Gunsteren, H. 1976. *The quest for control: a critique of the rational-central rule approach in public affairs*. London: John Wiley.

Wannop, U. 1981. The future for development planning. *The Planner* 67(1), 14–18.

Welsh Office 1988. *The Welsh language: development plans and planning control* [Circular 53/88]. London: HMSO.

— 1990a. *Strategic Planning Guidance in Wales: general paper*. Welsh Office, Cardiff.

— 1990b. *Strategic Planning Guidance, structure plans and the content of development plans* [PPG15 (Wales)]. Welsh Office, Cardiff.

— 1991a. *The structure of local government in Wales: a consultation paper* [June]. London: HMSO.

— 1991b. *The internal management of local authorities in Wales – a consultation paper*. London: HMSO.

— 1992a. *Development plans and Strategic Planning Guidance in Wales* [PPG12 (Wales)], Welsh Office, Cardiff.

— 1992b. *The role of community and town councils in Wales*. London: HMSO.

— 1993a. *Development control – a guide to good practice*. Cardiff: Welsh Office.
— 1993b. *Local government in Wales: a charter for the future* [Cm. 2155]. London: HMSO.
Wheatley, The Rt Hon. Lord 1969. *Royal Commission on Local Government in Scotland 1966–69: report* [Cmnd 4150]. Edinburgh: HMSO.
Wilcox, D. 1994a. Participation – sham or shambles? *Planning* **1074**(29 June), 7.
— 1994b. *The guide to effective participation*. Brighton: Partnership Books.
Wilding, P. 1992. The British Welfare State: Thatcherism's enduring legacy. *Policy and Politics* **20**(3), 201–12.
Williams, G., L. Strange, M. Bintley, R. Bristow 1992. *Metropolitan planning in the 1990s: the role of unitary development plans*. Occasional Paper 34, Department of Planning and Landscape, University of Manchester.
Wilson, B. 1990. Planning Policy Guidance. *The Planner* **76**(49)85–7.
WWF (World Wildlife Fund, Nature Conservancy Council, Countryside Commission, Countryside Commission for Scotland, The Royal Society of Arts and Council for Environmental Conservation) 1983. *The conservation and development programme for the UK*. London: Routledge & Kegan Paul.

Young, K. 1994. Local government. In *The Major effect*, D. Kavanagh & A. Seldon (eds), 83–97. London: Macmillan.

Index

253

258